THE INNER

The Mysticism of
Georges Bataille

FAUX TITRE

Etudes
de langue et littérature françaises
publiées

sous la direction de Keith Busby,
M.J. Freeman, Sjef Houppermans,
Paul Pelckmans et Co Vet

No. 189

Amsterdam - Atlanta, GA 2000

THE INNER SCAR.

The Mysticism of
Georges Bataille

Andrew Hussey

The paper on which this book is printed meets the requirements of "ISO 9706:1994, Information and documentation - Paper for documents - Requirements for permanence".

Le papier sur lequel le présent ouvrage est imprimé remplit les prescriptions de "ISO 9706:1994, Information et documentation - Papier pour documents - Prescriptions pour la permanence".

ISBN: 90-420-0629-3
©Editions Rodopi B.V., Amsterdam - Atlanta, GA 2000
Printed in The Netherlands

To John and Doreen Hussey,
and in memory of Doris and Vic Hussey (1922-1995)

Acknowledgements

This book began in discussion with Jeremy Stubbs, who steered it from Dijon to Paris and towards conclusion. It was further developed in conversation with James Eibisch in Barcelona and at Montserrat. Others who shared with me their insights on Bataille and related themes were David Bellos, Michèle Bernstein, Gavin Bowd, Michel Houellebecq, Isidore Isou, Francis Marmande, Malcolm Pollard, Jean-Claude Ranger, Ralph Rumney, Philippe Sollers, Glyn Williams, Richard Williams. I would also like to thank Monica Muñoz of the Fondació Antoni Tàpies, Barcelona for her help in organising a colloquium on Georges Bataille in Barcelona in 1998 and Margaret Parry of the Department of European Languages, University of Wales, Aberystwyth for her invaluable help in preparing the manuscript.

Andrew Hussey
University of Wales, 2000

Contents

'Le taureau affronté':
Georges Bataille and the problem of mysticism

Bataille, abattage d'un humain bétail
Michel Leiris,
Glossaire: j'y serre mes gloses

Since his death in 1962, Georges Bataille has acquired the status of one of the most influential thinkers of the age. It is an irony, however, that this status has been achieved despite the fact that, in his lifetime, Bataille's writings were known only to a relatively small number of people and that, in the years which immediately followed his death, much of his work remained either unpublished or, for other reasons, inaccessible. However, Bataille's current prestige is such that since the publication of the twelve volumes of his *Œuvres Complètes*, in the 1970s, almost all of his works have been translated into English and other major languages, whilst in France and elsewhere he has been the focus for extensive critical debate in the form of a plethora of essays, monographs and conferences.

It is a further irony that Bataille's posthumous fame, unlike that of former enemies such as André Breton or Jean-Paul Sartre, rests upon his perceived contribution to contemporary thought. The fact that this reputation has been established by the likes of Jacques Derrida, Michel Foucault, Roland Barthes and Philippe Sollers, indicates that Bataille, whose life and work intersect with the debates around the political and artistic avant-gardes of the first part of the century, is considered as a precursor of post-structuralism and post-modernism, the twin literary and philosophical movements which have, in recent years, dominated contemporary critical thinking in Europe and the United States.

The principal reason for this is that Bataille has often been perceived by contemporary critics as an avatar of limitless irrationalism.[1] This perception of Bataille is attractive to the post-

---

[1] A useful discussion of Bataille's status as a precursor of post-modernist thought can be found in the introductory chapter to Michael Richardson, *Georges Bataille* (London: Routledge, 1994). For a more detailed discussion of Bataille's relation to contemporary critical theory see also Geoffrey Bennington, 'Lecture: De Georges Bataille'in *Georges Bataille après tout*, ed. Denis Hollier, coll. L'Extrême contemporain (Orléans: Belin, 1995), pp.11-34. Also the introduction by Michel Surya

modernist imagination, first of all, because it establishes Bataille as a thinker whose work is emblematic of the post-modernist urge to separate meaning and function in language and philosophy.[2] Bataille's reputation as a precursor of post-modernism is further enhanced by the the fact that the essential content of his writings - which borrow ideas and terminology from the various and separate worlds of Hegelian philosophy, mysticism, ethnology and economics - is elision and paradox.

Despite Bataille's current prominence, however, few contemporary commentators have engaged with those aspects of Bataille's thinking which he discusses with reference to the language of mysticism. This is an omission which is all the more striking given that Bataille considered his thought to be not only opposite to the philosophical tradition which had its origins in the project of the Enlightenment, but also as a form of speculation which was intricately related to the religious exigencies of the Christian Medieval period. In the same way, Bataille not only was widely read in texts on Eastern mysticism but, as he pursued his interest in Hermetic philosophy and Gnosticism through the 1930s, also experimented with collective and individual forms of mystical practice based on Oriental methods.

Therefore the present study will address itself specifically to the question and the challenge of Bataille's relation to mysticism, the apparent blind spot for contemporary Bataille criticism. More precisely, this study is an examination of the relation between Bataille's account of an experience of loss of identity, which he describes as an 'inner experience', and the way in which Bataille parallels this experience to traditional forms of religious mysticism. This relation will be traced and defined in the texts Bataille wrote between 1938 and 1947 and which either precede or form the core texts of the unfinished series he entitled *La Somme athéologique*.

The difficulty of defining mysticism

The term 'mysticism' has commonly been the source of misuse or abuse. In the considerable literature of mysticism this difficulty is

---

to *Georges Bataille, une liberté souveraine*, ed. Michel Surya (Orléans: Ville d'Orléans/Fourbis, 1997), pp.7-11.

[2] This aspect of Bataille's contribution to critical philosophy is discussed in detail in Robert Sasso, 'Georges Bataille and the Challenge to Think', in *On Bataille: Critical Essays*, ed. Leslie Anne Bold-Irons (Albany: SUNY Press, 1995), pp.41-51.

generally acknowledged to be partly an inevitable result of the antiquity of the word, and partly because the ineffable nature of what is normally described as 'mystical experience' is inherently impossible or difficult to describe. As Bataille puts it in the opening section of *L'Éxpérience intérieure*, it follows from this central fact that one of the difficulties of reading the inner experience as experience rather than metaphor is that the term 'mysticism' very quickly loses any useful meaning.[3]

It is possible, however, to trace a pathology of mystical experience. In most instances, this means in the Christian tradition that mysticism is most often defined in relation to its original Greek cognate *muo*, 'to close up' or 'conceal', and that the mystic is one who is initiated and given access to visions of the unseen.[4] The methods which allowed access to these visions were, in the early Church, close to Oriental methods of meditation in that they were forms of ascetic practice which aimed at a separation between mind and body and, thereby, the negation of the individual, thinking subject.[5] The earliest accounts of Christian mystical experience, such as those given by Clement of Alexandria or his pupil Origen, also define themselves as 'allegories' in the sense that they provide - as in the Presocratic philosophy of Heraclitus so cherished by the Neoplatonic philosophers - a conduit to an occult relationship with the universe. Clement, in his *Stromateia* (Miscellanies) argued that there was in mystical experience a form of 'gnosis' (knowledge) which was a form of advanced Christianity. The secret, heretical tradition of what were termed the Gnostic Gospels was, in this sense, a key defining element in the formation of the early Church.[6]

It was an axiom of the Medieval Church, however, that true Christian knowledge was entirely separate from the hermetic

---

[3] This paradox is, indeed, the contradiction which defines the impossibility of writing about an 'inner experience'. Bataille writes: 'Mon livre fini, j'en vois les côtés haïssables, son insuffisance, et pire, en moi, le souci de suffisance que j'y ai mêlé encore, et dont je hais en même temps l'impuissance et une partie de l'intention.' *L'Éxpérience intérieure, Œuvres Complètes*, V, pp.10-11

[4] See *Oxford English Dictionary on Historical Principles* (Oxford: The Clarendon Press, 1973), p.1380.

[5] A famous account of Oriental influences on the early Church is given in Frederick Copleston, 'The Patristic Period', *A History of Philosophy, Medieval Philosophy*, vol 2 (Maryland: The Newman Press, 1962). See also Clement of Alexandria, *Opera Omnia*, trans. W.Wilson, 2 vols. (Edinburgh, 1867).

[6] Frederick Copleston, op. cit., pp. 34-36

philosophy represented by the Gnostics. The history of Christian mysticism during the Medieval period is, nonetheless, for the most part, a tradition which works against the hierarchical structures of the Church both as a political and philosophical body. This, clearly, explains Bataille's interest in mysticism as a process of thought which undermines or destabilises hierarchical forms of thinking.

Mysticism in the medieval period, particularly in Germany, France and Spain, was also concerned with forms of encounter or 'Union' which revealed God as within the body of the mystic as well as the external controlling principle of the universe. The law of the universe, it was implied, was also the law of the individual mind. In Germany and the Low Countries, for Meister Eckhart, Jan van Ruysbroeck, and the Blessed Henry Suso, this insight became the guiding theory of mystical speculation which sought to reconcile the themes of Neoplatonic contemplation with a spirit of analysis. In France, Aquinas' arguments for a separation between thought and feeling created a tradition which, in the Jesuit Jean-Pierre de Caussade or the Quietist Madame Guyon, sought 'abandonment' in the ecstasy of God.[7] This tradition also found its corollary in the Counter-Reformation where the Carmelite mystics, Saint Teresa of Avila and Saint John of the Cross, described their experiences in the erotic idiom of *The Song of Songs* as a series of encounters which induced an orgasmic, rapturous loss of self.

Jacques Lacan's remarks on Bernini's 'Ecstasy of Saint Teresa', describing the 'jouissance' which Teresa feels but does not know,[8] explain how, in the Christian tradition, mysticism has a dual status as the essential mystery of faith and as an interiority which defies the reductive narrative of the Church, thereby posing a threat to the fundamental principles of hierarchy and summit. This is a status which persists to this day and which, at least in part, explains the interest shown in Bataille's descriptions of the inner experience by thinkers

---

[7] The mystical principle of 'Quietism', a passive form of contemplation first advocated by the heretical Spanish priest Miguel de Molinos (1640-1697), had a widespread influence in the French Church during the period of the Counter-Reformation and its aftermath. The most important text of this period is François Fénelon's *Explication des Maximes des Saints* (1699) which defends Madame Guyon and 'Quietism' against the charge of heresy. See also Maurice Masson, *Fénelon et Madame Guyon* (Paris, 1907).

[8] For a discussion of these well-known remarks see Malcolm Bowie, *Lacan* (Fontana: London, 1991), pp.151-153.

such as Jean-Claude Renard or Le Père Daniélou who are operating within a Christian framework.

It is also important for this study that, like many of his generation, Bataille was widely read in the texts of Oriental mysticism. Indeed, as for the Surrealists, it seemed particularly significant for Bataille that in the Oriental tradition the participant in mystical experience did not aim at a summit which would be a point of encounter with God within a tradition, but at an experience in which the subject would be subsumed or literally dissolved into the movement of the cosmos. Bataille, in his mystical experiments during the late 1930s, specifically sought to enact this movement in real experience based on the techniques of Buddhist meditation.[9]

Most importantly, the object of mysticism - whether Eastern or Western - is practical and not theoretical. In her influential study, *Mysticism: A Study in the Nature and Development of Man's Spiritual Consciousness* - a work which is still a key point of reference for contemporary writers on mysticism - Evelyn Underhill says that it is the fact that mysticism is a concrete practical operation which makes it of such crucial significance in all religious systems of thought. It is, in this sense, she says, the fundamental reality of religion. [10]

In the same way, as the present study suggests, it is the inner experience which is the touchstone of Bataille's thought. It is therefore of singular importance for Bataille that the ecstasies of the Christian mystics, the meditative practices of Hindus or Buddhists, even the alcoholic intoxication which William James describes as 'a bit of the Mystic consciousness',[11] whether these experiences take the form of 'encounters', 'voices' or 'visions' all have in common a salient characteristic: they are all experiences which cannot be described adequately because they take place beyond language.[12]

---

[9] An account of these practices is given in Jean Bruno, 'Les Techniques d'illumination chez Georges Bataille', *Critique*, 195/196, 1963, pp.706-721.

[10] Evelyn Underhill, *Mysticism: A Study in the Nature and Development of Man's Spiritual Consciousness* (London: Methuen, 1930) p.45

[11] William James, 'The Drunken Consciousness is a bit of the Mystic Consciousness', *Varieties of Religious Experience* (New York, 1902) p. 387

[12] The attempt to fix thought beyond language is the first principle of inner experience: 'Le vrai silence a lieu dans l'absence des mots [...] Dans ce silence fait du dedans, c'est n'est plus un organe, c'est la sensibilité entière, c'est le cœur, qui s'est dilaté.' *L'Éxpérience intérieure, ŒC*, V, p.30

Reading the inner experience

One of the particular difficulties in reading Bataille is his notion that absence can be met directly in experience. This is the inner experience which is described in Bataille's 1943 book *L'Expérience intérieure* and it is, in many ways, the fundamental paradox of his philosophy.[13] Marguerite Duras elaborated this point, with reference to the problem of Bataille criticism, in an article written in 1958 for the journal *La Ciguë*.

> La critique, au seul nom de Bataille, s'intimide [...]. Les années passent: les gens continuent à vivre dans l'illusion qu'ils pourront un jour parler de Bataille [...] Cette abstention devient leur orgueil. Ils mourront sans oser, dans le souci extrême où ils sont de leur réputation, affronter ce taureau.[14]

For Duras, to confront Bataille's writing, and in particular his writing on inner experience, is to confront an assertion of pure negativity couched in terms which actively contradict each other and which seem to undermine or prohibit the analytical function of criticism. It is a further paradox, however, that despite these snares and impossibilities, within ten years of Duras' statement, Bataille's writing had taken on an almost canonical status in the French literary avant-garde.

This status was heralded by the special edition of the journal *Critique*, which was published in homage to Bataille in 1963, and in which articles from Bataille's friends and contemporaries, such as Maurice Blanchot or Pierre Klossowski, sat alongside articles from younger men such as Michel Foucault and Philippe Sollers. Through the subsequent course of the decade, a number of articles were published on Bataille's work by writers associated with the journal *Tel Quel*, which around the central figure of Philippe Sollers drew together a generation of writers and thinkers who saw the task of the avant-garde as matching theories of language and text to the practice of cultural subversion. In 1972, *Tel Quel* organised a conference on Bataille and Antonin Artaud under the rubric 'Vers une révolution culturelle'. This conference firmly installed Bataille as an exemplary

---

[13] This paradox is inherent in Bataille's thinking from his earliest essays. In the article 'La critique des fondements de la dialectique hégélienne' Bataille refers to the possibility of making a distinction between 'expérience' and 'valeur verbale' in the Hegelian dialectical method. *ŒC*, I, p.277

[14] Marguerite Duras, 'A propos de Georges Bataille', *La Ciguë*, 1 (1958), pp.32-33.

figure, whose practice as a writer and a thinker was to be followed and continued.

The reasons for the historical process which led to this status for Bataille were various and complex. In the first instance, however, as both Philippe Forest and Patrick ffrench have suggested in their histories of the journal *Tel Quel*, it is clear that Bataille played a prophetic role to a generation who were either hostile to the utopian demands of Surrealism, by now considered a pre-war antique, or suspicious of the lingering influence of Sartrean existentialism. [15] Secondly, as a writer who actively played upon the impossibility of bringing together meaning and form in text, thought or society, for those writers closely associated with *Tel Quel* as well others such as Michel Foucault or Jacques Derrida, Bataille anticipated the revolutionary tension of 1968 France.

According to Patrick ffrench, Bataille was also 'the acknowledged hero' of *Tel Quel* because his work 'rests on the ambiguous tension "between" Nietzsche and Hegel'.[16] More specifically, for the theorists of *Tel Quel* and associates such as Foucault and Derrida, Bataille's work represented a move beyond the totalizing demands of Hegelian philosophy towards a matrix of speculative theories which 'put the subject on trial'.[17] Above all, what brought Foucault, Derrida and the theorists of *Tel Quel* together was the common belief that there was a metaphorical parallel between the breaking of sexual taboos and revolt against technical constraints in writing and text. As Roland Barthes argued in his important and influential 1963 essay on Bataille for *Critique*, 'La Métaphore de l'œil', aesthetic transgession, the breaking with the forms and rules of language, is not only metaphorically equivalent to sexual trangression, but indeed may well be at the foundation of eroticism.[18]

This reading of Bataille was fundamental in his establishment as a thinker whose primary concern is the limits of language rather than real

---

[15] Philippe Forest, *Histoire de Tel Quel* (Paris: Éditions du Seuil, 1992), pp. 29, 31,41,111-114. See also Patrick ffrench, *The Time of Theory, A History of Tel Quel 1960-1983* (Oxford: The Clarendon Press, 1995), pp. 25-28. A parallel account of Bataille's importance for the *Tel Quel* group was also given by Philippe Sollers in an interview with the present author in Paris, February 11, 1996.

[16] Patrick ffrench, op.cit., pp.27-28

[17] An account of debates around this theme is given in Philippe Forest, op.cit., p.442-445.

[18] Roland Barthes, 'La Métaphore de l'œil', *Critique*, 195-196, 1963, p.771.

8

conceptual thought. This meant however that when Bataille's critical reputation was in the ascendant in the 1960s, Bataille's inner experience was in fact described in terms which were at some distance from the Surrealist generation to which Bataille had belonged. More precisely, the generation which posthumously made Bataille a culture hero described inner experience in metaphorical or metonymic terms. [19] The inner experience was read for the most part as a textual 'transgression', the term used by Bataille to describe an aesthetic, erotic or philosophical violation of law or limits. Bataille's writings on inner experience were discussed with exclusive regard to their theoretical implications for textual criticism, whilst the transgressive act of inner experience, which undermined ordered, discursive thought with the collapse of the subject, was seen as part of a textual game.[20] The actual experiences which lay behind the notion of inner experience, and which were described by Bataille with reference to the theories and experiences of religious mystics were, to a large extent, either overlooked or disregarded.

La Tache Aveugle

The generation which first read Bataille as a precursor of contemporary thought also privileged the term 'blindspot' as a

---

[19] The term 'metaphor' in this study is based on Aristotle's definition of metaphors as verbal phenomena which have a mimetic resemblance to experience ('To produce a good metaphor is to see a likeness', *Poetics*, 14591, pp.7-8). The term 'metonymy' is classically defined as a verbal figure which substitutes part for whole or evokes the whole by focusing on a salient aspect of it. See Christopher Norris, *Derrida* (London: Fontana, 1987, pp.113-114). It is important for this study that metaphor and metonymy represent thinking beyond the logic of ordered thought and experience. For a useful summary of the interplay between metaphor and metonymy see Martin Jay, *Downcast Eyes*, (Berkeley and Los Angeles: University of California Press, 1994),pp.33-34; Malcolm Bowie, op. cit., *Lacan*, p.68; Elisabeth Roudinesco, *Histoire de la psychanalyse en France*, tome 2, (Paris: Fayard, 1994), pp.315-316. The key source text for much contemporary debate on this subject, as well as being an important influence on Lacan and Derrida, is the seminal 1956 essay by Roman Jakobson and Morris Hall, 'Deux aspects du langage et deux types d'aphasie', initially published in the collection *Fundamentals of Language* (La Haye, 1957) and reprinted as 'Two aspects of language and two types of aphasic disturbances', in Roman Jakobson, *Selected Writings: Word and Language*, vol. 2, (La Haye, 1971), pp. 239-259

[20] It is the interplay between thought and language which is the essential characteristic of Bataille's discourse according to Maurice Blanchot in 'Le jeu de la pensée', in *Critique*, 195/196, 1963 pp. 737-738.

metaphor for unknowable and unreachable parts of a text which no amount of reading can fully decipher or reveal.[21] As the dizzying perspectives of Bataille's writing demonstrated for these readers, the 'blindspot' of the text has also dual status as the point from which the reader of the text cannot 'see' his or her own perspective, and also the point from which the reader's gaze, for reasons which may or may nor be innocent, has been averted.

For Susan Rubin Suleiman, it is highly significant that the body as represented in Bataille's erotic fiction is a notable 'blindspot' for this first generation which read Bataille. This is because, she argues, the body, and in particular the female body, 'is the very emblem of the contradictory coexistence of transgression and prohibition, purity and defilement, that characterises both the "inner experience" of eroticism and the textual play of the pornographic narrative.'[22] The mystical aspects of inner experience as a physical event, no less than its erotic content, are predicated upon a parallel contradiction which suspends thought. In this way they represent a form of poetic activity which actively works against the possibility of limiting inner experience to a textual process. The inner experience as a physical rather than a textual event, no less than the female body in Bataille's fictions, however marks a 'blindspot' for many of those critics who first announced Bataille as a contemporary.

In his essay,'Préface à la transgression', published in *Critique* in 1962, Michel Foucault makes the inner experience the central point of his argument.[23] Foucault describes the enucleated eye as the key motif of Bataille's thought. The blinded eye is an image which stands for the finitude of meaning, of language, in death. Foucault isolates erotic experience as the experience which takes the subject of Bataille's thought to these limits. This experience of the limit, for Foucault, is equivalent to the experiences of religious mystics because, like the modes of sexual ecstasy described by Sade or Freud, it is a form of experience which is beyond words. It is also therefore outside history. For Foucault it is through language that the human subject participates in the process of its own construction and therefore in history. It is also

---

[21] For a discussion of this point see Martin Jay, op.cit., *Downcast Eyes*, pp. 320, 355, 361.

[22] Susan Rubin Suleiman, 'Transgression and the Avant-Garde', *On Bataille: Critical Essays*, ed. Leslie Anne Boldt-Irons, (Albany: SUNY Press, 1995), p. 327

[23] Michel Foucault, 'Préface à la transgression,' *Critique*, 195-196, 1963, pp.751-769.

language which determines the limits of subjectivity. Mysticism, as such, can only be for Foucault one of a series of metaphorical experiences (blindness and violent orgasm are others) which represent the limits of the subject and the point of transgression. One of Foucault's main aims in 'Préface à la transgression' is to revolt against Hegelian philosophy. In particular, Foucault wishes to move away from the Hegelian dialectic as a model of mind. He therefore cites the inner experience as an exemplary analytical process, which undermines the Hegelian model of subjectivity, and, based on this, argues for a future 'discourse of transgression' which would replace the Hegelian logic of contradiction and the law of the dialectic.

Bataille's inner experience is then for Foucault an experience which marks a non-dialectical form of philosophical language. In this sense it is for Foucault no more metaphorical than Descartes' notion of 'acies mentis', the 'clear perception of sight' which Descartes makes a central principle of his method and which is not only a metaphor but also an intuition, that is to say an insight which is experienced before it is articulated in thought. Foucault notes that that the finitude and exhaustion of Bataille's language in this way reveal in L'Expérience intérieure a double language of philosophy which, in its self-reflective nature, lies beyond Christianity, religious feeling or the law of the Hegelian dialectic. Unlike the thought of Descartes, however, or the experiences of traditional religious mystics, Bataille's inner experience does not fit in with any categorical, transcendental or spiritual framework. It can then only function within discourse, like the enucleated eye, as an image of the experience of the limit which it announces. Ultimately therefore, for Foucault, Bataille's equation of mystical experience with erotic feeling, trapped as it is in discourse, can therefore only be, like all other forms of transgression, a metaphorical equivalent.

Similarly, for Philippe Sollers, in his essay 'Le toit', originally written in 1967, Bataille's inner experience represents an 'experience of limits', an encounter with 'le non-savoir', which opens up an infinite series of perspectives which redefine and reshape the subject.[24] Like Foucault, Sollers insists that the most important aspect of this experience is its textual value and Sollers therefore makes the point that this experience is not related to the Surrealist practice of poetry

---

[24] Also Philippe Sollers, 'Le toit', Tel Quel, 29, 1967, pp.24-45, reprinted in L'Écriture et l'expérience des limites, (Paris: Éditions du Seuil, 1971) pp.104-138.

which pursues a poetic ideal, the point which André Breton describes in mystical terms as the end of all contradictions. This is, says Sollers, because Bataille is concerned less with questions of 'spirit' or 'perception' rather than with 'space' and 'relations'. The inner experience is a dizzying experience of a summit which suspends the subject between discourse and silence and which prohibits all forms of action. The view from this summit cannot be described in mystical terms as 'vision' or 'encounter', however, but only in metaphorical terms as interplay between discourse and silence. The question which Sollers asks of Bataille, therefore, is not what can be seen from the summit, or 'the roof', but rather what is this 'roof' made of ('En effet, la question posée n'est pas seulement: que voit-on depuis le 'toit'? mais encore: qu'est-ce que ce "toit" lui-même?').[25]

Sollers examines Bataille's relation to language, eroticism and death. He finds that in each of these categories, Bataille holds a dualist position which rather than seeking to bring together opposites, meaning and non-meaning for example, actively embraces the paradox of separation. It is this irreducible position which, Sollers asserts, defines the movement of the subject towards its own death, the negative operation of inner experience. However, for Sollers, this experience cannot be properly mystical, although it is obviously related to traditional forms of Christian mysticism as an experience of silence, of wordless thought. It is the annihilation of language, and not the experience which follows this process, which counts most of all for Sollers. The significance of inner experience, the encounter with silence, is not in any real sense 'mystical' but rather a dialectical foil to discourse and reason.

Il [Bataille] admet la validité de la science et de la philosophie, mais l'espace commun, qu'il leur assigne doit être séparé sans retour de la philosophie, de la science. Il ne s'oppose pas au savoir (au contraire), mais il n'hésite pas à s'appuyer sur un 'non-savoir'. D'emblée la mise en forme extrêmement cohérente qui est la sienne prend donc le risque stratégique d'un malentendu: les accusations de 'mysticisme' et 'd'obscurantisme' ne peuvent manquer de lui être addressées.[26]

Inner experience is, then, like the 'roof', a metaphor for a perspective of high altitude which reveals a multiplicity of metaphorical systems and the impossibility of fixed meaning. Bataille's alleged 'mysticism'

---

[25] Ibid., p.107
[26] Ibid., p.110

12

is therefore, for Sollers, not a fixed state but, as it is for Foucault, only a passage towards a new theory of knowledge and discourse.

In his famous essay of 1967, 'De l'économie restreinte à l'économie générale: un hégélianisme sans réserves', Jacques Derrida presents an account of Bataille's 'mysticism' which, unlike either Foucault or Sollers, sets out to examine how Bataille's thinking corresponds to the conceptual language of Hegel. [27] Bataille's 'mysticism', for Derrida, is a metaphor which mediates the demands of the Hegelian system as an unrestricted negativity. The movement of inner experience can thus be traced as a movement beyond the Hegelian 'Aufhebung' - the term used by Hegel to describe the dialectical transition in which a lower stage is both annulled and preserved in a higher one and which is commonly translated as 'sublation'.[28] More specifically, although Bataille borrows the language of Hegel and engages with the dialectic, the possibility of the Hegelian sublation, as Derrida points out, is abolished by the self-destruction of the subject which occurs in inner experience. 'Quoi qu'il en soit, les pages qui vont suivre se situent au-delà du discours circulaire hégélien, writes Kojève in an abandoned preface for La Somme athéologique.[29]

As Derrida recognises, Bataille's version of Hegelian 'self-overcoming' or 'sublation' not only posits 'mystical' ecstatic experience as the central value of inner experience but also affirms a movement into radical negativity, 'négativité sans emploi',[30] which paralyses the movement of the dialectic. In this way, Derrida explains

---

[27] Jacques Derrida, 'De l'économie restreinte à l'économie générale: un hégélianisme sans réserves.' L'Arc, 32 (1967), pp.24-25, reprinted in L'Écriture et la différence (Paris: Éditions du Seuil, 1967) pp.369-409

[28] Ibid. p.376. A useful definition of Hegel's use of the key term 'Aufhebung', its use in The Phenomenology of Mind, and an explanation of the difficulty of its translation, can be found in Charles Taylor, Hegel (London: Cambridge University Press, 1975), p.119. See also 'Translator's introduction' and 'Translator's note', Jacques Derrida, Writing and Difference, trans. Alan Bass (Chicago: University of Chicago Press, 19780, p. xix, p. 335.

[29] 'Plans pour la somme athéologique', ŒC,VI, pp. 363.

[30] This is how Bataille describes the work of negativity in the Hegelian dialectic. In a 1937 letter to Alexandre Kojéve he writes that he sees this version of negativity as the endpoint of Hegel's discourse. 'Si l'action (le 'faire') est - comme dit Hegel -la négativité, la question se pose alors de savoir si la négativité de qui n'a 'plus rien à faire' disparaît ou subsiste à l'état de 'négativité sans emploi'. [...] Je veux bien que Hegel ait prévu cette possibilité: du moins ne l'a-t-il pas située à l'issue des processus qu'il décrit.' Georges Bataille, Choix de Lettres, ed. Michel Surya (Paris: Gallimard, 1997), pp.131-132.

inner experience as a textual experience of stasis which exceeds the logic of presence in a movement of self-annihilation which also annihilates all stable referents. Derrida describes Bataille's 'Hegelianism or anti-Hegelianism' as 'the displacement of the 'Aufhebung' and privileges the texts of *La Somme athéologique* as the locus of this displacement.

Derrida's real purpose in this essay is not however to discuss or engage with the first principles of thought and activity, that is to say the vocabulary and grammar of mysticism, which determine the content of inner experience. As Susan Rubin Suleiman has pointed out, Derrida is more concerned with the suggestion that 'transgression of rules of discourse implies the transgression of law in general, since discourse exists only by positing the norm and value of meaning, and meaning in turn is the founding element in legality.'[31] Transgression for Derrida can therefore only have significance as part of a general violation of discourse, which does not exclude mysticism, but which refuses all referents beyond the immediate experience of language and text.

Other theorists writing on Bataille in the 1960s and the 1970s also saw language as preceding experience and, from this insight, developed either theories of reading or action from Bataille's work. As in the critical readings described above, the mystical aspects of the inner experience were either dismissed or discarded as analogical or symbolic forms of language and thought with no currency beyond the allegorical value of the text. For Denis Hollier, for example, Bataille's inner experience represents a form of activity which, while not in any sense properly mystical, borrows the language of mysticism as part of a strategy which allows Bataille to resist the reductive authority of either spatial structures (this is the central theme of Hollier's book *La prise de la concorde*)[32] or symbolic dualities.

This theme is explored by Hollier in his influential article 'Le matérialisme dualiste de Georges Bataille' in which he describes how Bataille's thought is related to the dualist system of the Gnostic theologians, who emphasised the distance between opposites such as Good and Evil rather than their reconciliation.

---

[31] Susan Rubin Suleiman, op.cit., 'Transgression and the Avant-Garde', p. 316.
[32] Denis Hollier, *La prise de la concorde. Essais sur Georges Bataille* (Paris: Gallimard, 1974)

> Le Mal et le Bien ne s'opposent donc pas comme deux principes intérieurs au même monde, mais bien comme deux mondes étrangers et rivaux, quoique de leur impossible coexistence résulte entre eux une étrange complicité: monde d'une part de la raison et de la volonté, monde d'autre part de la fascination et de la séduction.[33]

It is this symbolic system, asserts Hollier, which allows Bataille to move away from the framework of dialectical thought. The significance of the inner experience within this system of thought is primarily as an assertion of separation or impossibility. However although this dualist system is, according to Hollier, related to mysticism or at least to deep religious feeling, this relation is still predicated upon a metaphorical usage of the term 'mysticism', used to signify simply the negation of thought rather than a real religious encounter.

Similarly, in her article 'Bataille, l'expérience et la pratique', given originally as a paper at the 1972 *Tel Quel* conference, Julia Kristeva finds in Bataille a constitution of non-meaning which undermines the Cartesian subject. For Kristeva, the central importance of Bataille's texts lies in the fact that their symbolic language is predicated upon a contradictory tension between the 'thetic', the controlling principle of discourse, and the 'semiotic', a heterogenous series of principles which disrupts the organizing function of the 'thetic'. Most importantly for Kristeva, the movement of inner experience is a movement backwards, or a traversal, which as the subject moves back towards itself, initiates a process of disintegration in the external world. The 'illumination' of inner experience is therefore a 'thetic' moment which introduces the subject back into the world.

> L'expérience intérieure consiste à introduire le savoir dans l'immédiateté [...] pour que le savoir traverse la vision, le spectacle, la représentation.[34]

The real significance of inner experience for Kristeva is that the collapse of the subject and the consequent paralysis of the Hegelian dialectic provide a guiding theory for rebuilding the exterior world in political action (she argues in this way, through a materialist formula, for an alignment of Bataille's inner experience and the political theory

---

[33] Denis Hollier, 'Le matérialisme dualiste de Georges Bataille', *Tel Quel*, 25 (1966), pp.44-45.

[34] Julia Kristeva, 'Bataille, l'expérience et la pratique', in *Bataille à Cerisy*, (Paris: U.G.E., coll.10/18, 1977), p. 290.

of Mao Tse-tung, then still the hero of the *Tel Quel* group).[35] It is most important for Kristeva, however, that Bataille's inner experience is a site where meaning is contested in a way which confronts conceptual thought. The 'traversal' of inner experience, argues Kristeva, can therefore only be 'mystical' in an analogous sense, mirroring the poetic logic of Christian humanism. In the same way that Christianity confused experience with discourse, thereby reducing mysticism to a pure text, the inner experience is a form of play, a 'fiction', which cannot be entirely separate from the language system which it seeks to undermine.

The critical reception of Bataille in France and elsewhere has inevitably been greatly determined by these critical readings of Bataille, published during the period in which he was 'the acknowledged hero' of *Tel Quel*.[36] Since the 1960s and 1970s, much critical writing on Bataille in the English-speaking world has indeed considered him almost exclusively in relation to those writers who established his posthumous reputation in France. In a brief survey of Bataille's legacy outside France, Fred Botting and Scott Wilson assert that Bataille's singular importance is 'in the mirror of post-structuralism.'[37] For Tony Corn, for example, this means that if there is a legacy which Bataille leaves us, it is as a thinker who marks a shift away from classical Hegelianism towards the 'post-Hegelianism' of post-modern thinking, thus prefiguring the inverted reading of Hegel which is one of the defining features of Derrida's *Glas* : 'Between "1945" and "1968",' writes Corn, '"Bataille" and "Derrida" mark decisive moments (as much chronological as logical) in the historicity of modernity's reading of Hegel.'[38]

The translation into English in 1984 of Jürgen Habermas's influential essay, 'The French Path to Postmodernity: Bataille between Eroticism and General Economics', similarly established Bataille's status as a precursor or even prophet of post-modern thought. Most importantly, Habermas reads Bataille as a thinker whose distance from

---

[35] A later analysis of inner experience as a 'traversée', which demonstrates how influential Kristeva's reading was, can be found in Bernard Sichère, 'L'écriture souveraine de Georges Bataille,' *Tel Quel*, 93 (1982), pp.58-75

[36] Patrick ffrench, op. cit., p.28

[37] Fred Botting and Scott Wilson, 'Introduction', *Bataille: A Critical Reader*, ed. Fred Botting and Scott Wilson (Oxford: Blackwell, 1997), p. 7

[38] Tony Corn, 'Unemployed Negativity (Derrida, Bataille, Hegel)' in op. cit., *On Bataille: Critical Essays*, p. 89

modernity is expressed in the way he 'oscillates between an incoherent attachment to the Hegelian project of the enlightenment, on the one hand, and an unmediated juxtaposition of scholarly analysis and mysticism, on the other.'[39]

For Habermas, mysticism signals failure, withdrawal and retreat; this is how Habermas is able to conclude that Bataille's final contribution to the development of post-modern thinking is as a writer who 'undercuts his own efforts to carry out the radical critique of reason with the tools of theory.'[40]

The prevailing view of Bataille, in France and elsewhere, as the above readings have demonstrated, is then as a thinker whose work has primarily a textual value. Few contemporary readings of Bataille have engaged with the language or content of mysticism in his writings in relation to lived experience. However, although aware of the theoretical implications and ambiguities he is exposing himself to, Bataille himself does not shy away from using the term 'experience' in discussion of 'inner experience' and nor does he hesitate to explain what he means with reference to real, lived activity. Indeed, the paradoxical relation between metaphorical language and experience, Bataille indicates, is analogous to the 'blindspot' which undermines all forms of knowledge which are limited to discursive activity rather than the lived poetic actions of vision and blindness:

> Il est dans l'entendement une tache aveugle: qui appelle la structure de l'œil. Dans l'entendement comme dans l'œil on ne peut que difficilement la déceler. Mais alors que la tache aveugle de l'œil est sans conséquence, la nature de l'entendement veut que la tache aveugle ait en lui plus de sens que l'entendement même. Dans la mesure où l'entendement est l'auxiliaire de l'action, la tache y est aussi négligeable qu'elle est dans l'œil. Mais dans la mesure où l'on envisage dans l'entendement l'homme lui-même, je veux dire une exploration du possible de l'être, la tache absorbe l'attention: ce n'est plus la tache qui se perd dans la connaissance, mais la connaissance qui se perd en elle.[41]

As this passage implies, as a close if not always faithful reader of Hegel, Bataille understood the relation between language and experience as based not on an opposition but rather, as it was for the

---

[39] Jürgen Habermas, 'The French Path to Postmodernity: Bataille between Eroticism and General Economics', trans. Frederick Lawrence, in op. cit., *Bataille: A Critical Reader*, p. 171

[40] Ibid., p.188

[41] *L'Éxpérience intérieure, ŒC*, V , p.129

Surrealists, a complicity between the self-reflective subject and symbolical and analogical forms of thinking. It is the mystical nature of the inner experience, in lived erotic feeling or meditation wherein the subject divides and collapses, which reveals this relation by undermining the possibility of any stable or mediated series of metaphorical relations. This is why Bataille refers to the limits of the Hegelian system in visceral terms as 'l'horreur de la tache aveugle'.[42] It is also for this reason that I have chosen to consider the mystical aspects of inner experience, and the writing of that experience, as the point where so many previous critical readings have encountered their 'blind spot.'

'...je n'aime pas le mot mystique':
Sartre's critique of Bataille's mysticism

It is therefore also significant to the present study that one of Bataille's earliest and severest critics was Jean-Paul Sartre whose attack on Bataille, 'Un Nouveau mystique', was first published in *Cahiers du Sud* in 1941 as a review on the publication of *L'Expérience intérieure*.[43] Although the reasons why Sartre should have launched such a sustained attack on Bataille are unclear, it is evident that Bataille reacted immediately, and with a certain amount of anger, to the piece. Indeed, although the subsequent texts of *La Somme athéologique* are not entirely conceived as a response to this piece, it is, nonetheless, true to say that Sartre's article had a direct influence on Bataille's own approach to the problem of 'mysticism' after that date.

In this article, Sartre made several accusations against Bataille, most of them concerned with the paradox of writing inner experience. Specifically, Sartre describes Bataille's inner experience as a form of mourning for God and accuses him of replacing the exigencies of existentialist thinking with a casuistry born of the religious vocabulary he parodies or appropriates.

Et l'on croirait, à lire plus d'un passage de *L'Expérience intérieure*, retrouver Stravrogine ou Ivan Karamazov - un Ivan qui aurait connu André Breton.[44]

---

[42] Ibid., p.130
[43] Jean-Paul Sartre, 'Un nouveau mystique', *Cahiers du Sud*, 260, 261, 263, (1943), pp.783-790, 866-886 and 988-994, in *Situations I*, (Paris: Gallimard, 1947), p.133-175
[44] Ibid. p.143

18

Sartre's scepticism, however, is not merely founded in his scorn for Bataille's rhetoric. The most serious charge which Sartre lays against Bataille is that inner experience, if it is concrete experience of absence, is an unreserved negativity which mitigates against the possibility of literature as it mitigates against the possibility of thought. Bataille's 'mysticism', says Sartre, is therefore no more than an artifice, in the same way that *L'Expérience intérieure* is an exercise in mourning which is a parody of the Pascalian 'essai-martyre'.[45]

In many ways, Sartre's attack on the sham or false aspects of Bataille's 'mysticism' represents a closer, or at least less partial, reading of Bataille than those which established his posthumous reputation. Still more importantly, as Bataille himself acknowledged, Sartre's attack asks many of the most important questions about the function and meaning of of inner experience.[46] Sartre does this without reference to a context framed by the authority of textual organisation or limited to the 'great irregularities of language'[47] privileged by Bataille's post-modernist critics.

In other words, the question Sartre asks, and which Bataille engages with in all of the texts of *La Somme athéologique*, is what the precise relation is between a mystical framework- either Christian or Oriental - which aims at a point of encounter with a transcendent beyond, and an experience which actively denies the possibility of transcendence. Is Bataille's inner experience merely a parody of mysticism? Or is it an experience of absence which has no other system of referents other than itself?

Sartre goes on to identify Bataille's negative theology as being placed in dialectical relation to the hierarchy it has replaced. This is how Bataille's 'mysticism', writes Sartre, is predicated upon an inverse hierarchical structure which is as inauthentic as the Hegelian idealism that it seeks to replace with the demands of inner experience.[48] It is

---

[45] Ibid. p.134

[46] 'L'opposition de Sartre m'aide à mettre l'essentiel en relief', 'Réponse à Jean-Paul Sartre', *Sur Nietzsche, ŒC*, VI, p.196.

[47] See Philippe Sollers, 'De grandes irrégularités de langage', *Critique*, 195/196, pp.795-802.

[48] Sartre explains this notion with reference to the apparent impossibility of reconciling inner experience with conceptual thinking: 'Vainement M. Bataille tente-t-il de s'intégrer à la machine qu'il a montée: il reste dehors, avec Durkheim, avec Hegel, avec Dieu le Père.' Jean-Paul Sartre, op.cit., 'Un nouveau mystique', p.154

above all to this interrogation of the substance of inner experience, 'the apparent blindspot of Bataille criticism', that this study addresses itself.

The language of transgression

Bataille describes his philosophical method as indistinguishable from eroticism. He also compares it to religious mysticism and describes it as an experience as well as a mode of thinking. Thinking is akin to eroticism and mysticism in that it is an experience which strips away layers of discourse in an elliptical movement which exceeds limits. This is the movement which Bataille himself terms 'transgression' - an excessive movement which brings together thought and experience in a moment which is both erotic and revelatory: 'Je pense comme une fille enlève sa robe. A l'extrémité, la pensée est l'impudeur, l'obscenité même'.[49]

One of the central goals of Bataille's thinking is to translate the experience of transgression into language which subverts the stable referents of philosophy. Bataille uses variously words such as 'communication', 'souveraineté', 'sacrifice' and 'nudité' to describe the experience of transgression. These terms are sometimes, but not always, interchangeable. The experience of transgression is also sometimes described as a 'blessure', which indicates that the experience of transgression is a form of auto-mutilation, a self-inflicted wound, as much as it is a revelatory experience of external reality. What each of these terms has in common is that they each give subjective accounts of transgressive experience. They are not fixed by objective criteria and are therefore able - as is the case with much Surrealist terminology - to slide into different meanings in the space of the same text, even within the space of a single page. This means that any critical reading of Bataille which, such as this thesis, seeks to engage with the problem of the relation between language and inner experience must simultaneously engage with the theoretical implications which inner experience has for a poetics of criticism.

For readers and critics of mystical authors in the Christian tradition, the central problem has been how to reconcile the authority of mystical texts, which by definition defy intellectual analysis, with the corporate authority of the Church. In the same way, the central challenge of

---

[49] *Méthode de méditation, Œuvres complètes, CEC*, V, p.200

writing about Bataille's inner experience is how to establish a critical position with regard to texts which actively seek to undermine the possibility of any fixed position or distance. Bataille's writing about inner experience, most importantly, is a radical provocation in which Bataille's own voice seeks to establish a series of fractures or points of slippage which undermine all exterior critical positions and the possibility of theoretical reading as a static, fixed perspective.

Bataille does this, first of all, by using language in a transgressive fashion to undermine the authority and value of critical language. As Bataille's own vocabulary of inner experience continually slides between meaning and silence, and is therefore subject to modification and nuance, so the language of the critic who engages with these movements cannot finally define inner experience, but only be part of a process of critical reading which works towards its possible definitions. It follows from this that the critical voice of this thesis will engage less with the narratives of interpretation which have been constructed around Bataille's texts, but rather with the subversion of the potentialities of theory as criticism, intervention or description which inner experience demands.

The relation between this thesis and the literary object it seeks to describe is defined by a necessary complicity with the demands of inner experience, rather than the establishment of a static critical position which would be dissolved or undermined by those exigencies. A primary example of this is represented by the obvious difficulty in fixing the relation between metaphorical terms used by Bataille, such as 'sacrifice', 'blessure', 'lacération' and 'cicatrice', and 'real' experience, that is to say experience which is felt and lived before it is codified in language. More specifically, Bataille uses these metaphorical terms to describe an experience which, because it is beyond discourse, establishes a limit to the multiplicity of meanings and their free play which is a defining characteristic of metaphorical language. This paradox is not resolved in Bataille's writings because, at least in one sense, the inner experience is itself a process which emerges from the dynamic tension which Bataille establishes in the text between meaning and non-meaning in thought and language. For Bataille, the 'real' experience which precedes the discourse of inner experience functions in an equal and equivalent manner: its purpose is to destabilise the possibility of a metaphorical language which might provide an organising pattern for inner experience at a textual level.

Ces enoncés ont une obscure apparence théorique et je n'y vois aucun remède sinon de dire: 'il en faut saisir le sens du dedans'. Ils ne sont pas démontrables logiquement. Il faut *vivre* l'expérience, elle n'est pas accessible aisément et même, considérée du dehors par l'intelligence, il y faudrait voir une somme d'opérations distinctes, les unes intellectuelles, d'autres esthétiques, d'autres enfin morales et tout le problème à reprendre. Ce n'est que du dedans, vécue jusqu'à la transe, qu'elle apparaît unissant ce que la pensée discursive doit séparer. Mais elle n'unit pas moins que ces formes - esthétiques, intellectuelles, morales - les contenus divers de l'expérience passée (comme Dieu et sa Passion) dans une fusion ne laissant dehors que le discours par lequel on tenta de séparer ces objets (faisant d'eux des réponses aux difficultés de la morale).[50]

The paradox of the relation of metaphorical terms to real experience is made even more 'impossible' by the fact the experience of trangression which Bataille undergoes in inner experience is not common experience but is 'erotic'. It is also related to traditional forms of mysticism in that it is 'ineffable' 'ecstatic' experience. It is therefore experience which defies reduction to language. The vocabulary which Bataille uses to trace this experience is, accordingly, language which cannot be wholly articulated or interpreted in textual terms. Bataille's poetry, it follows from this, is pared down to indicate all that is lacking in the texts of inner experience. Like the mystics who operate within a traditional religious framework, or indeed the Surrealists, Bataille seeks to endow or imbue his language with a quality which stands outside categorical discourse and which, like the living principle of poetry cherished by the Surrealists, has a religious meaning and context. Words such as 'sacrifice', 'blessure', and other terms which Bataille uses to transcribe the inner experience therefore necessarily function in part as metaphors (that they do so is a paradox as irreducible as it is inescapable). They also, within the framework of inner experience, have the status of liturgical language or prayer, that is to say language which escapes or exceeds a purely textual interpretation. This is how the vocabulary of transgression takes on the form of poetic experience and therefore takes on, in Bataille's terms, religious significance.

Si nous vivons sans contester sous la loi du langage, ces états sont en nous comme s'ils n'étaient pas. Mais si, contre cette loi, nous nous heurtons, nous pouvons au passage arrêter sur l'un d'eux la conscience et, faisant taire en nous le discours, nous attarder à la surprise qu'il nous donne.[51]

---

[50] *L'Éxpérience intérieure, ŒC,* V, pp.20-21
[51] Ibid., p.27

In the same way as the vocabulary of inner experience is subject to indeterminate meaning, Bataille's texts move uneasily between genres, ranging variously over essays, poetry and fiction in a way which demonstrates a profound suspicion of writing as a process. For those who have read Bataille through the prism of post-modernism this is how the defining feature of Bataille's work seems to be a movement between and displacement of literature and philosophy and it is these aspects of Bataille's work which have often been compared to the post-modernist urge to open up a space in which no one discourse can be privileged over another. This reading of Bataille has meant that in recent times, Bataille has been described not merely as a precursor of present conditions, but also as an active participant - albeit in a posthumous fashion - in contemporary debate. This is how, more precisely, his thinking, it was originally claimed by Foucault, Sollers and Derrida, not only presages present conditions but actively engages with the challenges set by the post-modernist interrogation of subjectivity.[52]

But although it is undoubtedly true that, as described above, Bataille has made a significant contribution to contemporary thought, this does not necessarily mean, however, that Bataille's work belongs exclusively to the present age anymore than it belongs to those who have contributed to his current high prestige. Bataille writes about many subjects and themes - from economics to religious mysticism, from political science to poetry - and is often described as a 'difficult' writer because his thinking deliberately embraces ambiguities and ellipses at the margins of these topics.

By seeking to establish a proximity to Bataille's own voice, this thesis will show that, although it is true that Bataille is deliberately unsystematic - and indeed sometimes obscure - to the point where he will admit to himself and to the reader that his text has no real point of

---

[52] It follows from these readings that Bataille is described by Jean-Michel Besnier as having 'fonction d'emblème' for thinkers such as Sollers or Derrida (Jean-Michel Besnier, *La politique de l'impossible, L'intellectuel entre révolte et engagement*, Paris: Armillaire, La Découverte, 1988, p.22). See also Jacques Derrida, op.cit., 'De l'économie restreinte à l'économie générale: un hégélianisme sans réserves', pp.369-409. Also Philippe Sollers, op. cit., 'Le toit', pp.104-138, and 'Une prophétie de Bataille', *La Guerre du Goût*, (Paris: Gallimard, 1997), pp. 480-482. See also Jean-Luc Nancy, 'La communauté désœuvrée', *Aléa*, 41 (1983), pp.11-49. This essay was later published in extended form as *La Communauté désœuvrée* (Paris: Bourgeois, 1986)

arrival, his work, nonetheless, exists as an organic whole which cannot be broken down into fragments of discourse. When Bataille discusses the psychological structure of Fascism, the use-value of the Marquis de Sade, inner experience, a theory of religion or Communism, there is a common thread which, although it is often difficult to discern, works through these texts holding them together and, most importantly, connecting ideas which are sometimes so diffuse or paradoxical as to seem entirely unintelligible.

Most significantly, if Bataille's thought is not always consistent it is, however, always made coherent by an aggressively anti-idealist philosophy which refuses all attempts at reduction or simplification. If this anti-idealism does not always shape his final position, it nonetheless determines Bataille's approach to philosophy from his earliest texts onwards. This means that his approach to problems of ethics, morality or rationalism is founded in real conceptual thinking. This a fact which evidently places Bataille at some remove distance from those post-modernist critics who have considered his work as merely a textual drama. And that is why the present study, therefore, will consider Bataille's thought as a dynamic movement whose 'difficulties', although they are founded on negative principles, are nonetheless, a direct engagement with the essential problems of existence. It is, most importantly, in this way that the experience of 'transgression', as well as the transgressive use of language which is related to that experience, comes to have a religious context and meaning for Bataille.

Atheology

Inner experience, as Bataille describes it, is an experience which eludes all categorical possibilities and is radically opposed to all forms of transcendence. But, at the same time, as a process, it separates the subject from the object in a movement which is akin to the religious ecstasy fundamental to mystical experience. Furthermore, although Bataille describes inner experience as a contradiction of the traditional meaning and function of the word mysticism, he nonetheless persists in defining inner experience with reference to Christian mystics such as Dionysius the Areopagite, Blessed Angela of Foligno, St. John of the Cross, and St. Teresa of Avila, or with regard to esoteric religions or practices such as Hinduism, Buddhism, Yoga or Tantrism.

In the same way Bataille conceived of the project of *La Somme athéologique* as an 'a-theological' version of St. Thomas Aquinas's *Summa Theologiæ*. In the *Summa*, which is considered by many to be the major contribution of Medieval philosophy to modern thought,[53] Aquinas sought to reconcile faith and reason by placing philosophical speculation alongside a belief in the Divine origin of the world and by arguing, with a dialectical method he inherited from Aristotle, that the human and the Divine although distinct were not separate.[54] In the texts of *La Somme athéologique*, Bataille asks the question: how is it possible to be religious and an atheist? This, says Bataille, is a contradiction which cannot be resolved. However, in imitation of Aquinas, Bataille posits the relation between man and the dead God as a contradiction which cannot be separated from its dialectical function in his thought. At the centre of this contradiction is the negative principle that inner experience is a form of communication with the dead God. 'Le parti pris de l'athéologie', Bataille writes, '[...] place la pensée devant le pire et le meilleur qu'est Dieu, mais du même fait devant l'absence de Dieu.'[55]

Although *La Somme athéologique* was unfinished, it is still possible to follow and respect Bataille's intentions for each volume. These fragmented texts, are in chronological order of publication: *L'Expérience intérieure* (1943), *Méthode de méditation* (1947), *Le Coupable* (1944), *L'Alléluiah* (1947), and *Sur Nietzsche* (1945). The chronology of their publication does not in all cases, however, match the chronology of their composition. Nor does the published version of each text correspond to the role Bataille had assigned it in his various plans for the finished *La Somme athéologique* - although the project was abandoned as incomplete, Bataille was still drawing up draft plans for publication as late as 1961. In the present book, however, each text will be considered as part of a totality - together with published and unpublished notes and addenda - because this is how Bataille how conceived of them.

More particularly, in reading these texts in this way, I will trace how these texts interact with the outer world of politics, social

---

[53] See Evelyn Underhill, op. cit., pp. 99, 111, 117, 190

[54] See St.Thomas Aquinas, 'What God is not', *Summa Theologiæ*, edited and translated by Timothy McDermott (Texas: Christian Classics, 1989), pp, 9-33. See also Frederick Copleston, 'Mediaeval Philosophy', part 1, in *A History of Philosophy*, vol 2 (Doubleday: New York, 1962), pp. 55-96.

[55] See *ŒC*, VI, pp.365-374.

relations and externalised discourse which Bataille sets up as the antipodes of inner experience. It will be further argued that the 'mystical' texts Bataille wrote during this period, whether critical, fictional, or poetic, like those of the Surrealists or Sade, are intended primarily as an interrogation of those conditions and an encounter with poetic experience. In the same way, although Bataille says that he has an aversion to the word 'mysticism' in its traditional sense, he is equally emphatic that this experience, which is a direct experience of absence, is predicated upon its dialectical relationship to traditional mystical experience. This is how inner experience becomes a 'religious' contradiction of philosophy.[56] It is is from this starting point that I will develop the central argument of the present study: that the inner experience of limits in Bataille's work, the movement which he terms 'transgression', is, unlike the textual dramas cherished by post-modernist critics, a non-metaphorical, even visceral event.

The encounter with Hegel

It is also of central importance to the present study that Bataille's intellectual itinerary traverses the period when the the avant-garde, in politics as in art, asserted itself as the redemptory force in the history of human affairs. Bataille's key ideas and central themes were thus shaped by a series of encounters with movements, writers or thinkers who had in common a belief in a radical interrogation of politics, art and metaphysics. Above all, in each of these encounters, Bataille demonstrated a preoccupation with the reintegration of religious values, and in particular direct experience of the sacred, into a social sphere which had lost all sense of transcendent purpose. In this way, his political ideas reflected a concern with the religious function of the collective unconscious. It is also clear that his later writings on economics have their origins in a parallel ambition to move the Marxist dialectic beyond its direct application to theory of surplus value and the alienation of labour.

---

[56] 'En dernier lieu je montrerai l'expérience intérieure liée à la nécessité, pour l'esprit, de tout mettre en question - sans trêve ni repos concevables. Cette nécessité s'est fait jour en dépit des présuppositions religieuses.' 'Notes pour L'Expérience intérieure', *ŒC*, V, p. 427

Bataille first emerged as a writer and thinker against the background of the Surrealist adventure in Paris. In his work for *Documents*, and then through the course of the 1930s, Bataille not only frequented circles associated with Surrealism but actively collaborated on projects with those close, or at least who had been close to Breton, such as Robert Desnos and, most importantly, André Masson. Moreover, aside from the apocryphal details of the fractious relationship between Breton and Bataille, it is significant that the origins of their rivalry lay in a fundamental disagreement over the meaning and function of poetic language. However, aside from the Surrealists, from the beginning of the 1930s onwards, Bataille also engaged with a variety of Left-wing circles engaged in the business of revolutionary politics. These ranged from the pro-Soviet group around Boris Souvarine and the 'Cercle communiste Marx-Lénine', to the 'groupe de réflexion spiritualiste', 'Ordre Nouveau', founded by Bataille's colleague at the Bibliothèque Nationale, Arnaud Dandieu - to whose journal, *La Révolution nécessaire*, Bataille contributed an anonymous collaborative article.[57] Bataille's final political position in the 1930s, however, developed separately from that of the groups he passed through. Like the anguished Tropmann, who in the novel *Le Bleu du Ciel* privileges his own suffering as a sole authentic value, by 1939, on the eve of war, Bataille had long since abandoned the utopian promise of the Marxist dialectic in favour of an interior experience.

The development of this position was partly determined by Bataille's encounter with the famous lectures on Hegel given by Alexandre Kojève at the Ecole des Hautes-Etudes between 1933 and 1939. In these lectures, Bataille, who had started reading Hegel at roughly the same time as the Surrealists, that is to say in the mid-1920s, found a version of Hegel which established him as a paradoxical, even violent thinker, who, like Sade, far from representing the 'monument of rationalism' and the avatar of Enlightment rigour, opposed cultural order in the name of 'sovereign' need and described history as a series of convulsions ordered, in equal measure, by the dialectical process of civilization and the paroxystic imperatives of desire. Most importantly, Kojève took as his starting point the

---

[57] Accounts of Bataille's relations with Arnand Dandieu are given in Michel Surya, *Georges Bataille, La Mort à l'œuvre* (Gallimard, 1987), p. 214, p.324, p. 456 (hereafter referred to as Surya), and Pierre Prévost, *Pierre Prévost rencontre Georges Bataille* (Jean-Michel Place, 1987), pp. 11-14.

distinction which Hegel makes in *Phenemonology of Spirit* between ego and substance. This distinction is for Hegel an 'inner distinction', 'negativity in general', which annihilates all other attempts to rebuild the movement of the dialectic.[58] Hegel also uses the term 'representation' ('Vorstellung') to describe 'transparent thought', that it is to say thought which is not based on clear concepts but images. Such thought is opposed to thinking. For Bataille, most importantly, the 'Vorstellung' is a mode of thought which is essentially religious. It represents, in this sense, a form of mysticism which functions as a contaminating force in the Hegelian body of thought.

These were the central ideas which, along with a refiguration of Surrealist principles, influenced Bataille's political and literary activities in the 1930s, from the secret society and journal *Acéphale* to the discussion group the 'Collège de Sociologie', and which shaped the direction of his movements between a series of eclectic collaborations with other journals and societies. In each of these projects Bataille's declared ambition was to reintroduce into French thought, via Kojève, a Hegelian vocabulary - negativity, alienation, sovereignty, sacrifice - without ever giving in to the demands of the Hegelian system.

Bataille's own iniatives, however, were not, at least on any practical level, a success. Although he founded both the secret society and the journal *Acéphale* to investigate the limits of experience in politics and religion, both ventures ended with Bataille as the sole driving force and participant. Similarly, Bataille's most notable political effort, his collaboration with Breton on the anti-Fascist project of *Contre-Attaque*, was characterised by personal rivalry and suspicion and consequently collapsed into recrimination and accusations made against Bataille of Fascist sympathies.[59] Given the political conditions in Europe in the late 1930s, it is hardly surprising that Bataille, who in the pages of *Acéphale* demonstrated an uncompromising admiration for Nietzsche and who argued for a sociology based on sacrifice and poetry found himself, at the outbreak of the Second World War, politically and philosophically isolated.

---

[58] Georg Wilhelm Friedrich Hegel, *Phenomenology of Spirit*, trans. A.V Miller (Oxford and New York: Oxford University Press, 1977), p.89
[59] See Robert Stuart Short, 'Contre-Attaque', in *Entretiens sur le surréalisme*, ed. Ferdinand Alquié (Paris, La Haye, Mouton, 1968), pp.144-175.

'Le point suprême':
Surrealism, mysticism and inner experience

The first two chapters of this study will argue first of all that Bataille is closer to the Surrealist generation than many of his post-modernist critics have allowed. Indeed, despite the overt antipathy famously shown to Bataille by André Breton in the *Second Manifeste du surréalisme*, Bataille, by his own admission, had often felt the need to define his ideas in relation to Surrealism and, if he was not actually close to those, such as Breton or Louis Aragon, who were setting the agenda for the Surrealist revolution, it is clear that he was nonetheless affiliated to the spirit of the movement. Indeed, far from being an enemy of Surrealism, as many of his recent critics have suggested, Bataille entirely shares the Surrealist ambition to restore myth as a central social value.[60] This determines his sociology as well as his attack on rational systems of thought. If Bataille's attitude to Surrealism in the course of the 1920s and 1930s was sceptical, this was not because he considered surrealism to be antipathetic to his own ideas but because he felt that Surrealist activity was, rather, a form of antithesis which, as he described it, stood in dialectical relation to his work: Bataille describes this relation as 'cette sorte de fumure qui nourrit une vérité toujours secrète.'[61]

In particular, the two opening chapters of this thesis will examine the language that Bataille uses to describe inner experience and its relation to Surrealist notions of transcendent poetic experience. As described above, Bataille in his exposition of inner experience draws

---

[60] Breton famously accused Bataille of being an 'obsédé' as well as 'malhonnête et pathologique' (See André Breton, 'Second Manifeste du Surréalisme', *Manifestes du Surréalisme*, Paris: Jean Jacques Pauvert, 1962, pp.215- 221) The reason for this was mainly because Breton feared that Bataille was setting up a rival group around the journal *Documents*. According to Michel Leiris the hostility between Breton and Bataille was based on personal animosity which dated from their first meeting in 1926 . Michel Leiris, *A Propos de Georges Bataille* (Paris: Fourbis, 1988, pp. 24-26). See also op. cit., Surya (Gallimard, 1987), pp.104-106, p.630.

[61] This is how Bataille announces the 1951 series of essays on Surrealism, *Le surréalisme au jour le jour*, (*ŒC*, VIII, p.169). This text was never published in Bataille's lifetime but, aside from some acerbic comments on Aragon and Breton, it is a broadly sympathetic appraisal of the movement's ambitions. For an account of Bataille's relations with the surrealists in the late 1940s see also Jean Wahl, in op. cit. *Entretiens sur le surréalisme,* ed. Ferdinand Alquié, pp.167-168 and Michael Richardson's introduction to Georges Bataille, *The Absence of Myth: Writings on Surrealism* (London: Verso, 1994), pp. 1-27.

upon the language of the Christian mystics and the methods of Eastern mysticism. However, his descriptions of 'mystical' states are couched in terms which are directly related to Breton's statement in the *Second Manifeste du surréalisme* of 1929 which describes how an individual, through the unconscious revealed in language, is enabled to fuse with the hidden nature of the cosmos in a form of mystic communion. This famous statement is itself drawn from the language of mysticism and Hermeticism.

> Tout porte à croire qu'il existe un certain point de l'esprit d'où la vie et la mort, le réel et l'imaginaire, le passé et le futur, le communicable et l'incommunicable, le haut et le bas cessent d'être perçus contradictoirement. Or, c'est en vain qu'on chercherait à l'activité surréaliste un autre mobile que l'espoir de détermination de ce point. [62]

Bataille often referred to this statement and, in many ways, it is a touchstone for many of the ideas which he develops in *La Somme athéologique* on the relation between language, experience and communication. The corollary of this, it will be argued in chapters three and four, is that Bataille's inner experience is predicated upon an inverse representation of the Surrealist notion that poetic activity is linked to the primal unity of the unconscious.

More particularly, for Bataille, the inner experience not only demonstrates the limits of metaphor as an expressive form of language but also the primacy of experience over the logic of linear or hierarchical thinking. The central movement of inner experience is, therefore, in Bataille's own terms, both a negation of action and a negation of itself.

In chapter three, this notion will be considered in relation to the early novels of Maurice Blanchot, *Thomas l'Obscur* and *Aminadab*,

---

[62] André Breton, *Œuvres Complètes*, tome 1 (Paris: Gallimard, 1988), p.781. This statement was obviously influenced by the famous sentence from the alchemical formula of Hermes Trismegistus, the 'Tabula Smaragdina', or 'Emerald Table' - 'What is below is like what is on high and what is high is like what is below, in order to bring about the miracle of a single thing' (trans. in E.J. Holmyard, *Alchemy*, London: Penguin, 1957), p. 97. Breton first refers to this sentence in some notes from the period 1920-1921 (see his op.cit, *Œuvres Complètes*, tome 1, p.617); he also cited it, terming it a dialectical principle when discussing the painting of André Masson in *Genèse et perspective artistiques du surréalisme* in 1941, reprinted in Breton, *Le Surréalisme et la peinture* (Paris: Gallimard, 1965), p.68. See also Andrew Hussey and Jeremy Stubbs, 'Tempête de Flammes: Surrealism, Bataille and the perennial philosophy of Heraclitus', 'Kojève's Paris/Now Bataille', *parallax, 4*, pp.151-167.

which were written at the time and partly as a result of, conversations between Blanchot and Bataille on the significance of inner experience. For both Bataille and Blanchot, inner experience is an 'expérience nue' which is a direct contradiction of the Surrealist belief in poetry as universal communication. This is not to say, however, that either Blanchot or Bataille disregard the Surrealist ambition to reconcile opposites. Rather, inner experience reveals that the textual reality is not distinct from metaphysical reality; this is, however, a negative rather than a positive movement.[63]

The negative movement of inner experience is also related to the Surrealist belief in the logic of contradiction which, as noted above, Breton also famously defined in the *Second manifeste du surréalisme* and which, invoking Heraclitus, he saw as the living principle of the universe. Indeed, for Bataille, the relationship between inner experience and the outer world is conceived in similar Heraclitean terms as a practical form of poetic activity in which 'Latent structure is the master of obvious structure.'[64] It is significant, therefore, that during the period that Bataille was planning and writing *La Somme athéologique*, he also wrote poetry as well as developing a theory of poetic experience .

Bataille's poetry is one of the most puzzling aspects of his work and has often been ignored or overlooked by critics who are unsure of its real status or significance. Chapter four will, therefore, consider the meaning of Bataille's ideas on the representation of the poetic image. These ideas are defined in *L'Expérience intérieure* with direct reference to Proust's Albertine and, in a more occluded fashion, throughout all of the texts of *La Somme athéologique*, with reference to Colette Peignot, Bataille's lover and collaborator who died in 1938 and whose death precipitated the crisis in Bataille's life which led directly to the writing of *L'Expérience intérieure*.

The poetry of inner experience, it will be argued, dramatises the death of the author, the thinking subject, in a literal experience which transgresses the textual surface of the poem. In the poetry of William Blake, Bataille saw a parallel movement into 'vision', or pure

---

[63] The point of connection between textual reality and metaphysical reality is also necessarily decribed in *L'Expérience intérieure* as 'échec'. 'J'échoue, quoi que j'écrive, en ceci que je devrais lier, à la précision du sens, la richesse infinie - insensée - des possibles', *L'Expérience intérieure, ŒC*, V, p.51

[64] Heraclitus, 'Fragment 54', quoted in Edward Hussey, *The Presocratics* (London: Duckworth, 1972), p. 35

subjectivity; Bataille's poetry, it will be argued, is an inverse form of Blake's 'Poetic Genius' who asserts the universe as his own centre.[65] This is how the poetry of inner experience, as a form of a-theological prayer, assumes the same 'religious' significance as the experience itself.

Like the Surrealists, from the beginning of his writing life Bataille had been concerned with expressing experiences which were either taboo or which defied expression at all and relating these impossibilites to collective, social space. He had come to writing after receiving psychoanalytic treatment from Dr. Adrien Borel and, although it would be a gross simplification to say that Bataille's work originates in the therapy administered by Borel, by Bataille's own admission, his work is determined by the 'obsessions' which led him to undertake treatment.[66]

These obsessions are represented in the form of allegories of sexual and religious transgression, most evident in his early fictions such as W.C. (later destroyed, although its opening chapter has been preserved in the first chapter of Le Bleu du Ciel), L'Histoire de l'œil (1928) and, then later, Madame Edwarda (1941), as well as early essays such as 'L'Anus solaire' (1927). Similarly, Bataille's work as editor and critic, firstly for Documents and then for the anti-Stalinist Marxist journal, La Critique Sociale, is characterised by a matrix of emotional responses to transgressive experiences which defy organization in the name of orgiastic liberation.

In chapter five these emotional responses are tested against the political context of Bataille's writings, and in particular his apprehénsion of the coming of the Second World War. In an autobiographical note, Bataille describes the writing of Le Coupable - a text in which he brings together the interior vision of mysticism and the agony of a Europe in flames - as 'une expérience mystique hétérodoxe'.[67] This chapter will consider how this experience exists, as one commentator puts it in a description of Bataille's relation to the

---

[65] Bataille makes frequent reference to Blake and, in particular, Blake's notion of 'Poetic genius'. The most extended discussion of this aspect of Blake's thought is to be found in the essay 'William Blake' in Georges Bataille, La littérature et le mal (Gallimard, 1957), pp. 84-101.

[66] A detailed discussion of Bataille's relationship with Borel and psychoanalysis can be found in Elisabeth Roudinesco, 'Bataille entre Freud et Lacan: Une expérience cachée', in, op. cit. Georges Bataille après tout, pp.191-212

[67] ŒC, VII, p. 462

work of Jean Fautrier, in 'a terrible and erotic universe' which parallels the experience of war.[68] Inner experience is both 'unformed chaos' and 'mystic despair': it is also a form of communication, or mediation, between subjective and objective realities.[69] In the same way, this chapter will argue, war is the highest form of irrational desire and is, therefore, a mirror image of the interior apocalypse of inner experience.

In chapter six, this collision between the inner and outer world, the interior world of radical alterity and the outer world of objective presence, is considered as a crucial defining factor in the development of the key Bataillien notion of 'souveraineté'. This is a term which Bataille alternatively uses to denote the disentanglement of the subject from the Hegelian dialectic of the master and slave, or to denote an assertion of freedom in the face of Divine absence. However, the 'sovereign' in Bataille's terminology is also often applied to erotic excess as a sacred experience of limits. In this chapter, I will argue that not only is eroticism central to Bataille's philosophical method - as Bataille himself pointed out (see p.19) - but that eroticism is itself a form of 'mysticism'.

This is how erotic experience can give substance to the 'mystical' encounter with Divine absence that Bataille posits as the central point of *La Somme athéologique*. It will therefore be argued that this is how inner experience - a 'mysticism' which contradicts the Surrealist notion of transcendence - functions as the defining paradox of George Bataille's thought.

'The enemy within'

As Breton pointed out, however, one of the principle reasons for Bataille's isolation in the late 1930s was that his relation to politics, as it was to Surrealism, was essentially parodic.[70] In the first instance, this meant that Surrealism, for Bataille, represents the pursuit of an ideal, the *Sur*real, which lies above and beyond language. The inevitable

---

[68] Sarah Wilson, 'Fêting the wound', in *Bataille: Writing the Sacred*, ed. Carolyn Bailey Gill (London: Routledge, 1995), pp.172-187.

[69] *ŒC*,VII, p. 462

[70] This, indeed, is the central thrust of Breton's argument in his famous attack on Bataille's anti-idealism in the 'Second manifeste du surréalisme'. See André Breton, op.cit, 'Second Manifeste du Surréalisme', *Manifestes du Surréalisme* (Paris: Jean Jacques Pauvert, 1962) pp.215- 221.

failure of Surrealism, for Bataille, is, therefore, inherent in its ambitions and the manner in which it is predicated upon the belief that poetic activity is the pursuit of a reconcilation of opposites which lies in a transcendent solution.[71]

For Bataille, on the other hand, the inner experience, which he describes as the first principle of knowledge or non-knowledge, is both irreducible and actively prohibits the generation of abstract or transcendent theories. In a secondary sense, therefore, a political conception of the world is also 'parodic' in the the same way. Bataille defines 'parody' as the inevitable result of the failure of language to carry any stable meaning. The Bataillien universe, therefore, is predicated upon a notion of parody or failure, 'échec', in which no true connection can ever be made between the contradictory forces of the dialectical process.[72]

For Bataille, therefore, the Surrealist notion of analogical thinking as revealing myriad hidden relationships was inseparable from the Medieval conception of the universe as a hierarchy of being. It was also equally devoid of any real content. Thus, although it is true, for example, that many of Bataille's themes are drawn together in a series of recurrent images - the sun, the eye, blindness, self-mutilation - which can be traced back to his earliest writings and which function as consistent metaphorical and metonymic patterns in his work, these key images are equally destabilised by the fact that, because God is dead, it is not possible to determine any linear form of meaning, either allegorically - that is to say, in the space of the text - or in terms of experience -that is to say in terms of religion or philosophy.

The logic of contradiction was something that Surrealism had come to associate with the unconscious through psychoanalysis. But Breton, differing from Freud and following Heraclitus, went so far as to see contradiction as the principle of the universe. It was by bringing together opposites and things normally unrelated to each other that the mind participated in the unceasing strife which drove the cosmos on.[73]

---

[71] Bataille discusses this notion most efectively in the fragment 'Surréalisme et transcendance', *Sur Nietzsche*, *ŒC*, V, p.205

[72] This fundamental principle is defined in by Bataille in the early essay 'L'Anus solaire': ' Il est clair que le monde est purement parodique, c'est à dire que chaque chose qu'on regarde est la parodie d'une autre, ou encore la même chose sous une forme décevante'. *ŒC*, I, p. 81

[73] Andrew Hussey and Jeremy Stubbs, op.cit., 'Tempête de Flammes: Surrealism, Bataille and the perennial philosophy of Heraclitus', pp.157-158

For Bataille, the 'parodic' nature of the universe did not so much bring opposites together, but emphasise their difference and reveal the essential discontinuity of language and experience.

> Depuis que les phrases circulent dans les cerveaux occupés à réflechir, il a été procédé à une identification totale, puisque à l'aide d'un copule chaque phrase relie une chose à l'autre; et tout serait visiblement lié si l'on découvrait d'un seul regard dans sa totalité le tracé laissé par un fil d'Ariane, conduisant la pensée dans son propre labyrinthe.
>
> [...] Le Soleil aime exclusivement la Nuit et dirige vers la terre sa violence lumineuse, verge ignoble, mais il se trouve dans l'incapacité d'atteindre le regard ou la nuit bien que les étendues terrestres nocturnes se dirigent continuellement vers l'immondice du rayon solaire.
>
> L'anneau solaire est l'anus intact de son corps à dix-huit ans auquel rien d'aussi aveuglant ne peut être comparé à l'exception du soleil, bien que l'anus soit la nuit.[74]

If the world is parodic, it also follows that the relationship between words and their meaning is also one of slippage and discontinuity rather than a fixed set of stable referents. The movement between opposites, the sun into night, is the central shift or displacement which occurs in the inner experience.

The movement between meaning and non-meaning, light and shade, however, is clearly not properly 'mystical' in the traditional sense of the word, and Bataille, in the opening section of L'Expérience intérieure writes that he not only opposes 'mysticism' but that inner experience is its polar opposite. However, in the same space Bataille moves to a discussion of St. John of the Cross and St. Teresa of Avila, arguing that although the content of Christianity may be lost, the framework which shapes faith and experience remains intact.

It will be one of the central arguments of this book that Bataille's relation to Surrealism is conceived in the same manner and that inner experience, although separate from the Hegelianism of the Surrealists, emerges from a parallel concern with the function of non-metaphorical experience.

Nonetheless, it is clear that it is not enough to emphasise the differences between Bataille and the Surrealists, but that, in many ways, as noted by Breton, the distinguishing features of the Bataillien mode of thinking are unrecognisable to the Surrealist.

---

[74] 'L'Anus solaire', ŒC, I, pp. 81-86.

Nous sommes de toute évidence dans un autre champ que celui constitué par le surréalisme. Breton (et que dire d'Eluard, d'Aragon, etc?), littéralement englué dans une fétichisation incessante, en reste à une poésie conservée, dont le surréalisme tout entier offre une sorte de résumé saisissant; il n'accomplit la poésie que dans son reflux (poésie comme 'échappatoire', comme 'issue'), dans sa réussite, non dans son échec, par où passe précisément le dépassement non-verbal du monde, dans la pratique réelle.[75]

Bataille's language is indeed, as Houdebine points out, language which conceives of itself as 'échec': it actively works against itself as it parodies and ultimately fails to carry the meaning of experience. Most significantly, for Bataille, this means that the language he uses to describe inner experience is undermined by both this parodic relation with meaning and by its exposure to the unstable universe of the heterogeneous - a term Bataille first uses positively (in the 1930s) and then negatively (in the 1940s) to describe essential discontinuity.[76] With the quotation from Nietzsche, 'La nuit est aussi un soleil,' Bataille announces the essential movement of inner experience; the shift from night into sun is a metaphor for the reversal of the subject into its own blinding self-reflection in which the self collapses and disintegrates.

The present study will argue that Bataille's inner experience, is, therefore, not only the point at which Bataille's thinking is entirely separate from Surrealism, but also the point at which the pursuit of radical subjectivity, the atheological system embraced by Bataille, becomes a renunciation of poetic ambiguity, as it is understood by the Surrealists, and the opening into the wound of the failure of the project of idealism.

In the first volume of Bataille's collected works - making the point that, in death, Bataille's works assume a totality which they did not have during his lifetime - Michel Foucault writes emphatically that 'Bataille est un des écrivains les plus importants de son siècle'.[77] However, like Nietzsche in *Daybreak*, who describes his work as mediating between necessity and chance, Bataille saw his writings as 'Untimely Meditations' in the sense that they defy all categorical systems of thinking but also collapse the distinction between temporal and infinite into an unresolvable contradiction.

---

[75] Jean-Louis Houdebine, 'L'ennemi du dedans', *Tel Quel*, 52 (1972) pp. 72-73.
[76] See, for example, 'La structure psychologique du fascisme', *ŒC*, I, pp.339.
[77] *ŒC*, I, p. 1

Inner experience is such a contradiction and this is how it comes to represent the the fundamental experience of irreligion or atheology. Bataille defines inner experience, thus, in conceptual terms:

L'expérience est la mise en question (à l'épreuve), dans la fièvre et l'angoisse, de ce qu'un homme sait du fait d'être. Que dans cette fièvre il ait quelque appréhension que ce soit, il ne peut dire: 'j'ai vu ceci, ce que j'ai vu est tel'; il ne peut dire: j'ai vu Dieu, l'absolu ou le fond des mondes', il ne peut dire que 'ce que j'ai vu échappe à l'entendement', et Dieu, l'absolu, le fond des mondes, ne sont rien s'ils ne sont des catégories de l'entendement.[78]

The purpose of this study, therefore, is not to seek any final argument which would fix inner experience as either a method or process which has a definite and immovable status in Bataille's thinking. Rather the book will present a series of commentaries on aspects of Bataille's writing which are most closely linked to the demands of inner experience. The aim is, therefore, to establish a complicity between the reader and the texts under discussion in a way that is faithful to Bataille's own notion that 'La littérature n'est pas innocente, et, coupable, devait à la fin s'avouer telle.'[79]

Bataille continues, in the same space, that 'L'action seule a les droits'. The writing of inner experience is an action which commands the same intensity as confessional religious experience. Furthermore, the confessional writing of inner experience is often described by Bataille as the opening of a wound. Michel Leiris' description of confessional writing as 'une tauromachie' can, therefore, be applied equally well to the 'mystical' writings of George Bataille.[80] There is, however, one singular difference: that in the process of vertiginous reversal - 'le vertige dionysiaque' which Leiris says is the central motif of Bataille's work[81] - which occurs reading Bataille's description of the inner experience, it is also the reader and the critic who finds himself confronted by Bataille.

---

[78] L'Expérience intérieure Œ C,V, p. 16

[79] La littérature et le mal (Paris: Gallimard, 1957), p. 8

[80] Michel Leiris, L'Age d'homme (Paris: Gallimard, 1988), p. 22

[81] Michel Leiris, A propos de Georges Bataille (Paris: Fourbis, 1988), p.40

Chapter One

'The Pathless Path':
Christian influences on the language
and process of inner experience

> I pray God that he may quit me of God
> Meister Eckhart, *Sermons*

The fact that the title of *La Somme athéologique* is borrowed from Aquinas' *Summa Theologiae* indicates how Bataille, although working beyond Christianity, still centres his language and thinking on the Western tradition. Similarly, although inner experience may borrow from the language of Christian mysticism, and in this sense parody it, Bataille still remains faithful to the distinction which Aquinas makes between direct experience of God and writing about this experience.[1]

More specifically, in the same way that Aquinas sought to construct the argument for existence of God in his *Summa* out of the separation of theology and philosophy, this chapter will examine the proposition that Bataille's inner experience is based on a process which offers a radical interrogation of the relationship between philosophy and atheology in religious terms as well as those of discursive thought.

It is the relationship between philosophy and atheology which is revealed in the movement of inner experience. In this sense, inner experience plays the same role as mysticism in Aquinas' *Summa*: mysticism is thus the central fact of a system which affirms that experience has a higher value than knowledge.

On the publication of *L'Expérience intérieure*, however, Bataille was criticised for asserting a form of meditation or spiritual thinking over analysis. Bataille was taken to task, in private by Jules Monnerot, and publicly by Patrick Waldberg, for producing a work which, in the

---

[1] This crucial emphasis on the distinction between 'real' and 'textual' value is, indeed, made by Bataille in the early essay 'La critique des fondements de la dialectique hégélienne', *ŒC*, I, pp.277-278. Aquinas uses this distinction to separate thought from its expression in the section 'We can talk about God but not define him'. St. Thomas Aquinas, *Summa Theologiae*, edited and translated by Timothy McDermott (Texas: Christian Classics, 1989), p.30

face of prevailing political conditions, seemed to advocate a form of quietism. Indeed, Boris Souvarine even went so as far as to suggest that whilst Bataille was not openly collaborating with the occupying German forces, the inward concerns of *L'Expérience intérieure* were, nonetheless, a form of collusion. Similarly, although the widely distributed tract *Nom de Dieu*, written and signed by 'un certain nombre de seconds couteaux surréalistes', stopped short of this accusation, and was aimed as much at Bataille's contribution to the journal *Messages* as at the 'mystical' content of *l'Expérience intérieure,* Bataille was, so his accusers claimed, culpable of 'idéalisme' in a situation which demanded pragmatic political commitment.[2]

The most serious attack on *L'Expérience intérieure*, however, was launched by Gabriel Marcel who in 'Le refus du salut et l'exaltation de l'homme absurde', considered the work from a Christian perspective. In this long essay devoted to considering *L'Expérience intérieure* against the atheist humanism of Camus' *L'Étranger*, Marcel objected not only to Bataille placing himself in the same tradition and, in Christian terms, on the same level, as great mystics of the Church like St. John of the Cross or Angela of Foligno, but also to Bataille's appropriation of the language of mysticism towards an end which denied the possibility of a transcendent God.

As a ' triste épigone de Nietzsche', Bataille's mysticism, for Marcel, could only be, as it was for Sartre, an empty parody of experience. Thus in the same way, as noted earlier, that Sartre reproached Bataille for 'mauvaise foi', which from an existentialist perspective is rooted in Bataille's 'refus de nommer Dieu', Marcel criticises Bataille for his 'nihilisme radical' which concedes no 'sommet'. Marcel goes on to describe *L'Expérience intérieure* as self-contradictory. More particularly, Marcel as a Christian is unable to admit Bataille's mysticism without mystery in theological or philosophical terms. From a phenomenonological point of view, Marcel is unable to concede the facts of Bataille's experience as anything other than pathological. Thus, when, in the opening section of *L'Expérience intérieure* called 'Principes d'une méthode et d'une communauté', Bataille compares the goal of inner exprience with the mystical aim of St. John of the Cross,

---

[2] Surya, pp. 402-411. See also Bataille's own response to early criticism which can be found in Georges Bataille, *Choix de Lettres*, ed. Michel Surya, (Paris: Gallimard, 1997), pp. 186-191.

'para venir a serlo todo' ('to become All'), he not only parodies religion, says Marcel, but degrades his own thinking. [3]

In the opening section of *L'Expérience intérieure*, however, Bataille explains that he uses the language of Christianity not merely to parody Christianity, but rather because the language of Christian mysticism gives to the essentially poetic activity of inner experience an extra-literary value. The aim of Christian mysticism to fuse subject and object in a divine encounter is, moreover, he states, an exact equivalent to the pursuit of 'le non-savoir' which occurs in inner experience. The relationship between the Christian tradition of mysticism and inner experience is, therefore, predicated upon a dialectical movement which is only parodic in the sense that, as noted earlier with reference to Bataille's relation to Surrealism, inner experience can only be defined by its function in an opposing system.

The use-value of Christianity

Bataille's first attested Christian mystical experience occurred in 1920 during a brief visit to the Benedictine Quarr Abbey on the Isle of Wight. He described this experience in *L'Expérience intérieure* as a kind of 'ravissement' and the beginning of his 'voyage à la limite du possible'.[4]

That he should undergo such an experience is hardly surprising, however, given the biographical facts: at this stage in his career Bataille was a student at the École des Chartes, a trained Medievalist, and a devout young man with notions of a monastic life or training to become a priest. His 'livre de chevet', as decribed by his fellow student André Masson (unrelated to the painter), was Rémy de Gourmont's *Le Latin mystique*, a compendium of neo-Latin poetry of the early church with an emphasis on the mortification of the flesh and torture scenes. Masson described the Bataille of this period as 'Romantique, sentimental et pieux.'[5] Another friend, Georges Delteil, describes the young Bataille in similar terms;

---

[3] It is this aspect of Bataille's thought, says Marcel, which leads him to 'un non-sens grandiloquent'. Gabriel Marcel,'Le refus du salut et l'exaltation de l'homme absurde', in *Homo Viator* (Paris: Aubier, 1945), p. 253.

[4] *L'Expérience intérieure*, Œ*C*, V, p.72

[5] Surya, op. cit., p. 41-44

A vingt ans, dans nos montagnes d'Auvergne, il menait une vie de saint, s'imposant une discipline de travail et de méditation. Il avait preparé seul son baccalauréat de philo, et en même temps il étudiait la religion et peut-être la théologie. [...] Quelques années plus tard, ses principes étaient à l'opposé, sa vie sentimentale et sexuelle toute différente. Mais si sa mystique religieuse avait disparu, il gardait encore le goût du mystérieux.[6]

In 1922, having successfully defended his thesis at the Ecole des Chartes, Bataille was still a devout Christian when he travelled to Madrid to pursue his studies at 'L'École des hautes études hispaniques'. At this stage Bataille was still a follower of the philosophy of Henri Bergson, as well as the Church. In Madrid, however, two key events occurred which had a definitive influence on the subsequent shape of Bataille's thought.

The first event was his attendance at a bullfight in which the bullfighter Granero was killed (an account and photographs of this incident appear in Hemingway's *Death in the Afternoon*): this moment, when the sun turned into night, became in both Bataille's fictions and other writings a key point of reference (as, indeed, does Hemingway whose *The Sun Also Rises* is cited several times in *La Somme athéologique*).[7]

The second key event was Bataille's first reading of Nietzsche at a time when his Christian faith was on the wane. The fact that Bataille read Nietzsche at such an important time in the development of his thinking meant that thereafter Nietzsche's writing and thought for Bataille did not simply become an intellectual phenomenon, but also took on a talismanic religious quality. Bataille's relationship with Hegel, whom he was yet to encounter, never equalled this relationship.

After 1922, Bataille further deepened his readings of Nietzsche, Dostoeveksy and Pascal under the tutelage of Léon Chestov, with whom Bataille proposed writing an article, and who provided Bataille

---

[6] Georges Delteil, 'Georges Bataille à Riom-ès-Montagnes', *Critique* 195-196, 1963, p.675. Also quoted in Surya, op. cit., p.36.

[7] For an account of Bataille's experiences in Madrid see *Choix de Lettres*, ed. Michel Surya, (Paris: Gallimard, 1997), pp. 26-31. A famous fictional account of Granero's death is given in *Histoire de l'œil*, *ŒC*, I, pp.52-57. Bataille also discusses photographic records of this event and his relationship with Spain in 'A propos de 'Pour qui sonne le glas d'Ernest Hemingway', in 'L'Espagne libre', *Actualité*, 1, 1945, p.194, reprinted in an abridged edition in *ŒC*, XI, pp.25-27 and reprinted in full in *Georges Bataille: Une liberté souveraine*, ed. Michel Surya (Ville d'Orléans: Fourbis, 1997), pp.41-47.

with a philosophical apprenticeship. Bataille at this stage described himself as being without God. Under Chestov's tutelage, however, Bataille was aware of metaphysical exigencies and experiences, although his loss of faith was now complete and irreducible.[8]

During the course of his studies with Chestov, Bataille was also developing a meditative method whilst undergoing psycho-analysis with Dr. Adrien Borel. It was at this stage that Bataille started to put together the symbolic language which became the language of his fictions and to describe the changes that he underwent in the meditative state. Most significantly, it was Borel who introduced Bataille to the series of photographs of the ritual slaughter, on grounds of deicide, of a Chinese youth, known as 'Le Supplice des Cent Morceaux.' This image was to have a decisive and long-lasting influence on the development of Bataille's ideas on mysticism; having been first used as a tool in psychoanalysis by Borel, it later became the object of great totemic significance for Bataille.[9]

Despite this intinerary, which took Bataille from Nietzsche's active hostility to Christianity to Chestov's critique of the first principles of Western religious thinking, when Bataille came to compose the first texts of *La Somme athéologique*, he did so by framing his thought with reference to the conceptual language of Christianity. Inner experience is, therefore, in the opening section section of *L'Expérience intérieure*, defined against the language of Christian mysticism.[10]

It is of key significance, moreover, that the references which Bataille makes to Christianity throughout *La Somme athéologique* suggest that, for Bataille, Christian mysticism, like erotic experience, reveals an experience which lies beyond language and which is occluded in discourse. This notion is fundamental in defining the textual surface of inner experience.

---

[8] A full account of the influence of Chestov on Bataille's thinking at this stage is given in Surya, op.cit., pp.79-86.

[9] Surya, op. cit, pp.120-127. For an account of Adrien Borel's relations with Bataille and the Surrealists, see also Elisabeth Roudinesco, *Histoire de la psychanalyse en France, tome 2* (Paris: Fayard, 1994), p. 21, p.24, p.25, p.33, p.36, p.42, p.48 and Elisabeth Roudinesco, 'Bataille entre Freud et Lacan: Une expérience cachée', in op. cit. *Georges Bataille après tout*, pp.191-212. This relationship is also discussed in Christophe Fiat, *Texte au Supplice* (Colleville-Montgomery: Éditions 23, 1998), p.11.

[10] *L'Expérience intérieure*, Œ C, V, p.15-17

42

Le christianisme n'est qu'au fond, qu'une cristallisation du langage. La solennelle affirmation du quatrième évangile: Et Verbum factum est, est en un sens, cette vérité profonde: la vérité du langage est chrétienne. Soit l'homme et le langage doublant le monde réel d'un autre imaginé - disponible au moyen de l'évocation -, le christianisme est nécessaire. Ou, sinon, quelque affirmation analogue.[11]

However, although inner experience is 'analogous' to but separate from Christian experience, inner experience is also an unresolvable and irrecuperable negativity. This means, in the first instance, that Bataille's relation to the language of Christianity is indeed, as was argued by Gabriel Marcel, essentially parodic. It also means, however, that Bataille's use of a specific system of references is also predicated upon the fact that inner experience parallels Christian mystical experience as a process.

Bataille is compelled, most importantly, to use the conceptual language of Christian mysticism to describe the interiority of his own experience because Christian mysticism offers a vocabulary which can apparently translate experience into language. As in the experiences of the Christian mystics, the movement of inner experience is one in which individual identity is lost. Bataille uses therefore the language of Christian mysticism to describe those aspects of inner experience which are parallel to the Christian experience of loss of selfhood and ecstasy.

However, it is also important for Bataille that Christianity offers a theoretical framework which, although it is subverted in the process of inner experience, is based on hierarchical thinking. Inner experience is the opposite of the Christian system in that, rather than aiming at a summit (God), it is a movement towards dissolution and disintegration. Inner experience can, then, be more precisely defined as a method and process which is analogous to Christian negative theology.

Most importantly, for the Christian, negative theology reveals the hidden God as 'darkness more complete than that conferred by the sharpness of sight'.[12] This method, it will be argued below, has an obvious metonymic resonance, for Bataille, whose experience reveals Absence as the central point of his 'revelation'.

---

[11] *Le Coupable, ŒC*, V, p. 382
[12] Evelyn Underhill, op. cit., *Mysticism, A Study in the Nature and Development of Man's Spiritual Consciousness*, p.367

Negative theology and atheology

It is significant, therefore, that the first and clearest Christian influence on Bataille's 'mysticism', and one referred to throughout the texts of *La Somme athéologique* as well as other writings, is *The Mystical Theology* by the unknown author - a supposed Greek convert of St. Paul - often called the Pseudo-Dionysius or Dionysius the Areopagite.

Since it was written in the late fifth or early sixth century, *The Mystical Theology* has enjoyed great influence on Christian spirituality, mainly for its alleged 'closeness to the spirit of apostolic witness.'[13] Dionysius was an important influence on the development of mystical thinking during the medieval period and, in particular, upon the Rhenish authors, Meister Eckhart, The Blessed Henry Suso and Jan van Ruysbroeck. The influence of his work, moreover, demonstrates how mysticism in the Medieval period persisted both as an affirmation of faith and a marginalized form of spiritual and intellectual experience aside from the corporate authority of the Church. Dionysius' work, however, also influenced Aquinas and the Spanish mystics, whom Bataille had studied as a young man, and who are also key points of reference in *L'Expérience intérieure.*[14]

Most significantly for Bataille, Dionysius describes the summit of the hierarchy of being as a God who is unknowable by discursive reason and apprehensible only in the intuition of ecstasy ('The wholly Unknowable'). For Dionysius this is opening of the negative way which leads to an encounter with the 'super-essential Darkness' which is the face of God. For Bataille, in a parallel manner, the negative way is an ascesis which annihilates discourse and asserts the Absence of God as the 'mystical' point of inner experience.

Je lis dans Denys l'Aréopagite (Noms Divins, 1,5): 'Ceux qui par la cessation intime de toute opération intellectuelle entrent en union intime avec l'ineffable lumière...ne parlent de Dieu que par négation'.[15]

---

[13] *The Fire and the Cloud, An Anthology of Catholic Spirituality*, ed. Rev. David A. Fleming S.M (London: Chapman, 1978), p. 56

[14] For a historical account of Dionysius the Areopagite's influence on Medieval thought see Frederick Copleston, *Medieval Philosophy, part 1* (New York: Image, 1950), pp. 106-116; Evelyn Underhill, op.cit., *Mysticism, A Study in the Nature and Development of Man's Spiritual Consciousness*, p.101, p.104, p.132, p.171

[15] *L'Expérience intérieure, ŒC*, V, p.16

As he begins to sketch out a method of inner experience, it is of central importance for Bataille that, there is a 'tension' in Dionysius' thought between relating Christian truth to philosophy and experience. According to Copleston, the 'Mystical theology' of Dionysius emerges as a monist revelatory experience which, in a dialectical relationship, confirms a neo-Platonic version of the Gospels. In *The Mystical Theology*, therefore, Dionysius posits that there are two ways of approaching God: a positive way (κατaφaτικη, kataphatic) and a negative way (aπoφaτικη: apophatic). In the first method the mind 'begins with the most universal statements', and then through intermediate terms proceeds to particular titles, thus beginning with the 'highest category'. In *The Divine Names*, Dionysius pursues this affirmative method showing how names such as Goodness, Life, Wisdom, Power, are applicable to God in a transcendental manner and 'how they apply to creatures only in virtue of their derivation from God and their varying degrees of participation in those qualities which are found in God not as inhering qualities but in substantial unity'.[16]

The importance of the negative way of 'apophatic mysticism', however, is that it stresses that God is beyond the power of the human intellect and that contemplation was a way of 'divine darkness' which, like the Baraillien 'non-savoir'which is analogous to it, can never be grasped in any adequate way by the human mind. The way to approach God is thus to strip away anthromorphic notions of the Deity 'by denying or removing all things that are - just as men who, carving out a statue out of marble, remove all the impediments that hinder the clear perception of the latent image and by this removal display the hidden statue itself in all its hidden beauty'.[17] When the mind has cleared itself of human thoughts, it may proceed to the 'Darkness of Unknowing'. This 'Darkness' is not due, however, to the unintelligibility of the Object considered in itself, but to the finiteness of the human mind, which is blinded by excess of light. In the famous second chapter of *The Mystical Theology*, Dionysius describes the mode of perception which he terms the Divine Dark:

Unto this darkness which is beyond Light we pray that we may come, and may attain unto vision through the loss of sight and knowledge, and that in ceasing thus

---

[16] Frederick Copleston, op.cit., p. 108
[17] Ibid., p.108

to see or know we may learn to know that which is beyond all perception and understanding (for this emptying of our faculties is true sight and knowledge), and that we may offer Him that transcends all things the praises of a transcendental hymnody, which we shall by denying or removing all things that are -like as men who, carving a statue out of marble, remove all the impediments that hinder the clear perception of the latent image and by this mere removal display the hidden statue in its hidden beauty. Now we must wholly distinguish this negative method from that of positive statements [...] in order that we may attain a naked knowledge of that Unknowing which in all existent things is enwrapped by all objects of knowledge, and that we may begin to see that super-essential Darkness which is hidden by all the light that is in existent things.[18]

For Bataille in the opening section of *L'Expérience intérieure*, Dionysius's 'apophatic method' is not only a constitution of negativity which paralyses thought but also a movement away from language into the paradox of silence: all categorical hierarchies of thought are negated in the movement towards 'silence voulu non pour cacher, pour exprimer à un dégré de plus de détachement.'[19] In the same way, the thinking subject of inner experience is caught in the voiceless snare which is the impossibility of its own expression. 'L'expérience ne peut être communiquée si les liens de silence d'effacement, de distance, ne changent pas ceux qu'elle met en jeu', writes Bataille.[20]

At the end-point of inner experience therefore, 'Dieu' is his own negation:

je meurs tu meurs [...] je suis mort
mort et mort
dans la nuit d'encre
flèche tirée
sur lui.[21]

God is, for both Dionysius and Bataille, an impossibility who abolishes speech in the same way that his absence deprives the world of intelligibility; the Divine Dark, 'nuit d'encre', is 'an ecstatic deprivation' which cannot be reduced to even the negative movement of human thought. This is how Bataille, in the same way, both abolishes God as

---

[18] Op. cit., *The Fire and the Cloud, An Anthology of Catholic Spirituality*, ed. Rev. David A. Fleming S.M , p. 58. See also *The Divine Names and Mystical Theology*, trans. by C.E. Holt (London: Methuen, 1920).

[19] *L'Expérience intérieure, ŒC*, V, p. 42

[20] Ibid., V, p. 42

[21] Ibid., V, p. 189

an object, and places the displaced object as the agent of his thought: God is literally unspeakable, a finitude at the limits of language, and, at the same time, an absence which overwhelms the logic of presence.

However, it is also important that although Bataille describes Christian mysticism as analogous to that of inner experience, he is also suspicious of analogical thinking as a stable system - this is, for example, one of the main reasons he is sceptical of the idealism of Surrealism. The negative way of Dionysius, however, offers Bataille a method which, as it assaults the stable referents of discourse and categorical thinking, becomes an assertion of impossibility. Most importantly, in the negative way which undermines all systems which lead to the logic of presence, Bataille finds a parallel of his notion, central to movement between night and sun and sun to night of inner experience, that the distinction between light and darkness, in a metaphorical and metonymic sense, is fundamentally unstable.

The use-value of Christian mysticism

In the introduction to *L'Expérience intérieure*, Bataille describes inner experience as a state of grace comparable to that achieved by the Spanish Mystics. Unlike the ecstasy experienced by St.Teresa or St. John of the Cross, inner experience does not, cannot, aim at a point already known to *ipse*, the term which Bataille uses in *L'Expérience intérieure* to describe the thinking subject.[22] Traditional forms of 'mysticism' take the participant into an experience which is 'unknowable' or 'ineffable' in the sense that it is transcendent and lies beyond ordinary experience; inner experience, in contrast, reverses all possible hierarchies and annihilates all that is known in the transgressive experience of 'l'état de nudité, de supplication sans réponse [...]'.[23]

Bataille is thus interested in how *Theologica mystica*, often called by the Spanish mystics *ciencia de amor* or *ciencia sobrenatural*,

---

[22] The term 'ipséité' is first used by Bataille to denote subjectivity in the essay 'Le labyrinthe', *ŒC*, I, p.435. The term is a borrowing from André Lalande's *Vocabulaire* which, according to Bataille, expresses an irreducible complexity in the subject: '(J'ai écrit pour ma part ipséité dans le sens du dictionnaire de Lalande à cause d'une équivoque sur l'individualité - identique en tous points, cette mouche-ci pourtant n'est pas celle-là'), 'Notes pour *Méthode de Méditation*', *ŒC*, V, p.474

[23] *L'Expérience intérieure*, *ŒC*, V, p. 25

dissolves into an erotic experience in which God has no form. The God of St. Teresa or St. John of the Cross is the God who is arrived at by negation, as in the apophatic experience of Dionysius, but he is also, for the Spanish Mystics, a negative presence who can give the mystical experience authority and value. Inner experience, in contrast, is its own authority;

> L'expérience intérieure ne pouvant avoir de principe ni dans un dogme (attitude morale), ni dans la science (le savoir n'en peut être ni la fin ni l'origine), ni dans une recherche d'états enrichissants (attitude esthétique, experimentale), ne peut avoir d'autre souci ni d'autre fin qu'elle-même.[24]

The value of inner experience, however, resembles the experience of the Spanish mystics in that it is a wound. St.Teresa famously describes her experience as 'dark ecstasy, or pain of God'.[25] In the same way, for Bataille, inner experience, is a dialectical inversion of the 'vision intellectuelle' of Saint Teresa; it is a vision which dissolves itself into a negative constitution of contradiction.

This central paradox of the inner experience has been identified, however, as one of the main flaws in Bataille's thinking. Most notably, in an article published four years after the publication of *L'Expérience intérieure*, Nicolas Calas wrote that he saw existentialism as fulfilling the function that mysticism traditionally had in the Christian tradition as the point of exchange between the interchangeable dualities of existence and essence. The atheistic (or, as Calas terms it, 'acephalic') mysticism of Bataille, at least in existentialist terms, was not only 'mauvaise foi' but also, argued Calas, literally meaningless in a social sense. For Calas, most importantly, Bataille's mysticism - as it is for Marcel - is a pathological state which, like the eroticism from which it is indistinguishable, cannot make religious sense in the framework of Bataille's negative theology.[26]

For Bataille, however, the inflicting of the wound, the self-lacerating central point of inner experience when the subject initiates its own destruction, is also a sacrifice. The meaning of this sacrifice is defined by the fact that it is an act which, analagous to the sacrifice of the

---

[24] Ibid., p. 18

[25] Op. cit., Evelyn Underhill, *Mysticism, A study in the Nature and Development of Man's Spiritual Consciousness*, p.394

[26] Nicolas Calas, 'Acephalic mysticism', *Hemisphères II*, no.6, 1945, pp.2-13

Christian Mass, has a social function as a point of mediation between two opposed dualities. Unlike the Christian Mass, however, the sacrifice of inner experience annihilates all other mediated relations.

This is, as observed earlier, opposite to the phenomenological core of the Christian mystical experience. The inner experience, in contrast, aims at a point, not of union, but of collapse. The authority of inner experience, for Bataille, however, originates not merely in the pathological experience of ecstasy, nor in the space of the text, but in the moment of the dissolution of the distinction between subject and object.

This moment is also a meeting with unknowing, 'le non-savoir', which has in common with Christian mysticism the notion that the goal of mystical experience is an encounter with a distinct and Divine idea. However, because God, as the object of Christian mysticism, necessarily negates the thinking subject which enters into mystical experience, Bataille does not see this as a negation which can complete itself.

> Aisément le chrétien dramatise la vie: il vit devant le Christ et pour lui-même c'est plus que lui-même. Le Christ est la totalité de l'être, et pourtant il est, comme 'l'amant' personnel, comme 'l'amant' désirable: et soudain le supplice, l'agonie, la mort. Le fidèle du Christ est mené au supplice. Mené lui-même au supplice: non à quelque supplice insignifiant, mais à l'agonie divine...[27]

Although the moment of communication is in itself 'sovereign' to the extent that it takes the participant outside the constraints of limited existence, the transcendent nature of the experience leaves the mystic consumating an empty union. The reality of the Christian experience of the Absolute, or God, is, however, separate from the finitude of the human imagination and represents, therefore, a sacrifice of both identity and knowledge.

Inner experience, in a parallel fashion, constitutes a sacrifice which denies the possibility of social meaning, as Calas rightly affirms, but which also undoes poetic or metaphorized versions of the experience of collapse. In this sense, inner experience is not merely a pathological state but also a literal encounter with the dead God. It follows from this that, although Bataille has discarded the transcendental version of a Deity integral to Christian hierarchical thinking, he is able to privilege

---

[27] *L'Expérience intérieure, Œuvres complètes*, V, p. 65

the language of Christian mystical experience as a way of preserving this transgressive space in his thinking.

Negative Silence

As Allan Stoekl has pointed out, the 'mystical' character of the inner experience is also, in large part, a result of Bataille's fascination with the Christian medieval allegorical imagination.[28] In the early essay 'Le bas matérialisme et la gnose', for example, Bataille develops the notion of matter as living principle in allegorical terms borrowed from the Gnostic theologians and which re-occur in Medieval mysticism. In particular he posits the autonomous existence of 'darkness' as an active principle in the Medieval imagination.[29] In specific terms, as in another early essay for *Documents*, 'L'Apocalypse de Saint-Sever', this means 'une expression immédiate des métamorphoses inintelligibles - d'autant plus significatives - qui sont le résultat de certaines inclinations fatales.'[30]

It is further significant, for Bataille, that the meaning of the word 'mystic' has its origins in words which describe hiddenness, closed doors. As observed earlier (see p.3), until the sixteenth century at least, the Christian usage of the term 'mysticism' had its origins in words deriving from the Greek *muo*, 'to close up' or 'conceal', and stayed close to this sense.[31] Inner experience is an occluded engagement with Absence which parallels this definition. It is crucial, however, that pursuit of the encounter with Absence, unlike the Christian experience, does not have as its goal any form of salvation; rather inner experience offers a dissolution of the subject into 'darkness' or 'night' which actively denies the possibility of transcendent salvation.

At this point, the 'mysticism' of inner experience seems to be closer to Oriental notions of mystic experience than the Christian tradition - a notion which will be pursued in the following chapter. However, although 'mysticism' in Eastern religions cannot always be discussed as

---

[28] Allan Stoekl, 'Introduction', in Georges Bataille, *Visions of Excess*, ed. Allan Stoekl, trans. Allan Stoekl, Carl Lovitt and Donald M.Leslie Jr. (Minneapolis: University of Minnesota Press, 1993), pp. ix-xiii

[29] 'Le bas matérialisme et la gnose', *ŒC*, I, pp.220-227

[30] 'L'Apocalypse de Saint-Sever', *ŒC*, I, p.169

[31] See *Oxford English Dictionary on Historical Principles* (Oxford: The Clarendon Press, 1973), p.1380

50

the 'unveiling of reality' or 'the opening of doors', and even less union with the One as defined in the Christian tradition, experience is, however, transcendental. Unlike Western hierarchical thinking which sees the believer moving vertically upward towards God, the aim of the Oriental mystical practice is the disintegration of spatial or temporal realities and collapse back into void.

In the movement of inner experience, it would appear that *ipse* is annihilated in a parallel manner. The authority 'de la part de l'inconnu' of inner experience, however, undermines the separate existence of the one and the other. As Stoekl indicates, inner experience receives its authority from 'la part de l'inconnu', a *gnosis*, from the Greek 'knowledge in the sense of interior certainty', rather than revelation.[32]

Inner experience, therefore, although it does not recognise the authority aimed at in the apophatic mysticism of Dionsysius the Areopagite or Meister Eckhart, nonetheless privileges the interiority achieved in the 'glissement des limites' in the 'apophatic' movement towards silence. Jean Bruno describes Bataille's experience, thus, as a drama which goes beyond the limits of discourse to reach an interior silence, a pure negative:

Si le silence et la dramatisation représentent des temps fondamentaux de la voie de Bataille, ils n'épuisent pas sa méthode. Il faut y ajouter la polarisation alternativement orientée vers l'intériorité ou le dehors.[33]

It is significant that Bruno is here specifically referring to the yogic practices in which the subject is consumed, or subsumed, in ' folds of consciousness' which are 'une présence sans bornes'. Inner experience, although it appropriates and assimilates the language of the Western tradition, nonetheless recognises no authority in the language of the Christian tradition.

Bataille, moreover, like Nietzsche, conceived of Christianity as being fundamentally anti-religious because it is predicated upon having established a hierarchy and therefore a transcendental summit. As observed above, Christian mysticism is therefore the exact antithesis of inner experience. In the movement of inner experience, in contrast to the encounters described in Christian mystical thought and experience,

---

[32] Ibid., p.863
[33] Op. cit., Jean Bruno, 'Les Techniques d'illumination de Georges Bataille', pp. 713-714

the subject not only consumes itself in its own unlimited freedom but also establishes immanence as the central principle of this movement.

In *The Tragic Sense of Life*, however, Miguel de Unamuno defines negative theology in Christian thinking in terms which can be matched to the method and vocabulary of inner experience. Unamuno writes, for example, that the God of theological philosophy, as defined by Aquinas in the *Summa*, and who is arrived at by 'three famous ways of negation, eminence and causality', 'viæ negationis', 'eminentiæ', 'causalitis'' is 'nothing but an idea of God, a dead thing'.[34] To make God an abstraction is, in the well-known definition of Meister Eckhart, equivalent to saying that God is nothing. The God of apophatic mysticism is therefore an unthinkable God who is himself pure negation.

Indeed, this is how the movement of inner experience, which parallels and assimilates the Christian experience, is in fact not only a subversion of that experience but also, as affirmed in the 'capital value' of Bataille's *gnosis*, a denial of the fact of that experience.

'Pourquoi je n'aime pas le mot mystique'.

Bataille's inner experience offers a metonymic and metaphorical movement from sun into night and night into sun which not only parallels the aspects of neo-Platonism which are preserved in Medieval philosophy but also reactivates those elements in theology which assert the fact of a living, subjective God who is separate from a human existence. God's presence, however, in the movement of inner experience, is Divine Absence. The movement and language of inner experience are nonetheless predicated on the apophatic method which aims at a mystical point where subjectivity is objectified.

It is significant that both Sartre and Marcel couch their objections to Bataille's inner experience with reference to Pascal. In particular, they refer to the Pascal of the opening section of *Pensées* who posits the absence of God as both thought and experience which precipitates a collapse of Absolute meaning and for whom 'l'homme dans la nature' represents 'Un néant à l'égard de l'infini, un tout à l'égard du néant, un milieu entre rien et tout.'[35]

---

[34] Miguel de Unamuno, *The Tragic Sense of Life* (London: Macmillan, 1921), p.163
[35] Blaise Pascal, *Pensées*, texte de Léon Brunschvig (Paris: Nelson, 1955), p.70

52

Inner experience, argues Bataille, although it is an encounter with a dead God, is still experience predicated upon the summit, the hierarchy of meaning integral to a Christian tradition. For Bataille, as for Pascal, however, God is an impossibility whose status cannot be defined by language and who, in fact, not only eludes definition in the positive constitution of meaning, but also cannot be properly defined as a negative proposition; the absence of God is not, therefore, in any sense, the same as atheism, which posits God as a negative entity. Marcel and Sartre see this as both a logical and metaphorical flaw in Bataille's construction of the 'topos' of inner experience, Sartre describing this as Bataille's 'panthéisme noir'.[36]

As observed in the introductory chapter, long before Bataille had articulated inner experience in mystical terms, André Breton criticized Bataille for the same apparent contradiction. For Breton, Bataille confuses the relationship between the inner and outer world by making it analogous to that between mind and body. In his attack on Bataille in the *Second manifeste*, Breton refers specifically to Bataille's article 'Le Langage des Fleurs' and says that Bataille's fundamental error is to conceive of rational thought as being separate from experience: 'Le malheur pour M.Bataille est qu'il raisonne: certes qu'il raisonne comme quelqu'un qui a 'un mouche sur le nez', ce qui le rapproche plutôt du mort que du vivant, mais il raisonne.'[37]

Similarly Breton's scorn for Bataille's 'bas matérialisme' was also due, in large part, to the fact that, for the Surrealists, the term mysticism was generally reserved for the communion with the Absolute which could be achieved through the Hegelian dialectical process.[38] As observed earlier, for the Surrealists, mystical communion with the primal unity, mostly in the form of poetry, is predicated upon a Hegelian dialectical movement which proceeds out of the relation between matter and mind and which aims at 'le point suprême'.

In inner experience, however, the encounter with the death of *ipse* overwhelms the dialectical process. This movement, says Bataille, transgresses both the Hegelian dialectical movement and the tradition

---

[36] Op. cit., Jean-Paul Sartre, 'Un nouveau mystique', p.171

[37] Op. cit., André Breton, 'Second manifeste du surréalisme', p.217

[38] The term 'mysticism' is indeed rarely used in Surrealism. However, Breton frequently refers to poetry with reference to mysticism, alchemy and Hermetic philosophy. One of the most famous examples of this tendency is to be found in a famous passage in the 'Second manifeste du surréalisme', op. cit., pp.206-209.

in French thought which is Pascal's final argument in *Pensées*, the ontological argument, first devised by Anselm in the eleventh century, which postulates that when we conceive of God we conceive that than which nothing greater can be conceived, or 'id quo nihil majus cogitari'.

Bataille's pursuit of 'non-savoir' is an inverse version of this ontological argument: inner experience reduces all moral categories to collapse and disorder which proceed from Divine Absence. It follows from this that, for Bataille, the vocabulary of Christian mysticism remains, in a refracted form, a finer vehicle for expressing the ambiguities of inner experience than the language of philosophy.

Inner experience, Bataille argues in the opening section of *L'Expérience intérieure*, is posited outside of all metaphysical authority. At the same time as it destroys the linear logic of the Hegelian dialectic, inner experience preserves, nonetheless, in the appropriated imagery of the Christian mystics, the Hegelian notion of the Absolute as a 'summit'. This summit is, however, one that is reversed before being displaced.

In this way, on Bataille's own terms, inner experience come to be a literal encounter with the blind spot of philosophy which dazzles the subject with its own reflection. This experience, in contemporary thinking is often termed 'aporia'. This term is a particularly apposite description of the central fact of the inner experience when it is remembered that this word in Medieval philosophy was often translated from the Greek as 'the pathless path'.[39]

---

[39] George Steiner puts much ironic emphasis on this translation as part of his attack on contemporary philosophy in his book *Real Presences* (London: Faber, 1989).

Chapter Two

'Je situe mes efforts à la suite, à côté du surréalisme':
Atheological theory
and methods of meditation

> Heroic love belongs to those superior natures called insane [insanno in the Italian], not because they do not know [non sanno] but because they more than know [sopresanno].
>
> Attributed to Giordano Bruno by Miguel de Unamuno in *The Tragic Sense of Life.*

For Hegel, as he was understood by Kojève and Bataille, mysticism is a central point in defining religious experience. Mysticism is, however, only part of the larger form of representation of religious feeling which Hegel calls 'Vorstellung' ('representation'; see above, p. 27). Most importantly, 'Vorstellung' exists as an inward form of consciousness which reconciles opposites. The central argument of this chapter is that inner experience is constructed out of the system which Bataille terms 'atheology' and which is equivalent to this Hegelian movement. Inner experience is, however, also a movement and activity which is opposite to the Hegelian concept of 'Vorstellung' in that it is predicated upon a separation between thought and feeling which undermines the thinking subject's own consciousness of itself.

In his description of Hegel's religious thinking, Charles Taylor describes how, for Hegel, the human subject is prey to an inner conflict, in which the conditions of his existence are at odds with with his essential goal.[1] This division is also part of the movement towards dissolution which occurs in inner experience. This process, for Bataille, like the Hegelian 'Vorstellung', is, moreover, a religious mode of consciousness in the sense that it can only be grasped in images and not conceptual language. This chapter will consider,

---

[1] A discussion of Hegel's use of the term 'Vorstellung' in this context can be found in Charles Taylor, *Hegel* (London: Cambridge University Press, 1975), pp.467-468.

however, the proposition that inner experience is a transparent or opaque representation of thought which is related to 'Vorstellung' only in the sense that it functions in a theological or atheological context. It will also consider how inner experience as the experience of unresolved and unresolvable negativity, is articulated outside and beyond the Hegelian definition of 'Vorstellung'.

Bataille's 'method of meditation' is thus less meditation as it is understood in the framework of mystical traditions of both East and West, but rather an elliptical form of mediation (in the Hegelian sense of an essential contradiction) which is also a deferral of 'experience'. Most importantly, in the contemplation of specific images, either real or imaginary, Bataille accedes to a state of consciousness which is properly mystical in that it exceeds all forms of discourse, although, as Bataille insists, it belongs to no tradition nor specific mystical idiom.

The present chapter will explore the notion that Bataille's methods of meditation are, unlike the automatic writing or trances of the Surrealists, experiences founded in a theory, that is to say atheology, which actively denies the possibility of transcendence at the same time as it posits itself as the sole authentic value.

Hegel and the Surrealist 'Religion'

The Surrealist discovery of Hegel, which began early (indeed for Breton as far back as his 'classe de philosophie' in 1913[2]), not only preceded Kojève's lectures which Bataille attended irregularly from 1933 onwards, but also, in many ways, pre-empted much of what Kojève had to say about Hegel as a philosopher of the revolutionary avant-garde.

In general terms, in the light of the events of history, most notably the Russian Revolution, and the high prestige accorded to Hegelian philosophy by Lenin, the Surrealists saw Hegelianism not only as a confirmation of their belief in the possibility of Absolute freedom, but also saw Hegel as a spiritual ancestor of Surrealism whose thinking, like that of Sade, Lautréamont, Marx, Rimbaud and Jarry, remained a living component of the Surrealist adventure. In particular, the

---

[2] Mark Polizzotti, *Revolution of the Mind, The Life of André Breton* (London: Bloomsbury, 1995), p. 13

56

Surrealists championed the Hegelian dialectic, which became a method central to the Surrealist endeavour.

Thus, in the first *Manifeste du surréalisme* of 1924, when Breton quotes Pierre Reverdy's dictum that 'L'image est une création pure de l'esprit' there is, in these 'mots quoique sibyllins' an echo of the Hegelian dialectic which seeks to transcend analytical reason in a way which annihilates the integrity of the rational thinking subject and confirms the status of conceptual thought.[3] For the Surrealists the Hegelian Absolute, and the dialectical process itself, thus existed as a reality and a confirmation of the Surrealist notion that the Absolute could be apprehended through myriad analogical relationships.

The Hegelian dialectic was, therefore, not only a predecessor to Surrealism which presaged its religious essence but also, from the group's earliest days, like the religious work of art, 'L'image [...] Création pure de l'esprit', an active method integrated into Surrealism and a key element in the movement which gave access to 'le merveilleux'.[4] Thus, when in the *Second manifeste du surréalisme* of 1929, Breton attacked Bataille's 'parodic' mode of thinking and, in the same space, defined the Surrealist overcoming of contradictions as 'un certain point de l'esprit d'où la vie et la mort [...] cessent d'être perçus contradictoirement',[5] he was echoing *The Phenomenology of Mind* in defining a mystic communion which does not exclude non-being from being.[6]

Towards the end of the 1930s, however, Bataille had not only developed a position which stood in direct contradiction to the

---

[3] Op. cit., André Breton, *Manifestes du Surréalisme*, p.34
[4] Ibid., p.34
[5] Ibid., p.154
[6] 'Ainsi, dit Hegel, la théologie chrétienne n'est pas une vérité tant que le Monde chrétien n'a pas réalisé l'Idée de l'Individualité c'est à dire la synthèse de la fusion du particulier et de l'Universel, de l'Homme réel et l'Esprit.' Alexandre Kojève, *Introduction à la lecture de Hegel* (Paris: Gallimard, 1947), p.238. Also '[in *The Phenomenology of Mind*] Hegel holds to the aspiration of the expressive unity ; it is this, of course, rather than a simple calculation of human fallibility which makes him unable to accept fully Kant's separation of reason and sensibility and cleave rather to Rousseau; it is this which will ultimately turn him against Kant.[...] in order to do this religion must be subjectivized: that is, it must be more than an external allegiance to certain doctrines and pieties and become living piety in order to unite man within himself.' Charles Taylor, op. cit., *Hegel* (London: Cambridge University Press, 1975), p. 54

'emmerdeurs d'idéalistes' of the Surrealist group, but also encountered, in Kojève's version of Hegel, an anti-idealist method, 'l'action négatrice,' which corresponded to his fascination, already expounded in *Documents*, and deprecated by Breton, with 'le bas matérialisme', 'bassesse'.[7]

Accused by Breton of advocating a 'retour offensif du vieux matérialisme',[8] Bataille nonetheless found in Hegel, particularly in Kojève's exposition of Hegel's notion of 'Vorstellung', confirmation that 'la souveraineté de la pensée' is a contradiction in terms.[9] Most importantly, thought, for Bataille and Kojève, cannot find synthesis, or 'souveraineté de la pensée' in any religious ('élevé, noble') mode of consciousness.

This means that when Bataille first comes to sketch out a theory of 'mysticism' in 1939, mystical experience is necessarily 'acephalous' or 'acephalic' in the sense that it has no summit, either Hegelian or Christian, to which it can aim itself; the 'certain point d'esprit' of ecstatic 'awakening' is the collapse of the thinking into radical heterogeneity, 'bassesse', which displaces authority.[10] Thus, in the movement of inner experience *ipse* cannot return to itself as an undifferentiated being, 'a rational necessity', once the wound of 'inner opposition' has been opened up.

Instead Bataille, as part of his 'méthode de méditation', describes how the movement from a Hegelian constructive dialectical mode of thinking which joins its *telos* to a transcendental logic is overwhelmed by a 'négativité sans emploi' which defies and denies recuperation.

This 'negativité sans emploi' both mediates and contradicts inner experience. The thinking subject of 'the practice of joy in the face of death' experiences beatitude in the experience of destruction which is it own negation. Inner experience, therefore, and in particular the

---

[7] 'La langage des fleurs', *ŒC*, I, p. 178

[8] André Breton, op. cit., p.216

[9] See Alexandre Kojève, op. cit., *Introduction à la lecture de Hegel*, p. 238.

[10] The term 'hétérogène' has a binary meaning for Bataille. Allan Stoekl explains this as 'two forms of heterogeneity [...] One [...] is imperative, associable with that which is noble, pure, superior, individual, and so on. The other is impure, involving untouchable things and people.' (Allan Stoekl, op. cit., 'Introduction', in Georges Bataille, *Visions of Excess*, ed. Allan Stoekl, trans. Allan Stoekl, Carl Lovitt and Donald M.Leslie Jr. (Minneapolis: University of Minnesota Press, 1993), pp. ix-xiii) Bataille makes this distinction clear in the article 'La structure psychologique du fascisme', *ŒC*, I, p. 344-350.

58

image of the 'Supplice des cent morceaux', unlike Hegel's religious 'Vorstellung', which is an intermediary representation of communication between two opposite poles (man and God, for example), is, in itself, a constitution of absent existence which contradicts the possibility of communication.

The practice of joy in the face of death

In the summer of 1939, Bataille gave a lecture, 'La joie devant la mort' to the Collège de Sociologie and, in the same month, published in *Acéphale* a long poem, 'La pratique de la joie devant la mort'. Although the notes to the lecture have been lost, the poem in *Acéphale* is preceded by an explanatory essay which, as the common title suggests, offers a theory for the experience of 'joy in the face of death'.

In the essay Bataille says that 'il y a lieu d'employer le mot mystique au sujet de la joie devant la mort et de sa pratique'.[11] He also says that the use of the word does not imply anything more than 'une ressemblance d'ordre affectif entre cette pratique et celle des religieux de l'Asie ou de l'Europe.' Although this excludes all hierarchical forms of religious experience from 'joy before death', this disclaimer, however, does not mean that the ecstasy experienced by Bataille, as he emphasises, was any less a concrete experience. Nonetheless, the lecture for Collège de Sociologie, of which Bataille was a founder member in 1937, aroused some controversy amongst fellow members of the Collège on account of Bataille's perceived 'mysticism' and, indeed, signalled the final break up of the group.

The origins of this break up lay in fundamental differences between Bataille, Leiris and Caillois about the aim and function of the group. Like the earlier project Contre-Attaque, the Collège was conceived, at least in part, as a response to what was perceived to be an insufficiency of both theoretical and practical rigour on the part of the revolutionary Left. In particular, the group, which included Michel Leiris, Roger Caillois, Jules Monnerot, Pierre Klossowski, and André Masson as members, was dedicated to exploring the limits and possiblities of a 'sociologie sacrée' which sought to reintegrate the sacred into the domain of the social and political; indeed Jules Monnerot's *La Poésie moderne et le sacré*, Roger Caillois's *L'Homme et le sacré*, Pierre

---

[11] 'La pratique de la joie devant la mort', *ŒC*, I, p.554

Klossowski's *Sade, mon prochain*, can all be traced back to this association.[12]

Like Contre-Attaque, the Collège de Sociologie was also founded as a reaction to specific political exigencies. As a climate of unrest and violence prevailed in France, the Spanish Civil War moved towards its final tragic climax, and, in the wake of Munich, a large scale European war seemed an inevitability rather than a possibility, the Collège defined its primary purpose, in 'Déclaration du Collège de Sociologie sur la crise internationale', as 'l'appréhension sans complaisance des réactions psychologiques collectives que l'imminence de la guerre a suscitées.[13] The Collège de Sociologie's role, therefore, was to analyse, in the face of the possibility of the annihilation of that society, the meaning of collective social relationships, or as a tract distributed by the Collège de Sociologie puts it, 'Le Collège de Sociologie regarde l'absence générale de réaction vive devant la guerre comme un signe de dévirilisation de l'homme.'[14]

Caillois and Leiris, who had a year earlier co-signed this tract, 'Déclaration du Collège de Sociologie sur la crise internationale', did not attend Bataille's final lecture to the Collège de Sociologie, partly due to personal reasons but also, in no small measure, as a reproach made in response to Bataille's practical interest in mysticism. Although Leiris had participated a year earlier (with René Allendy and Adrien Borel) in the activities of the 'Société de psychologie collective' who had discussed attitudes in the face of death, he was, as he wrote to Bataille, troubled by 'la rigueur avec laquelle a été menée cette entreprise'. Caillois was more specific: having prepared a text which explicitly attacked Bataille for the preoccupations he devoted himself to in the Acéphale community, Caillois accused Bataille of being intransigent about the notion of sacrifice having a practical as well as theoretical dimension. Thus Bataille ended the activities of the Collège de Sociologie outside of the collective authority of the group but within the framework of his own thinking. For Bataille, like the

---

[12] An account of the history of the Collège de Sociologie is given in Denis Hollier, 'Foreword: Collage', *The College of Sociology 1937-39* (Minneapolis: University of Minnesota, 1988), pp.viii-xxviii.

[13] *ŒC*, I, pp.538-541. For an account Bataille's influence on the politics of Contre-Attaque see also Robert Stuart Short, op. cit., 'Contre-Attaque', *Entretiens sur le surréalisme*, ed. Ferdinand Alquié (Paris: La Haye, Mouton, 1968), pp.144-175.

[14] 'La pratique de la joie devant la mort', *ŒC*, I, p. 539

60

community Acéphale, the purpose of the Collège de Sociologie from its inception was to function as a kind of Gnostic sect, devoted to the pursuit and creation of a 'sociologie sacrée' which would be practical as well as theoretical.[15]

Thus there is a particular emphasis in the *Acéphale* essay, 'la pratique de la joie devant la mort', on the sacrifice of selfhood which is not just political, or indeeed sexual stasis, but an ecstatic 'perte de soi'. This 'gnosis' is also the annihilation which *ipse* undergoes in inner experience. The 'souveraineté de l'être', which is opposed to the 'souveraineté de la pensée', is at the centre of Bataille's 'exercice d'une mystique'. It is a negativity which undermines all conceptual structures of the world which posit formal consistency or harmony as underlying principles or goals. In *Sur Nietzsche*, Bataille describes this as 'sommet immédiat'.[16] In *L'Expérience intérieure* he also writes that, at the centre of inner experience, the undifferentiated existence of the 'le moi' is predicated upon an 'abîme' of non-meaning which escapes both possession or appropriation: '[...] *l'ipse* cherchant à devenir le tout n'est tragique au sommet que pour lui-même...'[17]

For Bataille, this paradox is the essential point of 'joy before death'. The conflict between *ipse*, which in the essential movement of inner experience is isolated in its own discontinuity, and the night, the Absolute of 'le non-savoir', opens the wound which represents the Absent God.

If the opening of this 'wound', which is properly the 'mystical experience' of 'joy before death', can open up the blind spot of philosophy, this is because the rules of inner experience, as method and experiment, are predicated upon the paradox that inner experience is neither experience, in the terms ascribed to traditional forms of mysticism, nor is it a project which aims at closure or completion; Bataille writes: '[...] ce sacrifice que nous consommons se distingue des autres en ceci: le sacrificateur lui-même est touché par le coup qu'il frappe [...].'[18]

---

[15] Correspondance between Leiris, Caillois and Bataille is reprinted (in English) in *The College of Sociology 1937-1939*, ed. Denis Hollier (Minneapolis: University of Minnesota Press, 1988), p.353-359. See also Surya, op.cit., pp. 323-330, and Georges Bataille, *Choix de Lettres*, pp.161-176

[16] *ŒC*, VI, p.54

[17] *L'Expérience intérieure, ŒC*, V, p.105

[18] Ibid.,, p.176

This means, as Jean-Claude Renard points out, that the sacrifice of meaning at the centre of inner experience does finally take place beyond the textual drama of articulated language in a space where Bataille, as 'théoricien acharné', asserts 'la négation du mystère' as a contradiction which overwhelms the possibility of transcendence. Renard specifies, as Bataille himself does, that the refusal of closure also undermines Bataille's vocabulary in a way that undoes the project of inner experience:

> On peut également penser que ce n'est pas le 'voyage' lui-même qui devient l'unique valeur et l'unique autorité réelle - mais l'ensemble des valeurs nouvelles ou complémentaires que sa fonction continuellement désaliénante et modificatrice permet d'actualiser ou de découvrir sans limitation définie dans les profondeurs immanentes et/ou transcendantes de l'inconnu où il engage l'aventure humaine. [19]

The principles of an atheological method are thus predicated upon a sacrifice in which *ipse* annihilates itself in its assertion of itself as a 'negativité sans emploi'. 'L'homme athéologique', concludes Renard, is thus unable to use the term 'mystic' with the same authority as the Christian mystics because his sacrifice is constructed out of theory and not experience.

In the introduction to *L'Expérience intérieure*, however, although Bataille asserts that the 'théologie positive' of Christianity directly contradicts his own thought and experience, nonetheless, he is clear that he considers the end-point of Christian mystical experience - the journey to the stillness of God - as an authentic experience in itself and that the authentic nature of this experience is not merely recreated but also felt, in the most literal and concrete terms, as the central movement of inner experience. Thus the 'voyage au bout du possible' of inner experience is neccessarily defined in both Hegelian terms, as the 'Erfahrung' - an experience or journey which is the expansion of consciousness beyond the thinking subject into the object of its thought. Kojève describes the importance of this experience in the following terms:

> [...] Hegel écrit ce que j'ai déjà dit au sujet de la religion ou de la Théo-logie, en commentant le passage sur l'Erfahrung.

---

[19] Jean-Claude Renard, *L'expérience intérieure de Georges Bataille ou la négation du mystère* (Paris: Éditions du Seuil, 1987), p.29

'Dans le Temps, le contenu de la religion [chrétienne] exprime donc ce qu'est l'esprit [humain] avant la science [hégélienne]; mais cette dernière est seule [à être] le vrai savoir que l'Esprit [humain] a de lui-même.'

[...] Car, en réalité ou vérité, l'Esprit-Eternité est le résultat du Temps et de l'Histoire: il est l'Homme mort et non un dieu ressucité. Et c'est pourquoi la réalité de l'Esprit Eternel (ou absolu) est non pas un Dieu transcendant vivant dans le Ciel, mais un Livre écrit par un homme vivant dans le monde naturel.[20]

Bataille's version of inner experience is faithful to this notion of 'suppression of transcendence' in the experience of 'timelessness' but, as noted in the previous chapter, it is also constructed with reference to the apophatic methods of St. Teresa, St. John of the Cross, the Pseudo-Dionysius and Meister Eckhart. Thus, although in both the 'project' of the community and the published texts of the journal *Acéphale*, as well as those texts of *La Somme athéologique,* Bataille offers neither a method or principles of meditation, the enclosed drama of the text is nonetheless the space in which, as Blanchot puts it, sacrifice remains an irreducible instant of pure negativity, a supreme negation, which introduces Absence as the impossibility which negates all other possibilities.[21]

Le Fond des Mondes

In the poem 'La pratique de la joie devant la mort', however, the representation of an inverted image acts as a way of propelling the 'practitioner' into a vertiginous state where the 'locus of humanity' is quite literally turned on its head;[22] the immanent experience of the anticipated war is a concrete representation of this.

In this poem, Bataille is pursuing an 'impossible' experience which has at its centre a point where annihilation and dissolution of temporal

---

[20] Alexandre Kojève, op. cit., *Introduction à la lecture de Hegel*, ed. Raymond Queneau, p. 395

[21] '[...] le travail essentiel du vrai est de nier.' Maurice Blanchot, *L'Espace littéraire* (Paris: Gallimard), 1955, p.326.

[22] 'Like the insane among us, he [Bataille] raises, for the writer and the critic, the question of the locus of humanity, a humanity whose topology has become so shifting and uncertain that we are not sure whether it resides where it seemed to be, while we suspect ever more strongly that it is also located where it appeared not to be.' Michel Beaujour, 'Eros and Nonsense: Georges Bataille', *Modern French Criticism, From Proust and Valéry to Structuralism*, ed. John K.Simon (Chicago: University of Chicago Press, 1972), p. 152

and spatial realities are made real to the extent that not only does language break down altogether but comes to be replaced by silence, which is the central point of meaning. The first part of the leap into unknowing thus proceeds from watching language collapse into the void as do all other illusions of identity and personality:

> Je m'abandonne à la paix jusqu'à l'anéantissement.
> Les bruits de lutte se perdent dans la mort comme les fleuves dans la mer, comme l'éclat des étoiles dans la nuit. La puissance du combat s'accomplit dans le silence de toute action.
> J'entre dans la paix comme dans un inconnu obscur. [23]

The result of the pursuit of 'l'impossible' in inversion of thought and experience is then silence, the collapse of language into the void.

> Je tombe dans cet inconnu obscur
> Je deviens moi-même cet inconnu obscur [24]

Michel Foucault describes this experience of reversal as related to mysticism and as the transgression which opens a space for Bataille's philosophical language.

> L'œil énuclée ou renversé, c'est l'espace du langage philosophique de Bataille, le vide où il s'épanche et se perd mais ne cesse pas de parler - un peu comme l'œil intérieur, diaphane et illuminé des mystiques ou des spirituels, marque le point où le langage secret de l'oraison se fixe et s'étrangle en une communication merveilleuse qui le fait taire. [25]

The negative axes of inner experience, anguish and vertigo are the *gnosis* or recognition of silence, pure negativity, by the thinking subject of atheology: the method of meditation, or 'practice of joy in the face of death', is *ipse* complicit in its own self-destruction; 'une sainteté éhontée, impudique, qui entraîne seule une perte de soi assez heureuse.'[26]

Atheology exists, however, only in relation to its Other: the paradox is that the thinking subject, *ipse*, is also consumed by the

---

[23] 'La Pratique de la joie devant la mort', *ŒC*,I, p.555
[24] Ibid., p.555
[25] Michel Foucault, 'Préface à la transgression', *Critique*, 195/196, pp.765-766
[26] 'La Pratique de la joie devant la mort', *ŒC*,I, p.554

Other in a moment of 'negative mediation'. The mediating logic of the 'Aufhebung' is itself similarly consumed in 'le vertige' which annihilates the dialectical process and the mediating relationship between concepts out of which it has emerged:

> Lorsqu'un humain se trouve placé de telle sorte que le monde se réfléchisse en lui heureusement et sans entraîner de destruction ou de souffrance - ainsi par une belle matinée de printemps -, il peut se laisser aller à l'enchantement ou à la joie simple qui en résulte. Mais il peut apercevoir aussi au même instant la pesanteur et le vain souci de repos vide que cette béatitude signifie. A ce moment-là ce qui s'élève cruellement en lui est comparable à un oiseau de proie qui égorgerait un oiseau plus petit dans un ciel bleu apparemment paisible et clair.[27]

This is the 'le vertige dionysiaque', described by Leiris, 'le point où [...] haut et bas se confondent et où la distance s'abolit entre le tout et le rien';[28] it is the point at which Bataille's 'mysticism', which Caillois and Leiris objected to so much, is an 'experience which is not an experience'; it exists on a non-metaphorical level wherein 'la contemplation extatique et la connaissance lucide s'accomplissant dans une action' contradicts the possibility of recuperation by the Hegelian system.

However, unlike Surrealism, or more precisely Breton - who during the period Bataille contributed to the Collège de Sociologie was himself preoccupied by the ironies and ambiguities of Hegel's philosophy of religion as exposed by Kojève[29] - Bataille aims in inner experience at a transgression of the Hegelian system which annihilates the system itself. For Bataille, 'Joy before death', the explosion into 'béatitude', is a sacrifice which is a negation of both necessity and inevitability, and in which *ipse* wills itself to be sacrificed 'négativement' and 'pris de vertige' .

---

[27] Ibid.,552

[28] Michel Leiris, 'De Bataille l'Impossible à l'impossible Documents', *Critique* 195/196, 1963, reprinted in *A propos de Georges Bataille* (Paris: Fourbis, 1988), p.40

[29] The influence of Kojève's version of Hegel on Breton is most clearly demonstrated in his contribution to the Contre-Attaque project. Kojève is similarly a discernible influence on the contributions from Maurice Heine, Georges Ambrosino, Georges Gilet and Pierre Klossowski as well as Bataille. See 'Les cahiers de 'Contre-Attaque', in Maurice Nadeau, *Histoire du surréalisme* (Paris: Éditions du Seuil, 1964), p.438-446.

Aux antipodes du Yoga

In the same way that Bataille, via Nietzsche, aims at subsuming thought in Dionysian experience ('Le vertige Dionysiaque'), so the practice of Yoga aims at self-annihilation, revealing the illusion of personality which, like all else in the created world, is flux, the passage of events and not identity. It is significant, then, that the apparently textual dramas of the texts of *Acéphale*, and then *La Somme athéologique* are either contemporaneous or preceded, as Jean Bruno tells us, by yogic exercises which Bataille practised.

Not only do these experiences inform the language of *La Somme athéologique* but they also play a central role in what Bataille means by using the term 'mysticism' with reference to inner experience. In particular, the collapse of *ipse* which takes place in inner experience, and which is the same as the 'je' which, in 'la joie devant la mort', is 'rongé par la mort' and 'absorbé dans l'espace sombre'[30] appears to be closely related to yogic practice, and in particular the practices Bataille devoted himself to in late 1938 and early 1939 and of which Jean Bruno gives a full account.[31]

Indeed, although Bataille disparaged any appropriation of Eastern methods which recognised any form of cephalic 'sommet' as the 'point seul' of meditation, and although the vocabulary he uses to describe the movement of inner experience belongs largely to the Western tradition, Bataille was well-read in Classical Hinduism and Buddhism. In particular, an early text in *Documents*, Bataille demonstrates an academic expertise not only with Oriental themes but also the 'cauchemar inoubliable' of Hindu religious experience.[32] We know also that, as well as reading Alexandra David-Néel and Mircea Eliade's accounts of mystical practice amongst the Tibetans, Bataille was familiar with Romain Rolland's biographies of Ramakrishna and Vivekananda, *Essai sur la mystique et l'action de l'Inde vivante*, as well as possessing a heavily annotated copy of Vivekananda's *Raja Yoga ou conquête de la nature intérieure*.[33]

---

[30] ibid., p.555
[31] Op. cit., Jean Bruno, 'Les Techniques d'illumination chez Georges Bataille', pp.706-721
[32] 'Kali', *ŒC*, I, p.244
[33] Surya, p.425

The significance of the relation between the poem 'La pratique de la joie devant la mort' and Bataille's mystical techniques, as described by Jean Bruno, is that they disperse all categories of thought into the unknowable beyond which consumes human particularity. Indeed, we find this experience described by Swami Vivekananda in an essay in the collection *Les grands maîtres spirituels dans l'Inde contemporaine*, a book to which Bataille had been introduced to by Jean Bruno:

> L'homme réel se tient derrière l'esprit; l'esprit est l'instrument entre ses mains; c'est son intelligence qui filtre à travers l'esprit. Ce n'est que lorsque vous prenez votre place derrière l'esprit que celui-ci devient intelligent. Lorsque l'homme abandonne l'esprit, celui-ci tombe en morceaux et n'est plus rien. Vous comprenez ainsi ce que l'on entend par *chitta*. C'est le contenu mental, et les *vrittis* sont les vagues et les rides qui s'elèvent sur lui lorsque des causes extérieures viennent l'exciter. Ces *vrittis* sont notre univers.[34]

The 'Acephalic' experience of 'La pratique de la joie devant la mort' is similarly, as we have observed, a reversal of all systems or hierarchies of thinking. What is interesting in Bataille's version of the Yogic way is the aiming at the internalisation of an external experience of horror or terror: this leads to a 'vertiginous reversal' in psychic experience which is the first way into the encounter with the silence at the centre of inner experience; *ipse* overturns the 'le sommet' in a sacrifice in which it negates itself. This is the tragic or Dionysian experience which Nietzsche fixes as the central goal of his philosophy: a purposeless negativity which deliberately situates itself outside the aesthetic framework.

This is for Bataille a reversal aimed at in practice which is the internalization of horror, moving literally 'beyond good and evil', into an encounter with the void which heightens terror rather than dissipating it. This is quite separate from Classical Hinduism and closer to the esoteric teachings of Tantric literature.Yogic practice in Classical Hinduism teaches that the way towards enlightment is the dissolution of the self, which interests Bataille, but beyond this, Hindu philosophy, in the Upanishads and the larger part of the Tantras, points to a monistic conception of the universe: mystical experience is the

---

[34] Swami Vivekananda, 'Commentaires sur les aphorismes de Pantanjali', *Les grands maîtres spirituels dans l'Inde contemporain* (Bruxelles: Éditions Ayden, 1938), p.32. This text was quoted by Bataille in 'Expérience mystique et littérature', *ŒC*, XI, p. 85.

benign contemplation of a sacred experience of eternal Good which is
bliss.

Bataille's version of mystical experience is, however, much more
firmly rooted in the Nietzschean exigencies of a philosophical system
which has moved beyond hierarchies of thinking. Thus in the Tantrism
which attracted Bataille, whilst the identity between the souls and the
cosmos is essentially the same duality which occurs in Classical
Hinduism, the aim of the mystical experience is the internalization of
the cosmos, rather than the release of the soul to its natural state of
unity. The body is the microcosm, and the ultimate is not only
omniscience, but total realization of all universal and eternal forces.
The body is real, not because it is the function or creation of a real
deity, together with the rest of the universe. The individual soul does
not unite with the One; it is the One, and the body is its function.[35]

Bataille's 'joy before death', however, does not recognise the One;
instead, as an 'acephalic' state of grace it opens the wound of non-being
to unfathomable depths: illumination in the sense used by mystics is
impossible; the techniques of Eastern mystical practice serve only to
undermine the individualised thinking subject in a method which
recognises no other goal than the experience of alterity. The first step
towards an experience of the infinite is to be found in 'désordres
contraires', 'ivresse sacrée' or an exultation in 'excès': 'La pudibonderie
est peut-être salutaire aux malvenus: cependant celui qui aurait peur
des filles nues et du whisky aurait peu de chose à faire avec 'La joie
devant la mort''.[36]

'Joy in the face of death' is thus a transgression not only of moral
law, but an attack on the possibilities of philosophical language: a
dispersal of categories. In the same way as the central problem for
Nietzsche, according to Bataille in *Sur Nietzsche*, was whether a
Dionysian language could be created to express Dionysian thought, in
'La pratique de la joie devant la mort', Bataille, having defined reality
as formless and Dionysian, aims at an internalization of this truth
through a Dionysian method.

This method is, first of all, a reversal of all systems of thinking: the
encounter with the dead God, or Divine Absence, is an Absolute

---

[35] See Philip Rawson, *Tantra: The Indian Cult of Ecstasy* (London: Thames and
Hudson, 1993), p.12.
[36] 'La Pratique de la joie devant la mort', *ŒC*,I, p.554

experience which reverses all other categories of thought and is thus a passage to the 'impossible'. Most notably, the first aim of the poems of 'La pratique de la joie devant la mort' is a concentration upon the dissolution of fixed identity. Bataille describes these texts as 'moins des exercices à proprement parler que les simples descriptions d'un état extasié.[...] Seul le texte qui vient en premier pourrait à la rigueur être proposé comme un exercice'.[37] This first text, however, is worth pausing over. Like the rest of the poem, these lines, or 'mantra', are to be chanted by the adept as a way of entering the contemplative experience.

Je suis la joie devant la mort.
[...] Je demeure dans cet anéantissement et, à partir de là je me représente la nature comme un jeu de forces qui s'exprime dans une agonie multipliée et incessante.
Je me perds ainsi lentement dans un espace inintelligible et sans fond.
J'atteins le fond des mondes
Je suis rongé par la mort
Je suis rongé par la fièvre
Je suis absorbé dans l'espace sombre
Je suis anéanti dans la joie devant la mort.[38]

In an article devoted largely to the 'La fable mystique' of Michel de Certeau, Jacques Derrida analyses the substance of mysticism which refuses transcendence and asks the question, 'pourquoi faudrait-il choisir entre un espace 'divin' et un espace 'nietszchéen'?'.[39] Similarly, the meditation 'joy before death' embodies the unresolvable contradiction of 'ipse' caught between divine absence and a return to undifferentiated, continous being (death). The thinking subject, the 'je', of 'joy before death', however, chooses the anguish and agony of its own dissolution into chaos which is 'un espace nietzschéen.' Specifically, the collapse into catastrophe is Nietzschean in the sense that it echoes Nietzsche's desire to culminate philosophy in a tragic experience of self-annihilation: '[...] that is what I recognized as the bridge to the psychology of the tragic poet. Not so as to get rid of pity

---

[37] Ibid., p. 554
[38] Ibid., p.555
[39] Jacques Derrida, 'Nombre de oui', Psyché, Inventions de l'autre (Paris: Galilée, 1987), p. 642

and terror, not so as to purify oneself of a dangerous emotion through its vehement discharge -: but, beyond pity and terror, to realize in oneself the eternal joy of becoming - that joy which also encompasses joy in destruction.'[40]

It is specifically this Nietzschean account of tragic catastrophe which shapes the poetic vocabulary of the practice of joy before death:

> Je me représente un mouvement et une excitation humaine dont les possibilités sont sans limite: ce mouvement et cette excitation ne peuvent être apaisés que par la guerre.
>
> Je me représente le don d'une souffrance infinie, du sang et des corps ouverts, à l'image d'une éjaculation, abattant celui qu'elle secoue et l'abandonnant à un epuisement chargé de nausées.
>
> Je me représente la Terre projetée dans l'espace, semblable à une femme criant la tête en flammes.
>
> Devant le monde terrestre dont l'été et l'hiver ordonnent l'agonie de tout ce qui est vivant, devant l'univers composé des étoiles innombrables qui tournent, se perdent et se consument sans mesure, je n'aperçois qu'une succession de splendeurs cruelles dont le mouvement même exige que je meure; cette mort n'est que consumation éclatante de tout ce qui était, joie d'exister de tout ce qui vient au monde; jusqu'à ma propre vie exige que tout ce qui est, en tous lieux, se donne et s'anéantisse sans cesse. [41]

The Nietzschean language of this text does not, however, work against the Oriental basis of Bataille's method. Indeed, the 'excessive' source of the mystical experience, the point of transgression, belongs not so much to Classical Hinduism, but more especially to the esoteric Tantric literature which is shared and studied by Hindus, Buddhists and Jains.

Specifically, Bataille here draws upon the cosmology of Tantric literature and, in particular borrows from Tantric meditative practice which aims at the annihilation of perceived chronological realities in a manner not unlike Nietzsche's promulgation of the notion of the Eternal Return. In Tantrism, the consciousness is described as moving - driven by the repetition of the Mantra and by other disciplines. The image is of a serpent, coiled and dormant, driven upward in the body during the various stages of enlightenment until it reaches the brain:

---

[40] Friedrich Nietzsche, *Twilight of the Idols*, trans. R.J.Hollingdale (London: Penguin, 1979), p.110

[41] 'La Pratique de la joie devant la mort', *ŒC*,I, p.557

When the serpent is awakened, it passes gradually through various stages, and comes to rest in the heart. Then the mind moves away; there is perception, and a great brilliance is seen. The worshipper, when he sees this brilliance, is struck with wonder. The serpent moves through six stages and coming to the highest one is united with it. When the serpent rises to the sixth stage the face of God is seen.[42]

'La pratique de la joie devant la mort' is prefaced by a quotation from Nietzsche which echoes this image of the serpent ('Tout cela je le suis, je veux l'être/ En même temps colombe, serpent et cochon'[43]). But perhaps more significantly, Bataille appropriates the Tantric method of entering the contemplative state through the representation to himself of certain images. In Tantrism, as in Buddhist or Hindu yogic practice, the adept employs a 'yantra', which delineates a consecrated place and protects it against disintegrating forces represented in demonic cycles. The 'yantra' is the geometric projection of the universe, spatially and temporally reduced to its essential planes. It represents in a schematic form the whole drama of disintegration and reintegration, and the adept standing in its centre identifies himself with the forces governing these. Just as in temple ritual, a vase is employed to bring down the divine power so that it may be projected into the drawing and into the person of the adept, the 'yantra' becomes a support for meditation, an instrument to provoke visions of the unseen.[44]

More significantly, tantric meditation aims at not the 'vritti', which we have examined as described by Swami Vivekananda in *Les grands maîtres spirituels dans l'Inde contemporaine*, but what is termed a 'paravritti': in translation, 'turning back up'. What this means is that instead of considering himself as at the end of a sequence of chronological events which start in the past and lead to the present, the adept must consider himself at the centre of all creation and that the past, the present and the future flow out of him.[45] In the same way that Nietzsche's idea of Eternal Return posits that existence is an endless state of becoming which starts and leads nowhere, Bataille's mystical ambition in this text is to achieve a 'timeless' moment which is an encounter with this fact. The act of meditating upon the 'yantra' is

---

[42] Ananda Coomaraswamy, *The Darker Side of Dawn* (London: Abraxas, 1935), p.46

[43] 'La Pratique de la joie devant la mort', *ŒC*,I, p.552

[44] This aspect of Tantric ritual is explained in Philip Rawson, *Tantra: The Indian Cult of Ecstasy* (London: Thames and Hudson, 1993), p.12-15.

[45] Philip Rawson, op. cit., p.12

meant to drive the mind into taking a backward look, to stare straight back into the continuing face of creation: in Yogic meditation the highest aim is to achieve '*samadhi* (lit. 'concentration'), the 'sleepless sleep', described as ' a state of pure isolation in which there is no sense of 'I' or 'mine', a consciousness of pure detachment from the world and from other souls [...] detached both from the world and from God, he [the Yogin] abides in his own essence alone'.[46]

According to Bruno, the 'lucide somnolence' which Bataille achieved in his mystical practices of 1938 became, as he developed his mastery of technique over the following months, 'évanescense', an advanced form of illumination; Bataille then, says Bruno, made rapid progress towards the advanced states of 'samadhi' attained in *Vijñana Bhairiva*, a tantra from the Kashmir region, in which exterior and interior sensations are interchangeable.[47]

Like the Tibetan masters, who alternately annihilated and renconstructed the world to convince themselves of its unreal nature, Bataille, writes Bruno, 'avait spontanément redécouvert, après son illumination, la fantasmagorie de notre univers sensoriel'.[48] For Bataille, who rejected the monist or theist claims of traditional mystics of East or West, this experience is a reversal which is a negation of all other possibilities.

Beau comme une guêpe

In several essays which describe his experiments with mystical experience which took place around the time of the composition of 'La pratique de la joie devant la mort', Bataille describes the contemplation of an image of torture and death. This image was a series of photographs taken in China in 1905 and which depicted the dismemberment of Fou Tchou Li, the assassin of Prince Ao Han Ouan. Bataille had been introduced to these images in 1925 in the course of psychoanalysis under Dr. Adrian Borel and over the years these photographs of the 'Dionysos chinois', 'hideux, hagard, zébré de sang, beau comme une guêpe', took on various meanings.[49]

---

[46] Ibid., p.25
[47] Op. cit., Jean Bruno, 'Les Techniques d'illumination chez Georges Bataille', p.716
[48] Ibid., p.716
[49] *ŒC*, I, p.139

Most significantly, having been used by Borel as a psychoanalytical tool, these photographs play the same role as an aid to Bataille's meditation as the Gammadion, or 'swastika yantra', does in Tantric practice: illumination is produced by the concentration of sexual energies into psychic reversal, a *paravritti*. Bataille thus describes the image of the youth as an experience which undoes the boundaries of sense in a sacrifice which overcomes death as an abstract negation. In Hegelian terms, the spectacle of ritual slaughter, like the spectacle of the ritual slaughter of the bullfighter Granero, is religious in the sense that it is a 'representation' ('Vorstellung') which is oppposed to thinking ('Denken'). Thus, in Bataille's terms, the subject who contemplates the object of representation of the radical negativity of death experiences a movement from sun into night which overwhelms discourse in the blinding darkness of non-meaning: this is, as we have observed, the central metonymic shift of inner experience.

The 'Vorstellung', however, for Hegel, is 'a partly opaque medium'[50] which, although it provides images of God, contradicts those images because it refers to a domain which is unknowable; the religious imagery of the Bible, for example, is neccesarily reduced to a particular discourse which cannot carry the weight of the full meaning of the text. For Hegel, 'Vorstellung' is, thus, below thought, as religion is below philosophy. In the same way, for Bataille, at least on one level, the techniques of mysticism, and in particular the photographs of 'Le supplice de cent morceaux', are a banality: he writes 'La connaissance du monde, en Hegel, est celle du premier venu (le premier venu, non Hegel, décide pour Hegel de la question clé: touchant la différence de la folie à la raison: le 'savoir absolu', sur ce point, conforme la notion vulgaire, est fondée sur elle, en est l'une des formes).'[51]

Kojève writes how, for Hegel, the subject and the object have no empirical reality; this contradiction, revealed in the movement of the subject away from itself in inner contemplation, is for Hegel a mode of consciousness which is related and which mediates 'le concept Absolu'; for Bataille it is expenditure which cannot be recuperated or function as a mediator; the structural basis of the dialectic is undermined by radical subjectivity. The contemplation of the dismembered youth is a

---

[50] Op. cit., Charles Taylor, p. 467
[51] *Méthode de Méditation, ŒC*, V, p.205

gazing into oneself and the meditation upon the image of 'Le supplice de cent morceaux' is for Bataille, 'une destruction plus intime' which aids the 'glissement à l'immanence' of inner experience. The practical basis of the experiences provoked by the photographs is not in opposition to Bataille's refusal to admit either the Hegelian dialectal process or the architecture, as opposed to the techniques, of Eastern or Western mysticism to his thought.

La profondeur du ciel

It is, however, also significant that the concluding section of 'La pratique de la joie devant la mort', 'Méditation Héraclitéenne', embraces chaos and signals the dissolution of perceived chronological realities and moral categories as the highest form of irrational desire: in the same way that the contemplation of the 'Supplice des cent morceaux' provoked an internalisation of horror which was the first step towards silence, the irrational and poetic violence of the coming war, a world in flames, could be internalised as the largest Dionysian form of reality. Although appropriating the vocabulary and techniques of yoga, the reference to Heraclitus and the identification with the violent flux of the cosmos point to an engagement with a complex series of realities which are obviously not the same thing as the free communion implied by the orthodox Yogic way. Indeed, the absence of God is, for Bataille, a paradox, 'a vertiginous reversal', which, although dramatized in textual experience in the metaphor of the wound, in terms of literal mystical experience the experience of 'joy before death' can only function as a being in contradiction.

Moreover, although during the period he composed 'La joie devant la mort' for the Collège de Sociologie and 'La pratique de la joie devant la mort' for the final edition of Acéphale, Bataille had not yet met Maurice Blanchot, the themes of impossibility and silence are common to their respective writings at this stage. For Bataille, in particular, the poetic necessity for silence is at the centre of the experience of 'l'impossible'. Silence, for Bataille, is central to inner experience in so far as its halts the subjective consciousness's participation in the chronological unfolding of events: it effectively calls a halt to all movement in time and space. And in the same way that Mallarmé claims emptiness as the central point of his poetry, the participant in the practice of 'Acephalic' meditation has to claim

74

annihilation of self and consciousness of self as the central focus of being.

Je suis la joie devant la mort
La profondeur du ciel, l'espace perdu est joie devant la mort:
tout est profondément fêlé.
Je me représente l'instant glacé de ma propre mort [52]

In the light of this, the 'Acephalic' method of meditation described and advocated in 'La pratique de la joie devant la mort' seems to be not too far from the familiar and well-documented process of self-hypnosis which allows a certain regression into disordered states of mind.

L'existence mystique de celui dont la 'joie devant la mort' est devenue la violence intérieure ne peut rencontrer en aucun cas une béatitude satifaisante par elle-même, comparable à celle du chrétien se donnant l'avant-goût de l'éternité. Le mystique de la joie devant la mort ne peut pas être regardé comme traqué en ce sens qu'il est en état de rire en toute légèreté de chaque possibilité humaine et de connaître chaque enchantement accessible: cependant la totalité de la vie - la contemplation extatique et la connaissance lucide s'accomplissant dans une action qui ne peut pas manquer de devenir risque - est tout aussi inexorablement son lot que la mort est celui du condamné.[53]

The implications of this are that 'Sovereign' experience as an encounter with silence or emptiness as an Absolute experience apparently only makes sense in the context of an atheological framework, that is to say a system of thought which cannot offer the possibility of ascendance or transcendence. That is why Bataille, aware of both the 'impossibility' of sovereign experience also refers to 'opération souveraine' of inner experience as 'l'opération comique' (this description, he says, is also 'moins trompeur'; similarly he also refers to Hegel's spell of madness as a young man as 'petite récapitulation comique'[54]).

If 'l'opération souveraine' means the dominance of one man over men, or union with the Divine Being, or in any tangible sense for man to become as God, the notion of sovereignty is literally meaningless: all hierarchies are shattered in the negative mediation of inner experience. Unlike the mediation which Hegel posits as the necessary relation between opposites which is at the foundation of the Absolute,

---

[52]'La Pratique de la joie devant la mort' Œ̄C, I, pp. 555-556
[53] Ibid., pp. 553
[54] L'Expérience intérieure, ŒC, V, p.56

Bataille's inner experience displaces ultimate meaning into sacrificial effusion, 'joy in the face of death'.

However, although aware of the 'impossibility' of an experience predicated simultaneously on a transgression of the Hegelian dialectic and the techniques of Eastern mysticism, Bataille insists that man can experience sovereignty in the face of Absence. Moreover, in 'La pratique de la joie devant la mort' he insists that he had himself experienced the ecstatic truth of silence by overturning hierarchical or categorical systems of thought. This leap into impossible experience is a sort of revelation, or anti-revelation, in the original sense of an 'unveiling of truth' which annihilates all other truths. This is how 'Acephalic' mystical experience it comes to be Absolute and 'sovereign'.

Thus, the texts of *La Somme athéologique*, like the writings of saints in communion with God, are thus at once intended as not only an engagement with the drama of the extreme point of experience, where language and identity collapse into the Absolute, but also as texts which undermine themselves in a negative movement towards silence. In the absence of God, or, as is the aim of Eastern mysticism a transcendent experience of the Absolute, the term mysticism, seems redundant in atheological terms; Bataille's pursuit of silence is a contradiction which preserves intact all the other structures of traditional theology; his mysticism is in the terms ascribed by Christian thinkers an empty parody. Audoin, however, refutes this accusation;

> S'agit-il, comme on le dit souvent, d'un mysticisme sans Dieu?
> En aucune façon. Sartre, qui n'entendait rien à ces choses, a accusé Bataille de conserver intacts, au nom de Dieu près, et l'édifice de la théologie, et la croyance qu'il implique, en substituant simplement le mot Absence au mot Dieu. C'est pour le moins simpliste. C'est surtout un grave contre-sens. Lorsque le mystique rhénan, Maître Eckhart, affirme: 'Dieu est Absence', cela veut dire que par essence, il se dérobe (*Deus absconditus*). Mais quand Bataille dit: Absent, néant, vide..., il faut le prendre littéralement.[55]

As Audoin says, the words 'Absent, néant, vide' each have a literal meaning for Bataille. In the same way that *L'Expérience intérieure*, as

---

[55] Philippe Audoin, *Sur Georges Bataille* (Paris: Actual/Le temps qu'il fait, 1987), pp.30-31

76

the central text *of La Somme athéologique*, provides not only a theoretical, but a practical framework for his thought.

Morover, the texts which preceded the publication of *L'Expérience intérieure*, and which were partly consumed by it, not only mark a major shift in Bataille's development as a political thinker concerned with integrating the sacred into the social (one of Caillois's lesser objections to his 'mysticism' was precisely that such intransigence was unhelpful to collective effort[56]), but also, as he turns into his own 'interiority' - 'abandoned' by the community he had led - show him preoccupied with the 'violence intérieure' of identity and contradiction in a way which allows no way out: inner experience is not compatible with the unity of homogeneous existence. This, in essence, is a development of the anti-idealist 'bas matérialisme' which Breton had disparaged and which Bataille himself found to be incompatible with Surrealism.

Similarly, having moved away from the possibility of political 'work' in the Collège de Sociologie, and as the ultimate political solution of war looms on the horizon, Bataille finds that the practice of 'The joy before death' as method, in terms of Eastern techniques, and experience, a lacerating collapse of identity, is at the end-point of his encounter with Kojève's Hegel.

Inner experience, as Bataille begins to write almost immediately after the outbreak of war, is a journey towards the end of thought and language which ends in 'un arrêt dans le mouvement qui nous porte à l'appréhension plus obscure de l'inconnu: d'une présence qui n'est plus distincte en rien d'une absence.'[57]

However, the interrogation of totality which takes place in the movement of inner experience, the sacrifice of 'ipse', is a necessity which denies all form of reduction. The possibility of transcendence, as a movement towards God or Absence, is annihilated in the immanent experience of sovereign ecstasy. Thus, Absence is not simply a metonymic substitution for God: inner experience, unlike the 'Aufhebung', is not a process which can aim at or recognise the possibility of reconciliation, neither in the Hegelian sense, nor as the

---

[56] Bataille's response to this criticism can be found in Georges Bataille, *Choix de Lettres*, op. cit., pp.166-170

[57] *L'Expérience intérieure*, *ŒC*, V, p.17

'coincidentia oppositorum' of Nicholas of Cusa. All forms of reconcilation are transcendent in the sense that the dialectical movement is subordinate to the resolution of oppposites in a Hegelian triadic movement. This means that although, as Bataille recognised, 'joy before death' is not beyond expression - either distilled into poetry or explained in prose - it reveals nothing and no belief can be set out from it.

Most importantly, unlike Breton's conception of poetic experience as a method and process which emerges out of the Hegelian dialectic, inner experience is an unmediated contradiction which defies all systematic processes. As we seen, however, for Bataille, absence of method is also a method.

Chapter Three

Bataille and Blanchot:
The dialogue behind inner experience

> Le tout sans nouveauté qu'un
> espacement de la lecture.
> Stéphane Mallarmé, *Un coup de dés*
> *jamais n'abolira le hasard*

Bataille describes the inner experience as an experience which is accompanied by a sensation of inner emptiness. The point of arrival of the movement of inner experience is a state, equivalent to the Christian state of grace or the satori of Zen Buddhism, in which discourse is abolished. This is the experience which Bataille describes as the 'expérience nue' of 'le non-savoir'.

Bataille quotes St. Teresa to describes this movement. He does this partly to illustrate the extent to which the annihilation of the self which occurs in inner experience is also at the centre of Christian mystical experience: 'Ce qui me fait tressaillir d'amour n'est pas le ciel que tu m'as promis, l'horrible enfer ne me fait pas tressaillir..., s'il n'y avait pas de ciel je t'aimerais et s'il n'y avait pas d'enfer je te craindrais'. The loss of identity and the dispersal of categories described here by Teresa are, for Bataille, the central axes of the mystical encounter: all else in the Christian faith, writes Bataille, is pure commodity.[1]

The central argument of this chapter is that the 'expérience nue' finds, as observed in the preceding chapters, not only an equivalence in the writings of traditional mystics, but also a fictional corollary in the writings of Maurice Blanchot. Although there is a key distinction to be drawn between the fictional texts of Blanchot, who in his earliest novels, like Kafka, represents the act of writing as a static act rather than a transgressive one, there is also a sense in which Blanchot's concerns mirror Bataille's preoccupations with impossible experience. More can be revealed about the texts of *L'Expérience intérieure* in Bataille's conversations with his friend and by reading the latter's *récits* of this time.

---

[1] *ŒC*, V, p.32.

Most importantly, Blanchot, like Bataille, not only interrogates the substance of textual reality, but is suspicious of the act of writing to the extent that, as Bataille writes, 'seule la littérature pouvait mettre à nu le jeu de la transgression de la loi - sans laquelle la loi n'aurait pas de fin - indépendamment d'un ordre à créer [...] La littérature est même, comme la transgression de la morale, un danger.'[2] It is significant, then, that as Blanchot indicates, the relation between Bataille and Blanchot's thought has its origins not in the space of the written text but in the contiguities of both their meetings and conversations, which were sustained throughout the writing of *L'Expérience intérieure* and Blanchot's early fictions.

Both sets of work form an 'entretien' or interlocution which is related to and defines the other. Blanchot himself, commenting on the the elliptical nature of Bataille's inner experience, and his own conversations with Bataille on that subject, writes:

> Il me semble que, d'une manière peut-être unique dans notre société, Georges Bataille eut le pouvoir de parler, non moins que d'écrire. Je ne fais pas allusion à des dons d'éloquence, mais à quelque chose de plus important: le fait d'être présent par sa parole et, dans cette présence de parole, par l'entretien le plus direct, d'ouvrir l'attention jusqu'au centre.'[3]

For Blanchot, the presence of the spoken word of Bataille, which is simultaneously an absence in the written text of *L'Expérience intérieure*, is a paradox which, like *ipse*'s collapse into its own non-being, is both cause and effect of experience beyond language: this is how the 'livre [...] du desintoxiqué',[4] *L'Expérience intérieure*, comes to exist in a literary space created out of absence: this is also what Bataille means by describing the work as 'le récit d'un désespoir'.[5]

---

[2] Op. cit., *La littérature et le mal*, p.112.
[3] Maurice Blanchot, 'Le Jeu de la Pensée', *Critique*, 195-196, 1963, p. 734.
[4] *L'Expérience intérieure*, *ŒC*, V, p.10.
[5] Ibid., p.11.

L'Amitié

The initial meeting between Bataille and Blanchot took place in Paris at the end of 1940, where they were introduced to each other by Pierre Prévost. [6] It was, as they both later acknowledged, a pivotal moment in their intellectual itineraries which had a decisive and irreversible impact on the development of their respective ideas on subjective experience and, in a direct and immediate way, shaped the nature of their writings on the possibilities and impossibilities of communication. Indeed, the nature of their conversations, for Blanchot, was shaped by the very act of writing being separated from discourse; Blanchot insists upon the centrality of this notion to Bataille's discourse on inner experience:

> Parlant avec simplicité, avec cette gravité légère de la parole, présent par sa parole non pas en se servant d'elle pour exprimer une sensibilité pathétique, mais pour affirmer [...] le souci auquel ses interlocuteurs ne l'ont jamais entendu se dérober, Georges Bataille a ainsi lié les détours de l'entretien au jeu illimité de la pensée. Je voudrais insister sur ce point. Quand, en général, nous parlons, nous voulons dire quelque chose que nous savons déjà, soit le faire partager à quelqu'un d'autre, parce que cela nous paraît vrai, soit, au mieux, le vérifier en le soumettant à un nouveau jugement. Plus rare est déjà une parole qui, tandis qu'elle s'exprime, réfléchit - et peut-être parce que la disposition à parler ne favorise pas la réflexion qui a besoin aussi de temps, un temps vide, monotone et solitaire que l'on ne saurait partager, sans gêne, avec un autre interlocuteur à son tour silencieux. Pourtant, dans un certain genre de dialogue, il arrive que cette réflexion s'accomplisse par le seul fait que la parole est divisée, redoublée: ce qui est d'une fois d'un côté et non pas seulement réaffirmé, mais (parce qu'il y a reprise) élevé à une forme d'affirmation nouvelle où, changeant de place, la chose dite entre en

---

[6] This meeting is described in Surya, op. cit., p. 378-84 and also by Pierre Prévost in *Pierre Prévost rencontre Georges Bataille* (Paris, Jean-Michel Place, 1987) p.86. Bataille himself writes, in the third person, of the encounter and its context in an autobiographical note: 'Une mort l'a déchiré en 1938. C'est dans une solitude achevée qu'il commence d'écrire, dans les premiers jours de la guerre, *Le Coupable*, où il décrit à mesure une expérience mystique hétérodoxe, en même temps que certaines de ses réactions devant les événements. Dès la fin de 1940, il rencontre Maurice Blanchot, auquel le lient sans tarder l'admiration et l'accord.' *ŒC*, VI, p.486. Blanchot gives a detailed account of his relationship to Bataille in several texts, the most important of which are *Faux Pas* (Paris: Gallimard, 1943), *L'Entretien infini* (Paris: Gallimard 1969), *L'Amitié* (Paris: Gallimard, 1971), and *La Communauté inavouable* (Paris: Éditions de Minuit, 1983)

rapport avec sa différence, devient plus aiguë, plus tragique, non pas plus unifiée, mais au contraire suspendue tragiquement entre deux pôles d'attraction. [7]

The paradox of 'tragic' communication is that, as Blanchot decribes, the subject which speaks (Bataille) is necessarily caught in an apophatic movement to which the Other can only respond in silence; the 'redoubling' of the spoken word in the self-reflection of meaning is both a snare and a potential release of meaning into discontinuity. The nature of the dialogue between Blanchot and Bataille thus displaces the potential resolution of a dialectical movement into ellipsis and disperses meaning into fragments; as Bataille describes the 'tragic' communication in the movement of inner experience, ' Tu ne pourrais devenir le miroir d'une réalité déchirante si tu ne devais te briser...'. [8] This is how inner experience, for Bataille and Blanchot, is both experience of impossibility and the communication of this impossibility.

It is further significant that Blanchot's political background, at the stage in his career when he first encountered Bataille, was, to say the least, somewhat ambiguous. Sartre, in his review of *Aminadab,* refers to Blanchot as a 'disciple de Maurras' [9] and indeed, Blanchot had come to know Prévost through the 'Jeune France' movement - which included such disparate figures as Georges Pelorson, Emmanuel Mounier and Maurice Kahane (who would later change his name to Girodias and go on to finance the first issues of *Critique,* as well as running the Olympia Press) - and which despite its avowedly apolitical nature was, nonetheless, financed by Vichy and a vehicle for Vichy propaganda. [10] Bataille, however, was interested in Blanchot's insistence upon intellectual activity in the face of the immediate exigencies of the Occupation.

Although this was apparently in direct contradiction to the earlier, revolutionary Bataille who, as the leading influence upon the 'Collège de Sociologie', launched calls to action in the name of 'le sacrifice de

---

[7] Maurice Blanchot, 'Le Jeu de la Pensée', op. cit., *Critique,* 195-196, pp. 737-738.

[8] *L'Expérience intérieure, ŒC,* V, p.78.

[9] Jean-Paul Sartre, 'Aminadab, ou du fantastique consideré comme un langage.' *Situations 1* (Paris: 1947), p.114.

[10] Blanchot's relationship to 'Jeune France' is analysed by Patrick ffrench, 'The Corpse of Theory: Bataille/ Blanchot - excavation of an encounter', 'Kojève's Paris: Bataille Now', *parallax, 4,* 1997, p. 104.

la vie', the exchanges between Bataille and Blanchot were nonetheless political in the sense that they were both concerned with the meaning and function of a community which had collapsed into incoherence; the German Ocupation was a literal demonstration of Bataille's notion, expounded before the 'Collège de Sociologie', of how, lacking a religious centre founded on sacrifice, a society will commit suicide. As Sollers points out, inner experience is a renunciation which permits 'aucune issue collective' but which, like Tropmann's desire for suicide in *Le Bleu du Ciel*, stands as a metaphor for the individual responsibility for collective failure. [11]

Blanchot's pre-war activities, on the other hand, and in particular his contribution to the right-wing journal *Combat*, unlike those of Bataille, were predicated on an extreme form of nationalism, clearly following a lineage from Drumont to Maurras. These writings have provoked a great deal of discussion in recent years and unlike Céline, for example - whose pamphlets demonstrated as much an extreme horror of 'la patrie' as of anti-semitism - Blanchot's writings, although (like Céline) pacifist in nature, are explicitly faithful to an idea of France which excludes the possibility of failure. This is, obviously, an irony compounded by the fact that this version of France was about to collapse into the disaster of 1940.

Indeed, one of the most serious charges laid against Blanchot is that not only does his nostalgic and reactionary nationalism contradict his later position as a writer of metaphysical parables (How can a writer devoted to Maurrasien 'penser français' imitate the Central European mode of Kafka? asks Sartre[12]), but that, at the moment of crisis, he also disowned his past and disavowed all political commitment.[13] Although little is known of Blanchot's wartime career in the Resistance or

---

[11] Philippe Sollers, 'Une prophétie de Bataille', *La Guerre du Goût*, Gallimard: Paris, 1996, p.484.

[12] Op. cit., Jean-Paul Sartre, 'Aminadab, ou du fantastique consideré comme un langage', p.114.

[13] Blanchot's career as a right wing political journalist is discussed at length in Jeffrey Mehlman, *Legacies of Anti-Semitism in France* (Minneapolis: Minnesota University Press, 1983) and Philippe Mesnard, 'Maurice Blanchot: le sujet de l'engagement', *L'Infini*, 48, 1994. A letter from Jeffrey Mehlman to Maurice Nadeau on the same subject appears in *L'Infini*, 1, 1983. See also Leslie Hill, *Maurice Blanchot: Extreme Contemporary* (London: Routledge: 1997), pp. 36-45 and Patrick ffrench op. cit., 'The corpse of theory', pp. 99-119.

otherwise, this crucial period in his career remains both an enigma and a decisive turning point.[14]

However, although much of the facts of Blanchot's past remain obscure - largely because of Blanchot's own distaste for autobiography - it is clear that by the time he met Bataille his career as a political journalist played an important part in the development of his thinking, not only with respect to the immediate consequences of political action, but also upon the nature of language. In particular, as Blanchot moves from the verbal violence of right-wing polemic to fictions of a metaphysical nature, his relationship to the use of language becomes ambiguous and, indeed, one of suspicion and shame. Language, for Blanchot, especially in the specific context of Occupied Paris, but also in the context of the inner experience the character Thomas undergoes in his fictions, is a transgression which precludes all other ontological activity.[15] Thus, the language of Blanchot's fictions, partly conceived and written in response to Bataille's disquisitions on his own inner experience, demonstrates a central concern, above all, with the paradox of the impossibility of communication and its role in social space.

At this stage Bataille was similarly preoccupied with the working out of the notions of community he had developed before the war in the 'Collège de Sociologie' and *Acéphale*. Although, as he worked on the drafts of *L'Expérience intérieure* he came to see both these projects as relative failures, he also saw himself as cut adrift from the intellectual currents which were flowing in the direction of either Sartrean existentialism, which eschewed the interiority of Bataille's perspective in favour of direct political commitment, or the 'religious' humanism of 'la pensée praeterexistentielle'[16] represented, in differing

---

[14] Leslie Hill suggests that a rare autobiographical text, *L'instant de ma mort* (Montpélier: Fata Morgana, 1994) may be an account of how Blanchot faced a German firing squad at an unspecified date during the war. Leslie Hill, *Blanchot: Extreme Contemporary* (London: Routledge, 1997), p.12.

[15] Leslie Hill compares *Thomas l'Obscur* with Sartre's *La Nausée* and says that what they have in common is that they both represent 'a foundational philosophical enterprise'. Leslie Hill, op. cit., p.62

[16] This is a term used by Michel Surya to describe the grouping together of Gabriel Marcel, Camus, Unamuno, Kierkegaard, Dostoyevsky, Berdyaev and Bataille by Gérard Deledalle in *L'existentiel, philosophes et littératures de l'existence* (Editions Renée Lacoste, Paris: 1949), who opposes them to the 'penséee existentielle' of Heidegger, Jaspers and Sartre. Surya, op. cit. p. 492.fn.3.

forms, by the atheist Camus or the Christian Gabriel Marcel, but which Bataille considered separate from the concerns of atheology.

It is therefore unsurprising that Bataille should find in Blanchot - who had not passed through or come into contact with Surrealism - not only an ally but also, as he came to terms with his relative isolation and the failure of the projects of community, both concrete and theoretical, as incarnated in *Acéphale* and the 'Collège de Sociologie', someone who could not only explain this failure to him, but explain it in terms which, on a metaphorical and literal level, justified their performative as well as descriptive functions. In the same way that Bataille, in *l'Expérience intérieure* in particular, cites not only sections of Blanchot's work but also his conversations, Blanchot, in his first two novels, responds to and develops many of Bataille's notions on the impossibility of communication. In *La Communauté inavouable*, a late text from 1983, Blanchot, having recalled his own political itinerary of the post-War period, returns to the specific questions addressed by himself and Bataille before the war and at the time of their first meetings. Above all, Blanchot stresses the aspect of Bataille's thinking which privileges interiority over community and communication: inner experience is 'le glissement hors des limites' which at the same time as it founds itself in community, both attacks that community and exposes the possibility of its own finitude.

In the project of *Acéphale*, Bataille demonstrated the failure of community as an absence which is irreducible to the demands of social or political hierarchies. Inner experience, similarly, is a transgression of the possibility of communication at the same time as it presents itself as an impossibility and a movement towards the collapse into infinite exteriority. Thus inner experience, for Blanchot, is the expiation of all authority in the sacrifice of the subject in 'le non-savoir'; 'sacrifier n'est pas tuer, mais abandonner et donner.'[17] This, for Bataille, is the movement towards the reversal of summit and the collapse of *ipse* into itself.

---

[17] Maurice Blanchot, *La Communauté inavouable* (Paris: Éditions de Minuit, 1983), p.15

La nudité de la nuit

Blanchot's first two novels, *Thomas l'Obscur* and *Aminadab*, were published in 1941 and 1942 respectively. *Thomas l'Obscur* was originally conceived in 1932, published in 1941 and succeeded by an amended edition in 1950; according to Prévost, Blanchot burnt all his earlier fictions before submitting his first novel to his publisher in 1940. Both novels concern a central character, Thomas, who undergoes a series of allegorical meetings and experiences which are partly or never explained; although Blanchot denied the influence of Kafka - and there is little in his pre-war itinerary to suggest the influence of a Central European Jew - both novels have a clear parallel with Kafka's narrative technique and his concerns; in particular, many critics have been reminded of Kafka's metaphysical fable, *The Castle*. At the same time, 'as part inner experience, part self-reflexive *mise-en abyme*',[18] as Blanchot himself acknowledges, both these works betray the presence of Bataille as a presence and as an important influence in both the conceptual shape and textual surface of the works. In particular, the language used by Blanchot to describe Thomas' experiences not only parallels the vocabulary used by Bataille to describe his own inner experience, but also, in the expiation of authority which occurs at a textual and thematic level in these allegories, Blanchot matches Bataille's own reflections on the authority of inner experience; Bataille writes:

> Conversation avec Blanchot. Je lui dis: l'expérience intérieure n'a ni but, ni autorité, qui la justifient. Si je fais sauter, éclater le souci d'un but, d'une autorité, du moins subsiste-t-il un vide. Blanchot me rappelle que but, autorité sont des exigences de la pensée discursive; j'insiste, décrivant l'expérience sous la forme donnée en dernier lieu, lui demandant comment il croit cela possible sans autorité ni rien. Il me dit que l'expérience elle-même est l'autorité. Il ajoute au sujet de cette autorité qu'elle doit être expiée.[19]

In *Thomas l'Obscur* and *Aminadab*, the experiences undergone by Thomas are all associated with the passing away of meaning and authority into the metaphorized versions of the void; these metaphors are usually, the sea, the night, or a fading of light. The authority of

---

[18] Leslie Hill, *Blanchot: Extreme Contemporary* (London: Routledge, 1997), p.54
[19] *L'Expérience intérieure, Œuvres complètes, V*, p.67

Blanchot's texts themselves, as has been pointed out, is therefore predicated upon the opposite of what they can possibly represent;[20] at each stage in the allegory the narrative is undone by what is not said or represented; death is an absence which haunts the textual presence of both the author and his characters.

In particular, in the earlier version of *Thomas l'Obscur*, Thomas, in his encounter with his own non-being, passes through a partial suicide and encounters what Blanchot in a later work refers to as 'la mort impossible'. This 'death in life' appears mystical in that it is an experience which comes to Thomas as a significant moment of illumination about his own existence, although he does not grasp the meaning of this illumination. The absence of meaning is itself part of the moment of Thomas' inner experience; that there is no object for his inner experience means that the subject is thrown back upon itself in a movement of pure negativity. This is how, in *L'Expérience intérieure*, Bataille can describe *Thomas l'Obscur* as a volume which discusses questions of 'la nouvelle théologie (qui n'a l'inconnu pour objet)' in his own terms of reference;[21] for Bataille, both in conversation and in his novel, Blanchot incarnates the three principles of 'la vie spirituelle', which are absence of salvation, authority which expiates itself and non-knowledge ('le non-savoir').

Bataille quotes a section from chapter three of *Thomas l'Obscur* in which the image of the night, central for Bataille and Blanchot, represents the impossibilities of 'le savoir' and 'le non-savoir'in a metaphorical account of the self-wounding of inner experience. As Thomas peers deep into the gloom he can only make out an absence of vision; the 'moment tragique', where the subject, *ipse*, consumes itself as the object of its own gaze; the night is thus a pure and irrecuperable negativity which, as it is consumed by the subject, itself reverses the relation between subject and object and consumes both in the impenetrable impossibility of radical discontinuity.

> La nuit lui parut bientôt plus sombre, plus terrible que n'importe quelle autre nuit, comme si elle était réellement sortie d'une blessure de la pensée qui ne se pensait plus, de la pensée prise ironiquement comme objet par autre chose que la pensée. C'était la nuit même. Des images qui faisaient son obscurité l'inondaient, et le

---

[20] Leslie Hill, op.cit., *Blanchot:Extreme contemporary*, pp. 57-63
[21] *L'Expérience intérieure*, *ŒC*, V, p. 120

corps transformé en un esprit démoniaque cherchait à se représenter. Il ne voyait
rien et, loin d'être accablé, il faisait de son absence de visions le point culminant
de son regard. Son oeil, inutile pour voir, prenait des proportions extraordinaires,
se développait d'une manière démesurée et, s'étendant sur l'horizon, laissait la nuit
pénétrer en son centre pour se créer un iris. Par ce vide c'était donc le regard et
l'objet du regard qui se mêlaient. Non seulement cet oeil qui ne voyait rien
appréhendait la cause de sa vision. Il voyait comme un objet, ce qui faisait qu'il ne
voyait pas. En lui son propre regard entrait sous la forme d'une image au moment
tragique où ce regard était considéré comme la mort de toute image.[22]

The 'blessure de la pensée' which opens up the experience of night is
not simply a reversal of the Cartesian *cogito*, but rather a snare, an
ironic trap, in which thought is seized and paralysed in the gaze of the
Other;[23] thus thought which is conscious of itself as a process arrests
itself in a partial suicide and awakens the impossibility of that which
subsumes thought into the void. Thomas's collapse into himself finds a
parallel in inner experience in *ipse*'s inability to maintain itelf as a
stable thinking subject; the metaphor of light fading into darkness is
enclosed in a space which allows no exit.

La vie va se perdre dans la mort, les fleuves dans la mer et le connu dans
l'inconnu. La connaissance est l'accès de l'inconnu. Le non-sens est
l'aboutissement de chaque sens possible.
    C'est une sottise épuisante que, là où, visiblement, tous les moyens
manquent, l'on prétende cependant savoir, au lieu de connaître son ignorance, de
reconnaître l'inconnu, mais plus triste est l'infirmité de ceux qui, s'ils n'ont plus de
moyens, avouent qu'ils ne savent pas, mais se cantonnent bêtement dans ce qu'ils
savent. De toute façon, qu'un homme ne vive pas avec la pensée incessante de
,l'inconnu fait d'autant plus douter de l'intelligence que le même est avide, mais
aveuglément, de trouver dans les choses la part qui l'oblige d'aimer, ou le secoue

---

[22] Ibid., pp.119-120

[23] The use and definition of this term is for Sartre the source of the ontological
anxiety which characterises existentialist thinking (see, for example, the problem of the
Other as defined in the chapter 'L'existence d'autrui' in Jean-Paul Sartre, *L'Être et le
néant* (Paris: Gallimard, 1973), pp.275-276. The term 'Other' is used in this thesis,
however, in the Hegelian sense, as it was defined by Kojève and understood by
Bataille, of a objective and separate, real consciousness which defines the subject's
individual feeling of particularity. '[...] dans la terminologie de Hegel [...] l'Homme
vraiment humain, ou radicalement différent de l'animal, recherche toujours la
Reconnaissance et ne se réalise qu'en tant que reconnu effectivement.' Kojève, op. cit.
Introduction à la lecture de Hegel, p.507.

d'un rire inextinguible, celle de l'inconnu. Mais il en est de même de la lumière; les yeux n'en ont que les reflets.[24]

Thus, the inner experience of absence of vision, or 'death in life', is, for both Bataille and Blanchot, the most general category of being: the dialectic of subject and object, the progressive temporality of historical growth, are revealed as inauthentic experiences; inner experience reveals a more fundamental oscillatory movement in the realm of being. The 'mystical' nature of the experience is in both the apophatic movement away from language into the 'night', both metaphorical and real, where langage cannot name itself, and in the movement towards suicide or self-mutilation, which Thomas experiences as his loss of self, and which, in Bataille's inner experience, is not so much a fusion of subject and object in the experience of death but a wounding, 'blessure de la pensée', which is a sacrifice. Blanchot explains this in *L'Espace littéraire*:

> Celui qui se tue est le grand affirmateur du présent. Je veux me tuer dans un instant 'absolu', le seul qui triomphera absolument de l'avenir, qui ne passera pas et ne sera pas dépassé. La mort, si elle survenait à l'heure choisie, serait une apothéose de l'instant; l'instant, en elle, serait l'étincelle même des mystiques, et par là, assurément, le suicide garde le pouvoir d'une affirmation exceptionnelle, demeure un événement qu'on ne peut se contenter de dire volontaire, qui échappe à l'usure et déborde la préméditation.
>
> [...]On ne peut pas 'projeter' de se tuer. Cet apparent projet s'élance vers quelque chose qui n'est jamais atteint, vers un but qui ne peut être visé, et la fin est ce que je ne saurais prendre pour fin.[25]

More specifically, in *Thomas l'Obscur*, Blanchot sketches a map of poetic consciousness which leads back to the same negative act of dissolution and forgetting which occurs in the inner experience. Effectively, like *L'Expérience intérieure*, the novel is an ontological meditation which confirms the existence of a fundamental distance at the heart of all human experience. In the ascesis of depersonalization, Thomas frees his consciousness of inauthentic concerns and asserts the existence of a symbolic language which, like Bataille's inner experience, lies beyond the presence of the world. Blanchot aims, in

---

[24] *L'Expérience intérieure*, *ŒC*, V, p. 120
[25] Maurice Blanchot, *L'Espace littéraire* (Paris: Gallimard, 1955), p. 210

Thomas l'Obscur, and in fact all his writing, at a similar ascesis, both at the level of the text, and also (in a way which interested Bataille) in a less metaphorical sense. Blanchot is related to Mallarmé, whose themes of death, boredom and sterility are the corollary to Blanchot's own fascination with non-being and absence.

But for Blanchot, impersonality, the disintegration of the subjective consciousness, are less psychological concerns, but, as they were for Mallarmé, attempts to recapture the origin of the self: the moment of communication with the void is thus a moment which denies the possibility of subjective consciousness outside language.

> Autour de son corps, il savait que sa pensée, confondue avec la nuit veillait. Il savait, terrible certitude, qu'elle aussi cherchait une issue pour entrer en lui. Contre ses lèvres, dans sa bouche, elle s'efforçait à une union monstreuse. Sous les paupières, elle créait un regard nécessaire. Et en même temps elle détruisait furieusement ce visage qu'elle embrassait. Villes prodigieuses, cités ruinées disparurent. Les pierres furent rejetées au dehors. [...] Seul, le corps de Thomas subsista privé de sens. Et la pensée, rentrée en lui, échangea des contacts avec le vide. [26]

Similarly, the suppression of the subjective moment in *Thomas l'Obscur*, asserted in *L'Expérience intérieure* in the form of the categorical impossibility of self-reflection, is only a preparatory step in Thomas' hermeneutic understanding of the self. For Blanchot, the most important strategy against sinking, like the protagonist of Mallarmé's 'Un Coup de dés', into the 'ocean' of the natural world is the recognition of language as an autonomous and impersonal entity.

The mystical significance of the metaphor of 'night', for Bataille and Blanchot, is, therefore, that it destabilizes the logic of presence in the movement of inner experience towards self-annihilation. In the same way that Thomas in *Thomas l'Obscur* peceives his own non-being in the inner experience of staring into the night, or, in *Aminadab*, the shadows lengthen outside the house where Thomas wanders along the passages in the impossible search for himself, the experience of the night which reveals the unseeing eye is properly 'mystical' in the sense that it comes as a revelation, or anti-revelation, which undoes all categorical versions of 'truth'. 'La nudité du non-savoir' incarnate in

---

[26] Maurice Blanchot, *Thomas l'Obscur* (Paris: Gallimard, 1950), p.45.

the metaphor of the night is also a metonymic figure which opens the blank eye to its own blindness.

Ex-orbitant vision

Bataille and Blanchot are, however, not only concerned with the metonymic ambiguities of vision (night and day, blindness and insight, the eye) in the context of the 'religious' aspect of inner experience, that is to say the aspect which is concerned with the moment of communication between the thinking subject and the experience of its own nothingness, but also the relation of these ambiguities to language and the act of writing. Martin Jay, citing a paper by Blanchot, describes the textual blindness of inner experience as 'Orpheus' gaze [...] the founding act of writing because it crosses the threshold of death and seeks in vain to a return of visual presence that cannot be restored.'[27] As we have seen, this blindness is also, for Bataille and Blanchot, 'mystical' in the sense that it is an ecstasy which takes the subject across 'the threshold of death'. It displaces subject and and object in a 'timeless' moment which transgresses both the logic of presence and the possibility of writing as communication. Blanchot, in a recollection of his meetings with Bataille at the time he was writing *La Somme athéologique*, puts emphasis not only the importance of Bataille's presence as a speaker, as opposed to an *écrivain* at the meetings, but also on the way in which Bataille's language escaped the paradigmatic structures of philosophy and exposed itself a pure paradox.

The neutral, for Blanchot, represents an impossibility which overwhelms the act of writing. Literature, therefore, for Bataille and Blanchot, is a subjection to an impossible ethics which destroys the notion of textual authenticity in the same space as it affirms a responsibility to exhaust language in discourse. Inner experience, as discourse which seeks its own death, is thus, for Bataille and Blanchot, a form of aphasia which, like the graceful ellipses of Valéry's poetry which is in pursuit of an absolute mind, or Mallarmé's labyrinth of abstraction, emerges from the quest for impersonality: the collapse of

---

[27] Martin Jay, op. cit., *Downcast Eyes*, p.353.

'ipséité'. 'Le silence est un mot qui n'est pas un mot et le souffle un objet qui n'est pas un objet,' writes Bataille. [28]

At the centre of Bataille's inner experience, as Blanchot describes it, is thus the paradox of the impossibility of communication. At the centre of inner experience there is no underlying unifying force of universal consciousness to be revealed in the moment of communication, but instead, non-being or non-meaning, which is an absence which is distinct from nothingness. As an exercise in practical nihilism, Bataille's mysticism is based upon the recognition and acceptance of emptiness which will lead to a total negation; Bataille himself writes,

> J'entends par expérience intérieure ce que d'habitude on nomme expérience mystique: les états de l'extase, de ravissement, au moins d'émotion méditée. Mais je songe moins à l'expérience confessionelle, à laquelle on a dû se tenir jusqu'ici, qu'à une expérience nue, libre d'attaches, même d'origine à quelque confession que ce soit. [29]

Blanchot, similarly, emphasises the way in which, for Bataille, the act of enunciating thought is not only a paradox but also, as Bataille puts it 'immense aléa': Blanchot describes how this 'aléa' functions as '[...] la pensée même qui se joue en nous appelant à soutenir, en direction de l'inconnu, l'illimité de ce jeu, lorsque penser, c'est, comme le voulut Mallarmé, émettre un coup de dés'. [30] This deformation of the thinking subject in experience, whether in the fictive impossibility of Blanchot's early novels *Thomas l'Obscur* or *Aminadab*, or the 'extrême du possible' of inner experience, represents, for both Bataille and Blanchot, the central crisis of their thinking; what Paul de Man calls, with reference to Mallarmé and Blanchot, 'the *gageure* of letting the work exist only by and for itself.' [31] For Bataille, the essential feature of metaphysics is its concern with a supposed 'reality' which transcends experience and which is alleged to be accessible only to reason: inner experience is, therefore, the inversion of Kantian hierarchies of

---

[28] Op. cit., *La Littérature et le mal*, p.154.

[29] *L'Expérience intérieure* , *ŒC* V, p.15

[30] Maurice Blanchot, op. cit., 'Le Jeu de la pensée', *Critique*, 196-196, p. 738

[31] Paul de Man, 'Maurice Blanchot', *Modern French Criticism: From Proust and Valéry to Structuralism*, ed. John K. Simon, University of Chicago Press, Chicago and London, 1972, p.263.

thinking which hold that the Absolute is beyond negation and that reason is incompatible with knowledge.

Thus, when Kojève describes Hegel's 'madness' as intellectual self-mutilation in much the same terms as Bataille describes inner experience, that is to say a wound which opens up the possibility of an individuated will towards partial suicide, he is defining the 'self-that-dies' as an expenditure which cannot be maintained.

> La réalité humaine est donc en dernière analyse 'la réalité objective de la mort': l'Homme n'est pas seulement mortel; il est la mort incarnée; il *est* sa propre mort. Et, à l'encontre de la mort 'naturelle', purement biologique, la mort qui est l'Homme est une mort 'violente', à la fois consciente d'elle-même et volontaire. La mort humaine, la mort de l'homme, - et par conséquent toute son existence vraiment humaine, sont donc, si l'on veut, un *suicide*.[32]

Bataille himself comments in L'Expérience intérieure:

> Petite récapitulation comique. - Hegel, je l'imagine, toucha l'extrême. Il était jeune encore et crut devenir fou. J'imagine même qu'il élaborait le système pour échapper (chaque sorte de conquête, sans doute, est le fait d'un homme fuyant une menace). Pour finir, Hegel arrive à la *satisfaction*, tourne le dos à l'extrême. *La supplication est morte en lui.* Qu'on cherche le salut, passe encore, on continue de vivre, on ne peut être sûr, il faut continuer de supplier. Hegel gagna, vivant, le salut, tua la supplication, se mutila. Il ne resta de lui qu'un manche de pelle, un homme moderne. Mais avant de se mutiler, sans doute il a touché l'extrême, connu la supplication: sa mémoire le ramène à l'abîme aperçu, pour l'annuler! le système est l'annulation.[33]

This form of self-mutilation as inner experience, is thus apparently distinct from the pathological types, outlined in case histories by Adrien Borel, which had led Bataille to an initial description of inner experience. In particular, Bataille emphasises in these cases the importance of the feeling of insufficiency of being, which leads the auto-mutilator to a desire for identification with a totality which, on the brink of being realised, slips away into nothingness. The possibility of suicide, as Bataille explains in the text below, appears as a result of the self-mutilator, like Van Gogh whose autobiography the latter has been reading, being blinded by an excess of light: the self-mutilator, when

---

[32] Op. cit., Alexandre Kojève, *Introduction à la lecture de Hegel*, p.346.
[33] *L'Expérience intérieure, ŒC*, V, p. 56

blinded by the sun, perceives this as a consumate moment of self-annihilation.

Il (l'automutilateur) se promenait le matin du 11 décembre, sur le boulevard de Ménilmontant quand, arrivé à la hauteur du Père-Lachaise, il se met à fixer le soleil et recevant de ses rayons l'ordre impératif de s'arracher un doigt, sans hésiter, sans ressentir aucune douleur, saisit entre ses dents son index gauche, sectionna sucessivement la peau, les tendons fléchisseurs et extenseurs, les ligaments articulaires au niveau de l'articulation phalango-phalangienne, tordit de sa main droite l'extremité de son index gauche ainsi dilacéré et l'arracha complètement. Il tenta de fuir devant les agents, qui réussirent cependant de lui et le conduisirent à l'hôpital...

[...] Le jeune automutilateur, outre son métier de dessinateur en broderie, exerçait dans ses loisirs celui de peintre. Sans grands renseignements sur les tendances représentées par sa peinture, nous savons cependant qu'il avait lu des essais de critique d'art de Mirbeau. Son inquiétude se portait d'autre part sur des sujets tels que la mystique hindoue ou la philosophie de Frédéric Nietzsche.

[...] Dans les jours qui précédèrent l'automutilation, il prit plusieurs verres de rhum ou cognac. Il se demande encore s'il n'a pas été influencé par la biographie de Van Gogh dans laquelle il avait lu que le peintre pris d'un accès de folie, s'était coupé une oreille et l'avait envoyée à une fille dans une maison de protitution. C'est alors qu'en se promenant le 11 décembre sur le boulevard de Ménilmontant, 'il prit avis du soleil, se 'suggestionna, fixa le soleil pour s'hypnotiser devinant que sa réponse était oui'. Il crut recevoir ainsi un assentiment. 'Feignant, pas quelque chose, sors de cet état', semblait-il deviner par transmission de pensée. 'Ça me paraissait pas énorme', ajoute-il après avoir eu l'idée du suicide, 'de m'enlever un doigt. Je me disais: "Je peux toujours faire cela"'.[34]

In a second case history examined by Borel, however, Bataille makes the point that the insufficiency of being which leads the first self-mutilator to suicide, or the possibility of suicide, is also the same feeling which lead the isolated individual towards a desire to overcome its own discontinuity in a symbolic pattern which fixes itself again upon an excess of vision. More significantly, self-mutilation is not only a version of suicide, but also, in this case, the establishment of a symbolic language. In this case, however, the self-mutilation is resolved in an act which literally dissolves the metonymic relation of blindness and vision:

---

[34] 'La mutilation sacrificielle et l'oreille coupée de Vincent Van Gogh', *ŒC*, I,. pp.258-259.

94

[..] Une fille de trente-quatre ans séduite et rendue enceinte par son maître avait donné le jour à un enfant qui mourut quelques jours après sa naissance. Cette malheureuse était depuis lors atteinte du délire de la persécution avec agitation et hallucinations religieuses. On l'interna dans une asile. Un matin, une gardienne la trouve occuppée à s'arracher l'oeil droit: le globe oculaire avait disparu et l'orbite vide laissait voir des lambeaux de conjonctive et de tissu cellulaire, ainsi que des pelotons adipeux; à droite existait une exophtalmie très prononcée... Interrogée sur le mobile de son acte, l'aliénée déclara avoir entendu la voix de Dieu et quelque temps après avoir vu un homme de feu: 'Donne-moi tes oreilles, fends-toi la tête', lui disait le fantôme.[35]

The presence of God, summoned by the act of self-mutilation, shatters the discontinuity of the isolated individual at the same as it strips away categories of meaning. More significantly, self-mutilation is not only a version of suicide, but also, in this case, the establishment of a symbolic language which not only functions beyond the metaphorical limits of discourse, but also reintroduces the possibility of communication. Bataille thus equates this attempt at symbolic discourse with inner experience.

Inner experience is also, however, the pursuit of the displacement and dissolution of knowledge, 'sacrifice de la raison', at the same time as it posits divine absence at the centre of the meaning of sacrifice. The self-mutilator, in her blindness, has silenced the 'babble' of discourse and replaced it with a new language which 'celebrates the ex-orbitant, upturned eye, the poetic catastrophic image [...] discontinous being returned to NIGHT and radical continuity'.[36]

Blanchot's eschatological mysticism in *Thomas l'Obscur*, similarly, is predicated upon a stripping away of discursive layers to arrive at 'l'expérience nue'. This is a practice, in the negative theology of Bataille and Blanchot, which correlates to to the ambitions of Dionysius the Areopagite (see above, pp. 43-46). Moreover, the destruction of the subject under the impact of a reflective consciousness, *ipse*, annihilating itself in the blank violence of its own reflection, is not just a reversal in a spatial and temporal sense; it is literal experience of communion with the void. The dissolution of the self, when raised to an advanced level of self-reflection, becomes the

---

[35] Ibid., pp.263
[36] Leslie Anne Boldt, 'Translator's Introduction', in Georges Bataille, *Inner Experience* (New York SUNY, 1988), p. xxi

object of its own thought; this is what Bataille means by a 'mystical' experience; a form of self-wounding, that is beyond the parameters of metaphor.

In the section of *Thomas l'Obscur* where Blanchot describes the death of Anne the distinction, or rather movement, between absence and nothingness reveals a renunciation of *ipse* as it is trapped in discontinuity and a dissolving of subject and object in the abyss of non-meaning: the death of Anne is the direct confrontation of consciousness with the most general category of being; the temporal self abolishes itself in a spatial abyss which is total indetermination.

> Doucement, munie du seul nom d'Anne qui devait lui servir à la surface après la plongée, elle laissa monter la marée des premières, des grossières absences - absence du bruit le silence, absence d'être la mort; Mais après ce néant si tiède et facile où demeurait Pascal, pourtant déjà effrayé, elle fut happée par les absences du diamant, l'absence de silence, l'absence de mort, où elle ne pouvait reprendre pied que dans les notions ineffables, le je ne sais qui, sphinx du fracas inouï, les vibrations qui font éclater l'éther des sons les plus déchirants et font éclater, les dépassant dans leur élan, les sons mêmes. Et elle tomba dans les cercles majeurs, analogues à ceux de l'Enfer, passant éclair de raison pure, par le moment critique où il faut, un très court instant, demeurer dans l'absurde et, ayant quitté ce qui peut encore se représenter, ajouter indéfiniment l'absence à l'absence et à l'absence de l'absence de l'absence et, ainsi, avec cette machine aspirante, faire désespérément le vide. A cet instant commence la vraie chute, celle qui s'abolit, néant sans cesse dévoré par un néant plus pur. [37]

The paradox revealed in the 'nudity' of the 'impossible' inner experience is that *ipse*, the term used by Bataille for the subjective conciousness which orders or interprets being, is as alien an entity for Bataille as non-being is from being. The collapse of meaning in the textual nature of reality, which is achieved by the pursuit of impersonality by Blanchot and Bataille, is what lies at the heart of inner experience: a confrontation with the void which is a form of transcendent annihilation.

The project of destroying discourse, 'disintoxication' as Bataille terms it, is the most dramatic form of postponing the projection of existence into language and the way in which the wound is increased to surpass limited existence. Thus, in the same way, the reflective impulse of the self-mutilator to annihilate *ipse* in order to enter into

---

[37] Op. cit., Maurice Blanchot, *Thomas l'Obscur*, p.68.

communication is a dramatization of loss of self which overcomes absent existence. Loss of self becomes one with total sacrifice. The inner experience Bataile refers to in his commentaries on self-mutilation, therefore, is fundamentally the same as that described in *L'Expérience intérieure*: sacrifice which relinquishes any claim to hierarchical systems of thought or experience in favour of the lacerating experience of 'non-savoir', a stripping away of categories of meaning: this is what Bataille means by 'une expérience nue'.

De l'aveuglement

The purpose of self-mutilation is to make possible the apprehension of the experience of the sacred: thus, the inner wound stands outside of the authority of the social organization to which the mystic belongs. Self-mutilation is thus not only the way into insight, but also a meaningful response to the need for communication with the sacred. Like the experiences of the Christian mystics, this need finds its expression in a state which is at once pathological and a true experience of revelation. Thus, self-mutilation reconciles the contradiction between the ecstatic and the lower forms of the social.

Derrida sets out a version of Bataille's 'mysticism' which not only reveals it as working against the 'repressive' logic of presence, but which also posits the central operation of inner experience - that is to say the movement between blindness and vision - as the distancing of the self which creates the space which can be filled by 'souveraineté', a term which Derrida says is an elliptical translation of Hegel's term *Herrschaft* (Lordship), which is itself a demonstration of surpassing 'la singularité universelle d'être là.'[38] Blindness, in Bataille, and in particular in *La Somme athéologique*, Derrida takes to be part of a metonymic chain which affirms speech lost to the darkness of metaphysical experience. This movement is a virulent form of anti-Hegelianism which posits a break with any nonmetaphorical form of negative theology. The subversion or inversion of hierarchical categories of thought which occur in inner experience are thus only

---

[38] Op. cit., Jacques Derrida, op. cit., 'De l'économie restreinte à l'économie générale: un hégélianisme sans réserves', p.373.

performed at a textual level. Examining the metaphorical limits of 'non-savoir', Derrida writes in *De la Grammatologie*:

> L'écriture est dangereuse dès lors que la représentation veut s'y donner pour la présence et le signe pour la chose même.[39]

Derrida's version of Bataille, thus, slips away from the religious centre of Batille's project and inner experience is only an abstract negativity. Although Bataille stands poetic, ecstatic, sacred speech in opposition to 'significative discourse', like Breton's preoccupation with aphasia, and Mallarmé's version of 'le néant', Bataille's mysticism is a proposition which is confined by the limits of questions of textual authenticity, rather than being, as he conceived it, a 'way' which, as Jean Bruno suggests, leads to a sovereign form of revelation.

The fact that Blanchot, in *Thomas l'Obscur* and *Aminadab*, provides a fictive variation on experiences of 'la mort impossible' seems only further to justify this reading of the multiple significance of inner experience as being a disentanglement from language. Inner experience is, however, as has been demonstrated, a form of self-mutilation, which has as its goal the pursuit of varieties of heightened ontological anxiety which, having annihilated reason and abolished human particularity, mirrors and is related to other more protean forms of religious experience.

For Bataille, however, symbols of failure and negativity are also part of a wider symbolic language which, beyond the catastrophe of self-annihilation or 'inner experience', are the heroic and 'mystical' assertion of a 'will to nothingness'. Sartre suggests, however, that the experiences Bataille describes in *L'Expérience intérieure,* like the moments of transcendence ascribed to Thomas by Blanchot in *Aminadab*,[40] are merely forms of symbolic mourning for the death of God: '[...] l'on croirait, à lire plus d'un passage de *L'Expérience intérieure*, retrouver Stavrouguine ou Ivan Karamazov - un Ivan qui aurait connu André Breton. [...] cette expérience se retrouve, de façon ou d'autre, chez la plupart des auteurs contemporains: c'est [...] la mort de Malraux, le délaissement de Heidegger, l'être-en-sursis de Kafka, le

---

[39] Jacques Derrida, *De la Grammatologie* (Gallimard: Paris, 1967), p.214.

[40] Op. cit., Jean-Paul Sartre, 'Aminadab, ou du fantastique consideré comme un langage', p.128

labeur maniaque et vain de Sisyphe chez Camus, L'Aminadab de Blanchot'. [41]

Inner experience, however, unlike the experiences of Dostoyevsky's nihilist heroes, or indeed the Surrealist encounter with the primal unity described by Breton, is an experience which is specifically religious in both its shape and substance: atheology is a paradox founded on the death of God, but it is not a denial or abnegation of the reality of realigious experience. Bataille, thus, following Pascal, is able to posit the hiddenness of God, 'Deus Absconditus',[42] at the centre of his religious thinking. This is how, the words 'Absent, néant, vide', as Audoin posits, take on a literal meaning in the moment of communication with the void. [43]

Sartre points out that, however, that unlike Pascal, whose style of anti-Cartesian 'essai-martyre' he imitates, Bataille, in mourning for God, does not conceive of any metaphysical solution to the narrow potentialities of temporal existence. Sartre describes Pascal as 'le premier penseur historique, parce qu'il a saisi que, en l'homme, l'existence précède l'essence.'[44] Within the immanent condition of the 'misère de l'homme sans Dieu', Pascal is able to resolve the ambiguities of moral categories of collapse and disorder proceeding from divine absence, in the sublation of divine presence. This resolution is a transcendence which Bataille's anti-idealism has made impossible; nonetheless, in the state of anxiety which, for Sartre, is the 'mystical' centre of *L'Expérience intérieure*, Bataille has retained the dualist language of Christianity which, claims Sartre, although a contradiction in terms, allows him to claim a 'connaissance émotionelle commune et rigoureuse' of the absolute. 'Mais de quoi y-a-t-il connaissance?' asks Sartre: Bataille's experience, says Sartre answering his own question is that inner experience is pathological and that Bataille's 'mysticism' is

---

[41] Op. cit., Jean-Paul Sartre, 'Un nouveau mystique', p.124.

[42] '*Que Dieu s'est voulu cacher* -S'il n'y avait qu'une religion, Dieu y serait bien manifeste. S'il n'y avait des martyrs qu'en notre religion, de même. Dieu étant ainsi caché, toute religion qui ne dit pas Dieu est caché n'est pas véritable; et toute religion qui n'en rend pas la raison n'est pas instruisante. La nôtre fait tout cela: *Vere tu es Deus absconditus.*' Blaise Pascal, op. cit., *Pensées.* p.291.

[43] This point is made by Philipe Audoin, *Sur Georges Bataille*, Actual/Le temps qu'il fait. p.30. (See above, p. 75).

[44] Op. cit., Jean-Paul Sartre, op. cit.,'Un nouveau mystique', *Situations I*, p. 139

no more than an unstable metaphor for the paradoxical status of the negative in the movement of the Hegelian dialectic. The Bataillien notion of *ipse* as a 'négativité sans emploi' is, therefore, for Sartre, like 'le rire' an irony, that is to say an impossible negation which paralyses the movement of the dialectic: like the 'goût de se perdre' of the Surrealists, or the Dionysian excess advocated by Nietzsche, for Sartre the loss of self in inner experience is not only, as he puts it, 'daté', but also founded on a contradiction; as in the Hegelian dialectic all negative movement is met by its opposite; therefore the annihlation of *ipse* can only mean its replacement by another for of self-consciousness:

> 'Forte image, lâche penser' [...] Le rire de M.Bataille, en tout cas, n'est pas une expérience intérieure. Pour lui-même, l'ipse cherchant à devenir tout est 'tragique'. Mais, en révélant l'insuffisance de l'édifice total où nous croyons occuper une place rassurante et confortable, le rire, à son paroxysme, nous plonge soudain dans l'horreur: il n'y a plus de moindre voile entre nous et la nuit de notre insuffisance. Nous ne somme pas tout, personne n'est tout. Ainsi, de même que Platon double son mouvement dialectique par l'ascèse de l'amour, de même pourrait-on parler, chez M.Bataille, d'une sorte d'ascèse par le rire. Mais le rire est ici le négatif, au sens hégélien.[45]

Sartre is correct up to a point: in the Hegelian formulation of the negative, opposites which negate each other are ultimately associated with the subject, 'whose nature is to return to itself (self-consciousness); and in the case of the cosmic *Geist*, to posit its opposite'.[46] Kojève describes this movement as the necessary movement towards death: 'L'essence de la liberté individuelle est donc la Négativité, qui se manifeste à l'état pur ou 'absolu' comme mort.'[47] Bataille, however, describes negativity with reference to Hegel as one of the central axes of inner experience in terms of the 'death' and 'night', both as apophatic method and metaphor. For Bataille, as it is for Blanchot, the movement of *ipse* away from itself and into the night is a sacrifice which, although it has no meaning to be revealed as object, is, nonetheless, a form of communication. Although this communication is one in which 'the sender receives the message', that

---

[45] Ibid., pp. 159-160
[46] Op. cit.,Charles Taylor, *Hegel*, p.110
[47] Op. cit., Alexandre Kojève, *Introduction à la lecture de Hegel*, p.557

is to say it is a form of introjection wherein the subject does not meet the object but instead reflects back upon itself, it is a non-metaphorical experience which not only imitates and rebuilds the archaic experiences of heightened ontological disturbances described by Sartre as 'fêtes primitives', but posits at the heart of the experience a literal encounter with divine absence at the centre of inner experience. Bataille himself says:'[...] je tiens à l'appréhension de Dieu, fût-il sans forme et sans mode [...], pour un arrêt dans le mouvement qui nous porte à l'appréhension plus obscure de l'inconnu: d'une présence qui n'est plus distincte en rien d'une absence.' [48]

Among the variety of critical responses to *L'Expérience intérieure* on its publication, was a letter to Bataille from Artaud, in Rodez. According to Bataille, Artaud, for whom he had a high regard and sympathy, and whose own experiences in Rodez had an equivalent if not a parallel in Bataille's description of inner experience, had written to warn Bataille of the dangers of religious experience: as Bataille remarked, 'c'est que *L'Expérience intérieure*, qu'il venait de lire, lui montrait que j'avais à me convertir, à revenir à Dieu. Il devait m'en prévenir'. [49]

Bataille, however, in a text written shortly after the publication of *L'Expérience intérieure* and Blanchot's early fictions, was also concerned about the publication of writings which Artaud had written whilst in Rodez. In particular, whilst unsure of the morality of publishing work written under the great stresses of Artaud's breakdown, he found in these texts a form of disturbance equivalent to the process of inner experience.

Ce que ces écrits ont de singulier tient à l'ébranlement et au dépassement brutal des limites habituelles, au cruel lyrisme coupant court à ses propres effets, ne tolérant pas la chose même à laquelle il donne l'expression la plus sûre. Maurice Blanchot l'a cité disant de lui-même (1946): 'j'ai débuté dans la littérature en écrivant des livres pour dire que je ne pouvais rien écrire du tout; ma pensée quand j'avais quelque chose à dire ou à écrire était ce qui m'était le plus refusé. Je n'avais jamais d'idées et deux très courts livres chacun de soixante-dix pages roulant sur cette absence profonde, invétérée, endémique de toute idée...' Maurice Blanchot commentant ces quelques lignes écrivait: 'A de telles paroles, nous ne voyons pas ce qu'il serait convenable d'ajouter, car elles ont la franchise du couteau, et elles

---

[48] *L'Expérience intérieure*, *ŒC*, V, p. 17
[49] Surya, p. 352.

passent en clarvoyance tout ce qu'un écrivain a jamais pu écrire sur soi, montrant quelle tête lucide est la tête qui, pour devenir libre, a subi l'épreuve du Merveilleux.' Pour moi, cette dernière phrase de Maurice Blanchot me semble l'épilogue précis de l'aventure surréaliste toute entière, envisagée dès l'instant où elle a balbutie ses ambitions. Je crois que Maurice Blanchot a raison d'impliquer das ces derniers mots le principe même d'un mouvement qui a le plus souvent évité l'écueil et le naufrage spectaculaire que les dernières années d'Antonin Artaud offrent à nos yeux dans une lueur de désastre.[50]

Like Artaud's ambition to dismember language into component, and therefore magical fragments, Bataille's 'mysticism' is a way of dissolving and reconstituting binding myths of a community or a society in the most literal way. Thus, in *L'Expérience intérieure*, Bataille, like Blanchot's *Thomas l'Obscur*, abolishes discursive patterns of thought by applying a form of apophatic mysticism to the problem of knowledge: like Hegel, or at least Kojève's version of Hegel, who, in his alleged madness, annihilates humanity and reason in the experience of impossibility, Bataille asserts the failure of language at the price of sacred communication.

---

[50] *Le Surréalisme au jour le jour*, *ŒC*, VIII, pp.182-183.

Chapter Four

'Poèmes pas courageux':
The poetry of inner experience

The cut worm forgives the plow.
William Blake, *The Proverbs of Hell*

Inner experience and poetry are related in that they both represent for Bataille the most elusive and sovereign forms of individual activity. Poetry, moreover, like inner experience, is not merely a theoretical abstraction but a concrete experience. The demands of poetry are therefore, like those of inner experience, beyond the subordinate or utilitarian possibilities of language.[1]

However, apart from the anonymous publication of 'Fatrasies' in *La Révolution Surréaliste* in early 1926, Bataille concentrated his efforts in the early part of his career on fiction and criticism rather than poetry.[2] According to Michel Leiris, Bataille chose to publish these poems anonymously as a mark of his distaste for Breton and his followers on a personal level. This is borne out by Bataille's own accounts of his first encounters with Surrealism, where says that he distrusted both the Surrealist reading of Hegel and the Surrealist belief in the revelatory role of poetry.[3]

Thus, although Bataille's critical essays in *Documents* and elsewhere emphasised the importance of the sacred as poetic activity, and despite the fact his fictions were rooted in erotic and oneiric meditations which emerged out of his readings, amongst others, of Lautréamont and Rimbaud,[4] Bataille eschewed the Surrealist ambition

---

[1] Bataille emphasises precisely these aspects of poetic activity in the 1946 essay 'De l'âge de pierre à Jacques Prévert', *ŒC*, XI, pp.102-103.

[2] Bataille was asked to translate the 'Fatrasies', nonsense poems from the thirteenth century, having been introduced to the Surrealists by Michel Leiris. According to Leiris, Bataille had not yet publicly declared himself a writer, but had a considerable interest in Medieval poetry as demonstrated in his studies at the École des Chartes. Michel Leiris, op. cit., *A Propos de Georges Bataille*, pp. 21-25.

[3] 'Le surréalisme au jour le jour', *ŒC*, VIII, pp. 169-170

[4] Surya describes both of these poets as rare examples of poets admired by Bataille. Surya, op.cit., p.401. For wider discussions of Bataille's relation to other poets see also Jacqueline Risset, 'L'Écœurante sentimentalité poétique', op. cit., ed. Denis Hollier,

to bring together 'le réve et la réalité' in the Absolute reality of 'surréalité' . Consequently, during this period, he seemed to ascribe little importance to poets or poetry (the exception being his correspondance with Robert Desnos who after breaking with Breton in 1929 after the publication of the *Second Manifeste du Surréalisme*, like many other dissident Surrealists, found himself in sympathy with *Documents*).[5]

However, from the early 1930s onwards, as demonstrated in the rites of the Acéphale secret society and his experiments with yoga, experience of the sacred occupied an increasingly central place in Bataille's thought. It was during this period, therefore, that Bataille became interested in poetry not only as an abstract idea but as a practical technique. Moreover, it was during this period and throughout the composition of *L'Expérience intérieure* that Bataille wrote poetry which functioned as both a transcription of his experiences, and as he states as in 'La pratique de la joie devant la mort', a method of meditation. The poems of inner experience, in particular, resemble the songs which Nietzsche gives to Zarathoustra in that they are a response to experience as well as a way of mediating between experience and action; at the same time, unlike Nietzsche's poetry, which in form is conventional versification, and which in content is an overflowing from the main body of the text, Bataille's poetry stands in opposition to inner experience in the same way that inner experience is itself opposite to the notions of project or action; Bataille writes 'De la poésie, je dirai maintenant qu'elle est, je crois, le sacrifice où les mots sont les victimes.'[6]

There is a sense, therefore, in which engagement with Bataille's poetry involves the reader, as it does with the Surrealists and Sade, in participation in experience, although this does not mean that for Bataille, that the actual lived experience is to be relived or reenacted on a textual level. Rather the process of writing poetry is a form of communion which has as its goal the pursuit of absence. The central

---

Georges Bataille après tout, coll. L'Extrême contemporain, (Orléans: Belin, 1995) pp.147-160 and Jacques Cels, *L'Exigence poétique de Georges Bataille* (Brussels: Éditions Universitaires-De Boeck, 1989).

[5] Breton famously and publicly attacked Desnos in a note added to the 'Second manifeste du surréalisme', accusing him of plagiarism. See Desnos' correspondance with Bataille in *L'Infini*, 24, 1988-1989, pp.11-29.

[6] *L'Expérience intérieure, ŒC*, V, p.156

104

movement of inner experience is the vertiginous reversal which occurs as the subject annihilates itself in the shift into discontinuity which occurs in inner experience: poetry is, in the same way, an entering into experience of discontinuity which is both sovereign and ecstatic; in this the pursuit of poetry is, on a textual and non-metaphorical level, a fundamental part of the 'mysticism' of inner experience.

Poetic activity for Bataille is thus predicated on absence; it is a sovereign experience which negates itself in a circular movement. Bataille describes this when he traces the meaning and function of the poetic impulse:

> Les mots, nous les utilisons, nous faisons d'eux les instruments d'actes utiles. Nous n'aurions rien d'humain si le langage en nous devait être en entier servile. Nous ne pouvons non plus nous passer des rapports efficaces qu'introduisent les mots entre les hommes et les choses. Mais nous les arrachons à ces rapports dans un délire.[7]

The purpose of this chapter is to consider the nature of the paradox of poetry as pure negativity which is simultaneously an assertion of sovereignty. In particular, the poetry of inner experience functions as a series of moments of rupture with meaning. As Bernard Noël writes, the central challenge of Bataille's poetry is the same challenge inherent in the central movement of inner experience towards a pure subjectivity which has disengaged itself from the Hegelian dialectic. For Noël, inner experience and poetry represent equivalent forms of transgression which exceed and exclude the possibility of a dialectical synthesis. Noël also points out that all forms of discursive writing are a betrayal of inner experience in that they are predicated upon an organizational mode of thinking which is unfaithful to the instability of the subject; Bataille's poetry, as 'l'expérience de l'expérience', is, thus, characterised by an opacity of form, structure and meaning:

Silence
Dramatisation
Explosion
Transparence

---

[7] Ibid., p.156

Voici des mots: ils marquent une gradation de l'expérience; ils sont essentiels, et cependant ils ne disent rien. Qui les écrit se heurte aussitôt à l'indicible. Il faudrait un autre langage. On désespère de l'écriture et on choisit quand même d'écrire. [8]

However, although poetry is, as Noël asserts, 'transparent', and therefore irreducible to the linear temporality of discourse, inner experience is nonetheless sacred activity which returns to religion a sovereign liberty, and to transgression a religious sovereignty. Poetry, for Bataille, is an exercise in transgression which prefigures a slide into 'sovereign silence', and at the same time a manifestation of 'sovereignty' which cuts into the identity of the poet.

In the same way that the challenge of Sade, for Bataille, is that his work is a radical assertion of the negative which is a renunciation that withstands recuperation into the positive movement of the dialectic, the poetry of inner experience elides meaning and, in the same way that inner experience is neither project nor action, it reverses all textual experience ('Littérature n'est pas innocente, et, coupable, elle devait à la fin s'avouer telle'[9]). Unlike the Surrealists, Bataille refuses to ascribe any transcendent meaning to this movement. This is how poetry, for Batille, comes to represent, amongst all possible forms of sacrifice, 'le seul dont nous puissions entretenir, renouveler le feu.'[10]

Misère de la poésie

In an open letter to Breton, composed roughly around the time that Bataille became interested in poetry as practice as well as theory, Bataille cites Sade as an example of a thinker who represents in his work '[le] négatif tel quel'. Above all, Sade's texts, which pervert the the poetic image to the point where rupture with meaning is not only expected but inevitable, represent an absolute transgression or negation of the world as circumscribed within the ethical premises of literature. Moreover, writes Bataille, the specificity of poetic language as a negation, as exemplified by Sade, is a demonstration of the limits of

---

[8] Bernard Noël, 'Poésie et expérience', in Georges Bataille, *L'Archangélique* (Paris: Mercure de France, 1967), pp. 9-17. I have quoted this edition rather than the *Œuvres Complètes* because it contains the essay by Noël as well as a commentary and chronological structuring of the poems.

[9] Op. cit., p.8

[10] *L'Expérience intérieure*, *ŒC*, V, p.172

the Hegelian dialectic: this, he says, is the problem which Surrealism could not overcome.[11]

Sade's texts, in contrast, are an 'heroics of perversion' [12] in which aesthetic principles are reversed into a poeticized totality. This movement negates homogeneity at the same time as it ends the binary opposition of good and evil. For Bataille, the absolute failure of poetry is akin to this failure of meaning which occurs in Sade. The perversion of the enclosed space of the text, which for Bataille is the opening towards radical heterogeneity, is, however, the reversal of values, or the inversion, which Breton describes as 'un signe classique de psychasthénie.'[13]

It was an irony that Bataille's first published poem, 'Du haut de Montserrat', although written in 1934, appeared in 1938 in *Minotaure*, which was, ironically enough, a journal under the overall direction of André Breton.[14] This is an irony compounded by the fact that much of Bataille's thinking on the meaning and function of poetry was defined in relation to Breton's conception of poetic activity as the resolution of the contradiction of mind and matter in a synthesis which emerged out of the Hegelian dialectic as well as a more properly Surrealist version of the self expressed in terms of alchemical analogy.

The poem, 'Du haut de Montserrat', was intended as a companion piece to the essay 'Bleu du Ciel', which reappears in *L'Expérience intérieure* in almost the same form. The poem and essay are an explanation of and response to two paintings by André Masson, 'Aube à Montserrat' and 'Paysage aux prodiges'. These paintings by Masson had been inspired by his experiences whilst climbing with Bataille, and then spending a night outdoors on the summit of the mountain of Montserrat, near Barcelona. For Masson and Bataille, the experience on the mountain was comparable to a religious mystical ecstasy: the

---

[11] 'La valeur d'usage de D.A.F. de Sade', *ŒC*, II, p. 56

[12] David Hayman, introduction to Philippe Sollers, *Writing and the experience of limits*, trans. Philip Barnard and David Hayman, (New York: Columbia University Press, 1983), p.xxvvii.

[13] Op. cit., André Breton, *Second Manifeste*, p.219.

[14] *Minotaure* was, in fact, at the publisher Albert Skira's insistence, modelled on *Documents*. Indeed, Skira had at one stage suggested that the journal be co-edited by Breton and Bataille, to the inevitable disgust of Breton. Surya, op. cit., p.234. Also Mark Polizzotti, op. cit., *Revolution of the mind: The Life of André Breton*, pp.390-391.

poem stands as a textual version of the intensity of Masson's convulsed earth and sky, 'the latter filled with whirling suns, stars and planets'.[15]

For Masson, the meeting of heaven and earth takes the form of a fluid landscape which opens itself up to the sky; the paintings are 'filled with a pulsating energy'.[16] In Bataille's poem the central motif is also that of the oranges and reds which seem to glow from the paintings. In particular, Bataille traces a metonymic chain through the movement and colour of fire, 'Tempête de flammes',[17] which becomes emblematic of the Heraclitean flux at the centre of the 'mystical' experience; in a parallel image in the second painting, 'Paysage aux prodiges', one of highest peaks of Montserrat resembles a monk-like figure in communion with the whirling chaos of the open sky.[18]

In 'Du haut de Montserrat' Bataille calls upon Heraclitus, Paracelsus and Zarathoustra as intercessionary figures. It is of particular significance that Bataille, like Breton, finds a corollary of the Presocratic version of the relation between mind and matter in the langauge of hermetic philosophy, in this case Paracelsus. Indeed, the alchemical principles are precisely those which inform the dialectical relation between blindness and vision lying at the centre of the movement of inner experience: in the collapse of the subject, there is no conflict between internal being and external reality. The individual is the internalisation of the universe as the universe is the externalisation of the individual.

Any change in the substance of interior experience can therefore only be explained by the force of desire which acts (both within the individual and within the collectivity) on the chemical principle of precipitation. The thinking subject of poetry, therefore, is subsumed into the negative movement of energy which is at the centre of the experience of the poem. At the centre of the intense experience of

---

[15] Dawn Ades, *Masson* (New York: Rizzoli, 1994), p.18.

[16] Ibid., p.18.

[17] Op. cit., *L'Archangélique*, p.97.

[18] The original experiences which led to the 'Aube à Montserrat', 'Paysage aux prodiges', 'Le bleu du ciel' and 'Du haut de Montserrat' occurred in 1934 and 1935 when Masson and Bataille where drawing up plans for the journal and secret society 'Acéphale'. The acephal figure drawn by Masson for the journal is often illustrated in what are quite clearly the serrated peaks of Montserrat. See Andrew Hussey and Jeremy Stubbs, 'Tempête de Flammes: Surrealism, Bataille and the perennial philosphy of Heraclitus', in 'Kojève's Paris/Now Bataille', *parallax*, 4, 1997, pp. 151-167.

Montserrat is the experience of blindness from an excess of light: the eye is not an origin but an expenditure.

> Et toi ZARATHOUSTRA œil de lumière
> Au centre d'un monde terrible et joyeux
> Je vous salue des hauteurs de Montserrat[19]

Like the later poem, 'Pratique de la joie devant la mort', the poem is intended as a way of entering into experience rather than a transcription of experience. However, for Bataille, although the relation of poetry to the subject is posited on the fact that poetry, like mysticism, represents sovereign experience which defies recuperation, the autonomous or sacred nature of poetry is, nonetheless, inevitably subsumed in the movement of the historical dialectic. Poetry and religious experience are therefore predicated on their failure to withstand their historical meaning.

The central problem of 'Du Haut de Montserrat', however, is that its status as a poem also negates its status as an 'acephalic' prayer. Although the intensity of experiences undergone by Bataille and Masson was rooted in the non-metaphorical nature of meditative 'mystical' practices, their 'panthéisme noir' is, like erotic feeling, a breaking away from organized categorical thinking into limitless existence which contradicts the textual presence of poetry.

The 'vision' of 'Du haut de Montserrat' is thus a 'vision' which flows out of a negative movement away from a summit. Zarathoustra's 'eye of light' is also a blinding experience which trangresses all forms of mediation. As such, the blinding illumination of the experience of Montserrat, in which nature is in the poetic movement, reduced to a pure negativity which reflects the subject's own disintegration, is a paradox which contradicts its own presence as poetry. Bataille describes this experience as a wound.

> Mais de même que la réduction de la Nature à un vide, la destruction de celui qui a détruit est engagée dans ce mouvement d'insolence. La négation accomplie de la Nature par l'homme - s'élevant au-dessus d'un néant qui est son oeuvre - renvoie sans détour au vertige, à la chute dans le vide du ciel.[20]

---

[19] 'Du haut de Montserrat', op. cit., L'Archangélique, p. 98

[20] L'Expérience intérieure, ŒC, V, p.93

The eye turned upwards to 'le bleu du ciel' is a suspension of meaning in sovereign expenditure. In the same way, the wound opened by poetry is a contradiction in which meaning is suspended and then lost. The impossibility of communication in the process of pure negativity does not mean, however, that poetry, in relation to this process, can be fixed as a limit. The failure of poetry is that it is separate from the sovereign subject's existence as an unrestricted negativity. For Bataille, the absolute failure of poetry, therefore, is akin to the failure of meaning which occurs in Sade. The intense experience which is rebuilt in 'Du haut de Montserrat' can only have a religious function as it contradicts the first principles of presence or permanence. As in Sade, the work of the negative in poetry is to reverse values and then abandon them, having detached them from the structuring process in which they were originally created.

Moreover, although the reversal of values, or the inversion, which Bataille sees as fundamental to poetic activity depends on the failure of poetry as a way of exceeding the false reconciliation of the dialectic, poetry is still an assertion of sovereignty which opens the wound of being. This is how Bataille can describe the perversion of the enclosed space of the text as an opening towards radical heterogeneity, and most significantly how poetry, like the acephalic prayer 'Du haut de Montserrat, becomes 'absorption achévée.'[21]

Haine de la poésie

Inner experience is, however, poetic activity in the Surrealist sense that it is a movement in which the subject seems to overcome or overwhelm the objective world in a convulsive instant of illumination. Thomas' experience of blindness in Blanchot's novels or *ipse*'s self-destruction in the blinding glare of self-reflection are, to this extent at least, analogous to the Surrealist 'point d'esprit' where contradiction is abolished in the movement of the Hegelian dialectic toward what Breton calls 'l'anéantissement de l'être en un brillant, intérieur et aveugle, qui ne soit pas plus l'âme de la glace que celle du feu.'[22] For Bataille and Blanchot the movement towards the 'intérieur, aveugle' where the night moves into sun is an impossibility. Both inner

---

[21] Ibid., p. 156
[22] Op. cit., André Breton, *Second Manifeste*, p.154.

experience and the Surrealist 'point d'esprit', nonetheless, aim at the dissolution of the subject into a form of poetic activity which is based upon the free play of radical subjectivity.

For Bataille, however, inner experience is not only conceived as a shift into discontinuity which undoes poetic activity as a project, but also as a negativity which actively mitigates against the possibility of poetry as a transcendent activity. The notion of poetic activity as 'suprême connaissance' - the description Breton gives to the Surrealist moment when opposites cease to be in contradiction and the primal unity of the Universe is revealed [23] - is, for Bataille, not only a species of idealism which seeks resolution in the false reconcilation of subject and object, but also a misinterpretation of the role of the negative in Hegelian or Marxist terms. Specifically, the Hegelian notion of negation - which is at the origin of the Marxist version of the dialectic - is based on the premise that an essential opposition creates movement, and that '[the] link between negation and determinate being (*Dasein*) is a manifestation of the negativity whch is essentially in and constitutive of *Dasein*.'[24] For Bataille, however, negation represents a movement away from the dialectical process towards an unlimited subjectivity which consumes itself in an instant of sovereign communication. Bataille thus sees the Marxist dialectic as a movement which, like the Surrealist 'point d'esprit', aims at a transcendence emerging out of the unstable premise of Hegelian idealism. Communication, the centre of inner experience, is, however, not simply an inverse form of the Hegelian dialectic, but an exceeding of the limits of the relation between subject and object.

'Par 'négation du néant', je n'envisage pas quelque équivalence de la négation hégélienne de la négation. Je veux parler de 'communication' atteinte sans que l'on ait d'abord posé la déchéance ou le crime. Immanence signifie 'communication' au même niveau, sans descendre ni remonter; le néant, dans ce cas, n'est plus l'objet d'une attitude qui le pose. [25]

The abolition of the thinking subject in its own reflection which takes place in the movement of inner experience is not so much in opposition to Breton's 'l'anéantissement de l'être en un brillant,

---

[23] Ibid., p.154.
[24] Op. cit., Charles Taylor, *Hegel*, p.110.
[25] 'Sur Nietzsche', *ŒC*, VI, p.163.

intérieur et aveugle', but rather a contradiction which exceeds the Surrealist dialectic. The poetic activity of the Surrealists, for Bataille, is a work of 'escamotage'[26] which aims at a false moment of transcendence. 'La négation du néant', which takes place in inner experience is, however,'La négation accomplie de la Nature par l'homme - s'élevant au-dessus d'un néant qui est son oeuvre - renvoie sans détour au vertige, à la chute dans le vide du ciel.'[27]

Thus, in the same way that, as observed in the preceding chapter, Blanchot's early fictions immobilised the metonymic and metaphorical contiguities of 'le non-savoir' into allegorical patterns which, at the same time, aim at undoing the status of allegory as a fixed series of meaning, poetic activity, for Bataille, is a contradiction which is predicated upon a collapse of meaning. In the notes for L'Expérience intérieure, Bataille writes that his interest in Christian mysticism is that it is experience which lies beyond poetry as significative discourse and that this experience is its own authority and therefore opposed to 'philosophy'. This experience is also the reversal which occurs in the collapse of the poetic image into non-meaning in the night of 'le non-savoir'.

Moreover, Bataille asserts that poetry, as it carries within itself the trace of 'le non-savoir', overcomes and abolishes the movement of the dialectic in an experience which affirms the primacy of silence and absence. The experience of the subject returning to itself, 'déchirement intérieur', is a negation which is analogous to the ecstatic festivals which consecrate the living heart of all religions; at the same time it is an experience founded on absence and which, therefore, posits itself as a negative, a wound, which escapes Hegelian categories.

Nous sommes peut-être la blessure, la maladie de la nature.
Il serait pour nous dans ce cas nécessaire - et d'ailleurs possible, 'facile' - de faire de la blessure une fête, une force de la maladie. La poésie où se perdrait le plus de sang serait la plus forte. L'aube la plus triste? annonciatrice de la joie du jour.

---

[26] Bataille often accuses the Surrealists of artificial practice or 'conjuring tricks' as part of their poetic method. In particular, he famously described Aragon as an 'escamoteur' at one of his early meetings with the Surrealists. See Œ C, VII, pp. 174-175, or Alain Jouffroy , 'Un Aragon, des Aragons' in Louis Aragon, Du surréalisme au réalisme socialiste, Du libertinage au mentir vrai, des incipit à la posterité, eds. Gavin Bowd and Jeremy Stubbs (Manchester: Aura, 1997), p.11.

[27] L'Expérience intérieure, Œ C, V, p. 93.

La poésie serait le signe annonçant des déchirements intérieurs plus grands. La musculature humaine ne serait en jeu tout entière, elle n'attendrait son haut degré de force et le mouvement parfait de la 'décision' - ce que, quoi qu'il soit, l'être exige - que dans la transe extatique.

Ne peut-on dégager de ses antécédents religieux la possibilité demeurée ouverte, quoi qu'il semble, à l'incroyant, de l'expérience mystique? la dégager de l'ascèse du dogme et de l'atmosphère des religions? la dégager en un mot du mysticisme - au point de la lier à la nudité de l'ignorance? [28]

The role of poetry is therefore to stand for the failure of poetic activity as a project. In the same way that inner experience is opposed to itself as both action and project, for Bataille, poetry, the sovereign perversion of language, stands as a negativity in its purest form.

L'image poétique, si elle mène du connu à l'inconnu, s'attache cependant au connu qui lui donne corps, et bien qu'elle le déchire et déchire la vie dans ce déchirement, se maintient à lui. D'où il s'ensuit que la poésie est presque en entier poésie déchue, jouissance d'images il est vrai retirées du domaine servile (poétiques comme nobles, solennelles) mais refusées à la ruine intérieure qu'est l'accès à l'inconnu. Même les images profondément ruinées sont domaine de possession, mais ce n'est plus rien posséder, c'est retenir d'une main ce que l'autre donne. [29]

Poetry represents a transgression which undermines all notions of metaphorical stability: it occupies a space which is both the locus of aporetic vision and a movement towards dispersal which constitutes a sacrifice, like Blanchot's description of 'le regard d'Orphée' as 'le moment extrême de la liberté, moment où il se rend libre de lui-même'. [30]

Exquisite Corpse

The poetic image for Bataille is, then, the representation of a moment which cannot be reduced to language. It is, in this sense, opposed to the ordering function of language and conceptual thinking. The poetic image, most importantly, has a religious function in that, like eroticism or mysticism, it transgresses limited existence and opens up a wound in being in the real experience of silence or death. In notes made during the composition of *Le Coupable*, Bataille gives an account

---

[28] Ibid., 'Par-delà la poésie', p.422

[29] Ibid., *L'Expérience intérieure*, p. 170

[30] Op. cit., Maurice Blanchot, *L'Espace littéraire*, p.231.

of how, several weeks before she finally died in November 1938, he had brought a rose to Laure, his lover and collaborator on the Acéphale project, who had been slowly dying from tubercolosis for some months. This account was originally intended to form a central part of *Le Coupable*, but was withdrawn by Bataille shortly before publication. Nonetheless the Orphic image of the the dying lover and her last words ('La rose'), although not present in the text, resound as a metonymic echo through the texts of *Le Coupable*. Most significantly, in his account of the death of Laure and his role as witness to her agony, Bataille emphasises that the spectacle of the death of the Other is an experience which, in a visual and textual sense, lies beyond metaphor. It is an encounter with absolute silence which immobilises discourse in a moment which is 'déchirant': the experience tears apart the fabric of language and exposes the irreducible work of radical negativity. Poetry, therefore, is a paradox which, emerging out of such an experience, can only be realised as a literal impossibility. At the same time, the encounter with the death of a loved one is a transformative experience. In the same way that Anne, in *Thomas l'Obscur*, represents Eurydice for Thomas in the metonymic figure of a 'cadavre, néant inassimilable [...] suprême moquerie à la pensée de Thomas', [31] the image of the dead lover represents for Bataille an irreducible transgression in which the subject and the Other destroy each other in a moment of convulsive poetic activity. The blinding interior vision of inner experience has its origin in this point of dissolution: like the 'formless vision' and 'formless word' of Angela of Foligno, Bataille's inner experience, although definite, is an illumination which is beyond definition. The word 'déchirant' is a naming of a shift into alterity which is both an assertion of the sovereignty of poetic feeling, and an experience which annihilates the possibility of poetry.

12 octobre
Hier, dans le bureau d'un camarade de travail, alors que celui-ci téléphonait, j'éprouvais de l'angoisse et sans que rien puisse être aperçu, je me trouvai absorbé en moi-même, les yeux fixés sur le lit de mort de Laure (celui-ci où je me couche maintenant chaque soir). Ce lit et Laure se trouvaient dans l'espace même de mon coeur ou plus exactement mon coeur *était* Laure étendue sur ce lit - dans la nuit de la cage thoracique - Laure achevait de mourir à l'instant où elle éleva l'une des roses qu'on venait d'étendre devant elle, elle l'éleva devant elle avec un mouvement excédé et elle cria presque d'une voix absente et infiniment

---

[31] Op. cit., Maurice Blanchot, *Thomas l'Obscur*, p.70.

douloureuse: 'la rose!'. (Je crois que ce furent ses derniers mots.) Dans le bureau et pendant une partie de la soirée la rose élevée et le cri restèrent longuement dans mon coeur. La voix de Laure n'était peut-être pas douloureuse, elle peut-être simplement *déchirante*. Au même instant je me représentais ce que j'avais éprouvé le matin même: 'prendre une fleur et la regarder jusqu'à l'accord...'.[32]

The evidence of this account is that the death of Laure, or at least the memory of her death, is, for Bataille, an exposure to a transformative experience which is unmediated by the logic of presence. The poetic image of Laure is, like Nietszche's abyss which stares back at him who gazes at it too long, a vision which is both impossible and a limitless transition.

C'était là une vision, une vision intérieure maintenue par une nécessité subie en silence; ce n'était pas une réflexion libre.[33]

In the same way that poetic sensation, when expanded into spiritual sensation, dislocates and overturns reason and immobilizes the syntax of philosophy, the absence of Laure becomes a non-metaphorical enunciation of discontinuity. In the collection *L'Archangélique*, published in 1944, the central image is, therefore, of the tomb: an impossible (and impassable) negation of language; 'je suis le père/ et le tombeau/du ciel.' [34]

The relation between the tomb and the possibility of language is, moreover, opposed to any form of dialectical movement; the sovereign expenditure of poetry can only be maintained in experience which is analogous to traditional forms of mysticism. Thus, in the introduction to *L'Expérience intérieure*, Bataille defines the 'emanation' in terms which, if not entirely acceptable, are nonetheless accessible to the Christian imagination:

Dieu diffère de l'inconnu en ce qu'une émotion profonde, venant des profondeurs de l'enfance, se lie d'abord en nous à son évocation. L'inconnu laisse froid au contraire, ne se fait pas aimer avant qu'il ne renverse en nous toute chose comme un vent violent. De même les images bouleversantes et les moyens termes auxquels recourt l'émotion poétique nous touchent sans peine. Si la poésie introduit l'étrange, elle le

---

[32] *ŒC*, V, p. 512. The date of Laure's death, 12th October, and the image of the rose are also significant in Maurice Blanchot's narrative *L'Arrêt de Mort* (Paris: Gallimard,1948) pp.43-44.

[33] Ibid., p.512

[34] 'Le tombeau', op. cit., *L'Archangélique*, p.36

fait par la voie du familier. Le poétique est du familier se dissolvant dans l'étrange et nous-mêmes avec lui.[35]

The dissolution of the familiar into the unknown is, like the 'impressionism' of Mallarmé, founded upon an essential flaw in the structure of language and existence. This movement is separate from poetic emotion, however, which is a movement towards 'l'appréhension divine ou poétique'.[36] Thus far, therefore, poetry may be equated with the poetic image of Christ's wound on the cross, which, for the Christian, reaches beyond metaphor into real experience of sacred communication.

As observed above, Bataille found an equivalent to the image of Christ's agony in the series of photographs of a dismembered Chinese youth, originally shown to him by Dr.Adrien Borel. These photographs were also shown to the poet Pierre Jean Jouve in the course of psychoanalysis and appear in a fictional form in his novel *Vagadu*. Most importantly Jouve, who embraced a fervent if unorthodox form of Catholic mysticism, similarly ascribes transformative qualities to this image. Indeed, although after his spiritual crisis of 1924 Jouve's poetry was shaped by his interest in traditional Christian forms of mysticism, his belief in the potency of these photographs as a psychoanalytical tool and as a way into a concrete experience of self-annihilation mirror Bataille's notion of the images and shed light on Bataille's formulation of inner experience as a negative form of communication.[37]

Je ne peux aller plus bas.
[...] Un de ces jours-là elle vit 'le Chinois'. Il faut bien décrire le Chinois. Dans ce moment où elle ne supportait la compagnie de personne, elle feuilletait les journaux illustrés. La revue à la mode 'Bateau Ivre' lui apporta ce dont elle avait besoin. Au milieu - le Chinois. La tête d'un martyr chinois. Le masque de cet homme couvrait la page entière, sans marges.
Quelle précision dans le rendu! On ne voit aucune blessure car c'est le 'corps' qui fut torturé mais on voit sur chaque trait, chaque ride, dans toutes les nuances de ces yeux ouverts. l'effet psychologique et l'émotion qui ont accompagné l'agonie.
[...] Son effroi prit une force d'ouragan quand elle aperçut que l'expression du malheureux n'était celle de l'épouvante. Il ne pleurait pas. Autour de cette bouche

---

[35] *L'Expérience intérieure, ŒC*, V, p.17
[36] Ibid., p.17
[37] An account of Jouve's relation to psychoanalysis is given in Elisabeth Roudinesco, op. cit., *Histoire de la psychanalyse en France*, tome 2, pp. 110-115.

116

ouverte, qui exprimait de si longues affres, une sorte de délicatesse heureuse, de félicité régnait...sous les gouttes de sueur, de sang...il y ouvrait une joie céleste. Ah double horreur! C'était magnifique. Catherine prit la parole. 'Non je ne peux pas voir ça!' 'Montre encore!' C'était si hideux, comme elle avait peur. 'Que veux-tu me dire, ô Chinois, que veux-tu me dire?'
D'autres motifs passaient dans son esprit: instruments, troncs d'arbres, danses, cris, parties arrachées. Le sang sur le sol, et une éternelle chaleur humaine. C'était sur un autre continent beaucoup plus ancien.
Catherine eût voulu crier d'horreur, mais comment, comment expliquer le mécanisme, et qu'une horreur si personnelle, mélangée de plaisir, sortît de la photo du Chinois? Comment expliquer que l'extase du Chinois fût un des états à elle et se communiquât à son âme de l'intérieur vers l'extérieur? 'Cachez-le, je ne veux plus, je ne veux plus, j'ai envie de vomir?' Cependant le Chinois qui était ainsi arrivé en elle ressemblait à Luc Pascal, mais en sens contraire.
Une matière psychologique d'une extraordinaire densité, d'une complexité extrême, dont le traduction en langage clair me paraît même pas toujours possible, est sous les yeux. [38]

The photograph of the Chinese youth, in *Vagadu*, reduces those who see the image to silence. As a poetic image, it trangresses all possible assimilation and, in its blinding atrocity, breaks with language and is an opening into 'impossibility'. It is, therefore, an experience analogous to inner experience. As the wounded Christ on the cross is the poetic image which breaks with the movement of existence and ruptures being into transcendence for the Christian saint, so the contemplation of the dismembering of the Chinese youth is an act of self-mutilation which is the beginning of the poetic activity of of inner experience.

The poetry of sacrifice and catastrophe, however, does not function for Bataille, as it does for Jouve, as an affirmation of transcendent meaning. Rather, for Bataille, although it is the non-servile creation which is at the origin of religious feeling and meaning, the poetry of inner experience can only be 'parodic' of meaning or hierarchy at a transcendental level; in this sense it is 'arch-angelic'. The poems of inner experience are thus forms of prayer which have a non-metaphorical relation to the Christian mystical experience. However, instead of functioning as doxology, that is to say an affirmation of metaphysical presence, the poems have a 'parodic' relation to the logic of presence and therefore function as 'a-doxology'; the reversal of the

---

[38] Pierre- Jean Jouve, *Vagadu* (Paris: Gallimard, 1985), p. 98

subject into itself is asserted in Bataille's poetry as a moment of ecstatic non-being.

> Au plus haut des cieux
> les anges, j'entends leur voix, me glorifient.
> Je suis, sous le soleil, fourmi errante, petite et noire, une pierre roulée
> m'atteint,
> m'écrase,
> morte, dans le ciel
> le soleil fait rage,
> il aveugle,
> je crie:
> 'il n'osera pas'
> il ose.[39]

Inner experience, however, is not a representation or dramatization of the death of the Other, although it is a method. Like the bullfight, it is a tragic ritual which communicates the experience itself of the other's death. Thus, the sovereign operation breaks with mediation in the same way that the bullfighter, at a given moment of his choosing, breaks with the tragic spectacle of the corrida to move into the 'impossible experience' of killing and communicating the anguish of that act. Laure, in one of the fragmented texts assembled by Bataille writes:

> La corrida relève du sacré parce qu'il y a menace de mort et mort réelle, mais ressentie, éprouvée par d'autres, avec d'autres.
> Imaginez une corrida pour vous tout seul [40]

The reversal of the subject into itself is thus, like the bullfight, also an experience which can be visualised in the death of the Other. The poetic image of the lover's tomb is one of the ways way out of the labyrinth of discourse into the open wound of inner experience. The poem 'Dieu' (already quoted above, see p. 45), is a version of *ipse*'s double encounter with the death of the subject as also, and simultaneously, the death of the Other:

> A la main chaude
> Je meurs tu meurs

---

[39] *L'Expérience intérieure, ŒC*, V, p.185
[40] Laure, *Écrits, fragments, lettres*, ed. Jérome Peignot (Paris: Jean-Jacques Pauvert, 1978), p.112

où est-il
où suis-je?
sans rire
je suis mort
mort et mort
dans la nuit d'encre
flèche tirée
sur lui[41]

There are two important points about this poem: firstly, it is significant that the unlimited moment of a sovereign communication is, first of all, defined by the fact that its meaning is subverted and lost in the discontinuity of 'night'; secondly this encounter with nothingness appears in a textual space opened up by the infinite void of death.

Bataille's meditations upon the body of Laure - which are at the centre of inner experience and the central object of his practice of joy in the face of death - are thus an inversion of the method of 'intersubjective' and 'trans-personal' experiences revealed to the Surrealists in games like 'Cadavre Exquis' and in which the poetic image was a a self-sufficient representation of symbolic or magical meaning. Within the process of inner experience, the poetic image of Laure, for Bataille, annihilates all systems of meaning and transgresses the closure of knowledge. Like the Surrealist ambition to dissolve the unity of the self into the free and limitless play of analogical thinking, Bataille's poetic method aims a central point of illumination; inner experience seeks, however, to shatter subjective experience into fragments, shards of light which wound and blind the 'I- who-sees'; the 'supreme point' is replaced by 'le miroir de la mort.' This fundamental premise of inner experience is explained by Bataille in 'La pratique de la joie devant la mort':

Je fixe un point devant moi et je me représente ce point comme le lieu géométrique de toute existence et de toute unité, de toute séparation et de toute angoisse, de tout désir inassouvi et de toute mort possibles.
    J'adhère à ce point et un profond amour de ce qui est en ce point me brûle jusqu'à refuser d'être en vie pour autre chose que ce qui est là, pour ce point qui, étant ensemble vie et mort d'un être aimé, a un éclat de cataracte

---

[41] *L'Expérience intérieure, ŒC,* V, p. 189

119

Si je me représente dans une vision et dans un halo qui le transfigure le visage
extasié et épuisé d'un être mourant, ce qui irradie de ce visage éclaire de sa nécessité
le nuage du ciel, dont la lueur grise devient alors plus pénétrante que celle du soleil
lui-même. Dans cette représentation, la mort apparaît de la même nature que la
lumière qui éclaire, dans la mesure où celle-ci se perd à partir de son foyer: il
apparaît qu'il ne faut pas un moindre perte que la mort pour que l'éclat de la vie
traverse et transfigure l'existence terne, puisque c'est seulement son arrachement
libre qui devient en moi la puissance de la vie et du temps. Ainsi je cesse d'être
autre chose que le miroir de la mort de la même façon que l'univers n'est que le
miroir de la lumière. [42]

In this way poetic activity, 'the mirrror of death', escapes the dialectic
of possibility imagined by Hegel, and is a sovereign negativity which
displaces the subject in a movement towards dispersal.

The poetic experience is, however, also erotic: like wounding,
laughter or abandonment, it is a violent disruption to the organization
of philosophical thinking; it is predicated upon the desire of the subject
to be ecstatically abandoned in the object and, as such, is erotic.
Bataille's central purpose, however, is to examine the relation between
inner experience and poetry, not only as a form of exclusion, but also
to consider the function of the poetic as a pure negativity which
destroys the subject in the moment of erotic abandonment. Poetic
experience is, for Bataille, therefore, a negative form of the mystical
transformation described by St. John of the Cross, wherein the
'perfect' joining of the lovers in union is a loss of identity and
transfiguration.

Quando tu me mirauas
, Su gracia en mi tus ojos imprimían
(When you looked upon me
your eyes gave to me your Grace)[43]

Thus, in the same way that Albertine for Proust represented a
'lucidité désagrégeante' qui 'le déchirait',[44] Laure represents for
Bataille an absence who, beyond the opposition of presence and loss,
ruptures the symmetry of inner experience in a poetic awakening.

---

[42] 'La pratique de la joie devant la mort', Œ C, I, pp.556-557
[43] St. John of the Cross, El Cántico Espiritual, coll. Clásicos castellanos (Madrid:
Espasa- Calpe, 1944) p. 245
[44] L'Expérience intérieure, Œ C, V, p. 161

At the end of discourse, *ipse* negates itself in the movement towards its reduction to silence. What remains of this shattered subjectivity is an image which, reflected back upon itself, is both *sacrificier* and sacrificed: this is what Bataille finally means by the poetic image: a negative reflection of *ipse* which confronts its own discontinuity.

The Marriage of Heaven and Hell

David Gascoyne describes the poetic activity of Breton and Soupault in *Les Champs Magnétiques* as 'paroxysmic death-birth' in which 'an id [is] no longer subservient to a super-ego'.[45] This is also true of the movement of inner experience in which *ipse* moves away from its origin towards it own annihilation; Bataille describes this as a textual, poetic experience, 'mise à mort de l'auteur par son oeuvre',[46] which undermines not only language, but in a dialectical reversal, perverts and dissolves the subject in the negative work of poetry. *Ipse*'s encounter with the night of 'le non-savoir' is therefore a paradoxical experience which presents itself, in the form of poetry and in the vocabulary of negative theology, as 'a-doxology', that is to say poetic activity which goes beyond dramatisation and experience into the lightning flash of illumination: 'je me représente l'instant glacé de ma propre mort.'[47]

Poetry, for Bataille, is also sovereign in the sense that it is pure expenditure and, as it is for Blanchot, 'la purification de l'absence'.[48] It follows from this that poetry is a sacrifice which is a sovereign renunciation of recognition which erases meaning and abolishes individuality. In this sense, it is a form of sovereign communication of absence which is a transcription of 'mystical' experience to the extent that it rebuilds the possibility of communication at the same time as it abolishes the thinking subject.

Bataille (and Laure) particularly admired William Blake as the supreme example of a writer whose poetry emerged out of and actively played on the tensions between mystical experience and language rather than seeking reconciliation in the synthesis of a poetic image

---

[45] David Gascoyne, 'Introduction', in André Breton and Philippe Soupault, *The Magnetic Fields*, trans. David Gascoyne (London: Atlas, 1985), p.15.

[46] *L'Expérience intérieure, ŒC*, V, p.174.

[47] 'La pratique de la joie devant la mort', *ŒC*, I, p.556

[48] Op. cit., Maurice Blanchot, *L'Espace littéraire*, p.136

which can be subordinated to meaning. More specifically, in the texts of his *Doctrine of Contraries*, Blake asserts an anti-materialist perspective which (emerging out of Blake's preoccupation with the mysticism of Swedenborg) seeks to put together the opposing forces of rational and irrational 'energies' in a vision which is akin to the Spinozan *sub specie humanitatis*. For Blake the free-play of inter-acting contraries, rather, is the source of the vital 'Energy' of Being and is, indeed, like the Heraclitean vision of a cosmic unity, the source and end of Creation.

> As a new heaven is begun and it is now thirty three years since its advent, the Eternal Hell revives. And lo! Swedenborg is the Angel sitting at the tomb; his writings are the linen clothes folded up. Now is the dominion of Edom, and the return of Adam into Paradise; see Isaiah xxxiv & xxxv Chap;
> Without contraries is no progression. Attraction and Repulsion. Reason and Energy, Love and Hate, are necessary to Human existence.
> From these contraries spring what the religious call Good and Evil. Good is the passive that obeys Reason. Evil is the active springing from Energy.
> Good is Heaven. Evil is Hell.[49]

There is a circularity to this motion, however, which Bataille acknowledges as an abstraction inscribed into Being: 'mysticism' disrupts discursive knowledge but is related to nothing else other than the unlimited exteriority of the impossible. For Blake, this paradox is inscribed into the nature of what he terms the 'four-fold vision' of the poet. For Bataille, however, the 'Poetic Genius' is both a parody of spiritual sensation and a system, or transcendence of a system, which is able to integrate the abstract negativity of thought which abolishes itself into the sovereign displacement of meaning which takes place in poetry. Blake's 'four-fold' vision is, in fact, 'une expérience nue' which refuses to submit to profane value systems.

Although Bataille's notion of sovereignty originated in the Hegelian dialectic of slave and master, Bataille goes beyond Hegel and beyond meaning in his determination to destroy purpose and live entirely in an instant in which utilitarian principles are obliterated   by the 'awakenings' of laughter and poetry. Bataille's version of non-knowledge, or un-knowing - which has the same dialectical relation to knowledge as anti-matter bears towards matter - is predicated upon

---

[49] William Blake, 'The Proverbs of Hell', *Selected Poetry*, ed. W.H Stevenson, (London: Penguin, 1988), p.66

displacement and sacrifice of meaning: as soon as knowledge is asserted it simultaneously moves away from itself. Bataille himself sees this slippage into silence as the central point of the sacred experience of poetry, as, in fact, the sacrifice of teleological purpose .

Unlike the Surrealists, who aim at a 'Golden Age' predicated upon what Bataille sees as their misunderstanding of Hegel,[50] Bataille sees poetry as a necessary sacrifice in which the destruction of the subject also brings into ruin the possibility of language.

> Le sacrificateur, le poète, ayant sans relâche à porter la ruine dans le monde insaisissable des mots, se fatigue vite d'enrichir un trésor littéraire. Il y est condamné: s'il perdait le goût du trésor, il cesserait d'être poète. [51]

Thus far the notion of sovereignty thus far mirrors the absolute revolt of Surrealism. Writing poetry (which is, after all, the only form of writing Bataille admits), however, involves not only the iniatives of sovereignty, but also the imperatives of the sovereign experience. Moreover, the refusal to subordination, in the first instance, is a break with the ontological unity of 'le don verbal'; in the second instant, the 'poetic Genius' shatters the paralysis of meaning in the assertion of 'non-savoir' in the metonymic figure of death.

In Blake, however, Bataille sees not only a paradigm of sovereign experience, but a Gnostic vision and a method which is a dédoublement of the 'discipline' of 'Méthode de méditation'.[52] Although, he is suspicious of the word 'mysticism' itself, he is in favour of analogical thinking as a method which exceeds the Hegelian system. This Gnostic method indeed transgresses the entire project of knowledge in History and, in poetry, leaves traces which lead beyond meaning to an unresolved and unknowable Beyond. For Bataille, this is a touching upon impossible experience in the sovereign form of poetic experience.

Bataille's declaration in his text of 1947 of a 'hatred of poetry' is a hatred, first of all, for any aesthetic practice which originates in the false promise of Hegelian idealism. In the second instance, it is, more properly, a hatred of the lacerating paradox ('Déchirement') which is the central movement of inner experience. More specifically, as

---

[50] *L'Expérience intérieure, ŒC,* V, p.173.
[51] Ibid., p. 172
[52] *Méthode de méditation, ŒC,* V, pp.218-219

negativity, poetry overwhelms the dialectic, exceeds presence and sacrifices meaning and knowledge in the opening of a sacred wound. This how it becomes the founding point of, in Nietzschean terms, a negative theology which seeks to account for a loss of meaning in categorical terms. Bataille's 'hatred of poetry', as one commentator puts it, has 'ontological implications' since, as observed, 'the aesthetic part of literature, put on trial by the impossible and by death, finds itself confronted with the limits of being. This investigation meaures beauty (the aesthetic) in the light of evil and thus raises the crucial question of ethical exigencies.' [53]

The impossible ethics of poetry are also, however, inscribed into the 'mystical' premise of inner experience. In 1942, on the publication of *L'Expérience intérieure*, Kojève wrote to Bataille that 'Toute la mystique est le mot Nobodaddy' - Blake's God who, in *Songs of Experience*, is nobody's father and has replaced, with his priests and kings, Christ, the poet and the child, the Gods of Innocence. Bataille's 'searching eye', the eye of the poet in search of sacred experience, is analogous to Blake's 'four-fold vision', and, like Blake's Gnostic method, extends the trope of blindness and vision into the realm of sovereignty in a manner which undoes all the dialectical strength of dualist thinking. Poetry is the encounter with Noboddady, or the absent God, which releases *ipse* from the constraints of dialectical movement: at the same time, poetry is also an opening to annihilating vision.

Thus, when Bataille writes, 'Le sacrifice est immoral, la poésie est immorale',[54] he is asserting a paradox which affirms poetry as sacred activity and, like Blake, he announces the impossibility of bringing together text and vision in mystical experience.

In the poetry of inner experience, Bataille stresses the primacy of an ethics which privileges the death of the Other and our responsibility for it. Bataille is thus able to compare the non-metaphorical encounter with alterity which takes place in inner experience with the 'déchirements intérieurs plus grands' signalled in the poetic experience of the Other's death. In literal terms, Bataille's inner experience begins in his meditation upon the corpse of Laure and then, as Bernard Noël

---

[53] Marie-Christine Lala, 'The hatred of poetry in George Bataille's writing and thought', in *Bataille: Writing the Sacred*, ed. Carolyn Bailey Gill (London : Routledge, 1995), p.115.

[54] *L'Expérience intérieure, ŒC,* V, p.158

suggests, moves beyond language into an encounter where the sacred and sovereign status of poetry saves the experience from recuperation in 'l'écriture'. Thus, at a non-metaphorical level, as well as a textual level, in the 'opération souveraine' of inner experience, the impossible ethics of writing poetry is the same 'angoisse la plus folle imaginable' in which God prays to *ipse*, who also occupies a summit, but an inverted one. Poetry, however, is, for Bataille, evidence that the sovereign operation, the sacred collapse into the void, can traced through fragments of language, even though discursive meaning has long since been discarded.

Chapter Five

'Le combat intérieur':
war as inner experience;
inner experience as war

> Quae conventio luci ad tenebras ?
> (What Conformity is there between
> light and darkness?)
> St. Paul, *Corinthians*

This chapter will examine the relationship in Bataille's thought between inner experience and the outer social world of politics. Although inner experience is, in many ways, opposite to the externalized discourse of politics, it is of crucial significance that Bataille formulated his ideas on the mystical aspects of his thinking in a political context. Indeed, from the early 1930s onwards, Bataille, at varying levels of activity and commitment, involved himself in overtly political struggles which aimed at deflecting the threat of coming war, as well as establishing specific anti-capitalist and anti-Fascist positions. In 1933 and 1934, Bataille was not only actively involved in Boris Souvarine's Cercle communiste démocratique and the journal *La Critique sociale*, but was also a member of the group Masses, which brought together Jean Dautry, Édouard Lienert, Paul Bénichou and, to a lesser degree, Simone Weil, and which sought to establish a theoretical position on the spontaneous movement of the revolutionary classes.[1] In 1936 and 1937, at the same time as he was pursuing the Nietzschean exigencies of Acéphale, in articles such as 'Le Front populaire dans la rue' for *Cahiers de Contre-attaque*, and in his contributions to the public meetings of the Contre-attaque group held at the Grenier des Augustins on place Saint-Michel, Bataille was not only to collaborate with those, like Breton, who had earlier attacked him, but also to engage with debates about the theory and representation of revolution with members of the revolutionary Left who had recently emerged from Surrealism or the Parti Communiste

---

[1] Op. cit., Surya, p.227. See also Francis Marmande, *Georges Bataille Politique* (Lyon: Presses Universitaires de Lyon, 1985), p.49-50

Français, or both, and who stressed the primacy of experience over Marxist theory.[2]

Although Contre-attaque was divided into two camps, grouped around Bataille (Ambrosino, Klossowski, Dubief, Chavy) or Breton (Eluard, Péret and Gillet), Bataille was effectively the intellectual leader of the group.[3] In the first instance, this meant that, as Bataille put it in the first tract which signalled the activities of Contre-attaque, the opposition to fascism was predicated on the perceived failure of communism.[4] In the second instance, this meant that - as defined in a text signed by both Bataille and Breton - the principal aim of the of the group was to call for a renovation of the language and content of revolutionary violence.[5]

There were, nonetheless, fundamental and irreconciliable differences between Breton and Bataille around the concept of revolutionary violence. Breton at this stage in his career defined himself politically as anti-Stalinist but also as a revolutionary thinker faithful to the demands of dialectical materialism and the spirit *of The Communist Manifesto of 1848*.[6] Bataille, on the other hand, sought to call for revolutionary violence in the name of desire and radical subjectivity.

Most importantly, however, the central premise behind Contre-attaque was to turn the weapons of fascism upon itself. This was not only the central idea developed by Bataille during the meetings of Contre-attaque, but also a notion entirely in concord with Bataille's concerns, reflected in the community Acéphale, of exploring the potential of violence and sacrifice in real paroxystic experience and transferring these concerns to the domain of the social and political.

---

[2] The group included, for example, Maurice Heine, Adolphe Acker, Benjamin Péret, Jean Bernier and Henri Dubief. See 'Cahiers de Contre-Attaque', in Maurice Nadeau, *Histoire du surréalisme* (Paris: Éditions du Seuil, 1964) pp.452.

[3] Op. cit, Surya, pp.266-277. See also the authorative and detailed account of Bataille's political development at this period and his relation to members of the Cercle communiste-démocratique as well as members of the Surrealist group given in Robert Stuart Short, 'Contre-attaque', *Entretiens sur le surréalisme*, ed. Ferdinand Alquié (Paris: La Haye, Mouton, 1968), pp.144-175.

[4] Op. cit., Georges Bataille, *Choix de Lettres*, pp.105

[5] 'Contre-Attaque, Union de lutte des intellectuels révolutionnaires',*ŒC*, I, pp. 379-383

[6] André Breton, 'Position politique du surréalisme', op. cit., *Manifestes du surréalisme*, pp.240-241

Thus, at the same time as Bataille turned his attentions to the 'outward' problems of history, and in particular the rise of Hitler and possibility of a European war, he never lost sight of the fact that 'war' was a religious, rather than political or economic problem. To this extent, the world of 'outward' experience, of economic and social struggle, as Bataille later defines it in *La Part Maudite*, is inextricably related to the problems of 'inward' experience; the 'violence intérieure', which exceeds and contradicts 'la violence révolutionnaire', and which, in the movement of inner experience, leads to annihilation of the self, is also the experience out of which proceeds any definition of a political economy which bases itself in metaphysical values .

This notion is a key motif in Bataille's writings of the period leading up to the Second World War: in 'Le bleu du ciel'(the fragment published in *Minotaure* in 1934, as distinct from the novel), Bataille describes his experiences on Montserrat in the shadow of the Spanish Civil War as 'mystiques'; in the novel *Le Bleu du ciel,* Tropmann, who is, or has been, a Left Wing activist, asserts the importance of the inner experience of 'le désir d'aller à la mort' over the historical materialism of his supposed and possibly abandoned Marxism. No less important, is the way in which in 'La Conjuration sacrée', a text contemporaneous with those of Contre-Attaque, and published in the first edition of *Acéphale*, Bataille describes the project of the 'communauté' of Acéphale is a kind of 'holy war'. In this text, citing Sade, Kierkegaard and Nietzsche as witnesses to the decomposition of a society which has no religious centre, Bataille argues, as he would do at the colloquia of the Collège de Sociologie, for the restoration of the sacred, of inner experience, to political life. Although Bataille emphasises, first of all, that the project of Acéphale is situated beyond art, beyond the limits of metaphor, it is significant that the metaphorical use of 'guerre' in this text does not stand in contradiction to his declaration that the centre of all political activity must be founded upon what he terms 'les difficultés que rencontre le passage du chaos à l'existence organique'.

NOUS SOMMES FAROUCHEMENT RELIGIEUX et, dans la mesure où notre existence est la condamnation de tout ce qui est reconnu aujourd'hui, une exigence intérieure veut que nous soyons impérieux.
Ce que nous entreprenons est une guerre.[7]

---

[7] 'La Conjuration sacrée', *ŒC,* I, p.443

The 'exigence intérieure' - the sovereign need, or need for the sovereign experience - is at the centre of the 'acephalic' sacrifice of meaning in radical discontinuity. 'La guerre' or 'la nuit', is here, then, not only a mirror of 'la violence intérieure' of inner experience, but also a sacrifice which, as a paradoxical negation, establishes the fundamental importance of the disjunction between the sacred and the transcendental substance of sacred experience.

This shift between metaphor, metonymy to experience, raises the question, however, to what extent the sovereign operation of inner experience, refracted through the analogical sacrifice of 'war', can have meaning and value as the representation - or in Hegelian terms 'Vorstellung' - of the self-destruction of *ipse* in inner experience.

Most significantly, by the summer of 1939, in the fifth and final number of *Acéphale*, 'war', for Bataille and the rest of his generation, had become *the* war - the coming apocalypse of the Second World War. As such, in the texts 'La menace de guerre', 'La pratique de la joie devant la mort' and 'Méditation Héraclitéenne' - the first texts which Bataille explicity describes as 'mystiques' (although he does so with certain misgivings)[8] - 'war' is both a description of given conditions and a metonymic figure which is the object of Bataille's project of dissolving philosophy into impossible experience. The aim of this chapter, therefore, is to trace the movement between the subjective and objective realities of war as they are described in the texts of *La Somme athéologique* and to provide a commentary on the relation between inner experience as, in the language of the Spanish mystics, 'interior combat', and war as a mirror image of the collapse of identity into irrational, erotic desire .

The inner experience of Nietzsche

Throughout the 1930s and in particular the second half of the decade as the skies blackened with the threat of war, Bataille devoted several articles to Nietzsche. In these articles Nietzsche was not only defended against those, on the Right and Left, who associated him, like Wagner, with 'Hitlérisme', but also, more significantly, described less as a philosopher and more as the emblem of 'an aesthetic pessimism' which combined an adoration of Greek civilization, and in particular the pre-Socratics, with a tragic attitude to life.

---

[8] 'La Pratique de la joie devant la mort', *ŒC*, I, p. 554

Nietzsche, according to Bataille, substituted a search for truth in philosophy for a search for aesthetic phenomena which transcended the limits of traditional versions of Neo-Platonic dualism: this is how Nietzsche's thought, in political and philosophical terms, is an assertion of sovereignty which admits no possible or potential subordination. 'L'enseignement de Nietzsche [...]', concludes Bataille in an article 'Nietzsche et les fascistes', 'élabore la foi de la secte ou de l'ordre dont la volonté dominatrice fera la destinée humaine libre, l'arrachant à l'asservissement rationnel de la production comme à l'asservissement irrationnel au passé.'[9]

As Bataille began to write *Sur Nietzsche* in the early spring of 1944, he had already concluded that the project of *La Somme athéologique* would remain unfinished. Although *Sur Nietzsche* was to play an important role in later, revised plans for republication of the texts which Bataille had written during the war,[10] it is of significance that this text is conceived as a necessarily incomplete work which both reflects and bears witness to the reality of war in France in 1944 and the collapse of Germany. Most importantly, Bataille, like Klossowski, sees Nietzsche as one who refuses all possibility of transcendental experience whilst admitting the possibility of religious feeling. Inner experience is, thus, both the dissolution of the thinking subject and, as *ipse* wounds itself and wills its own destruction, a breaking with consciousness of individuation which opens the way to communication.

In *Sur Nietzsche*, Bataille places an account of torture in *Le Petit Parisien* against his own inner experience of 'nudité'; this is, he writes, a moment of tragic communication:

D'un récit de torture (*Petit Parisien*, 27-4):'... les yeux crevés, les oreilles et les ongles des mains arrachés, la tête fracassée à coups de bûche et la langue coupée avec une tenaille...' Enfant, l'idée du supplice me rendait la vie à charge. Je ne sais, encore maintenant, comment je supporterais... La terre est dans le ciel où elle tourne... La terre aujourd'hui, de toutes parts, se couvre de fleurs - lilas, glycine, iris - et la guerre en même temps bourdonne: des centaines d'avions emplissent les nuits d'un bruit des mouches.

La sensualité n'est rien sans le glissement louche, où l'accessible -quelque chose de gluant, de fou, qui d'habitude échappe - est soudain perçu. Ce 'gluant' se dérobe encore mais de l'entrevoir, nos coeurs battent d'espoirs déments: ces espoirs mêmes

[9] 'Nietzsche et les fascistes', *ŒC*, I, p.465
[10] 'Plans pour la somme athéologique',, *ŒC*,VI, pp. 360-363

qui, se bousculant, se pressant comme à l'issue, font jaillir, à la fin...Un au-delà insensé souvent nous déchire alors que nous semblons lascifs.

'Au-delà' commencant dès la sensation de *nudité*. La *nudité* chaste est l'extrême limite de l'hébétude. Mais qu'elle nous éveille à l'étreinte (des corps, des mains, des lèvres humides), elle est douce, animale, sacrée.c'est qu'une fois nu, chacun de nous s'ouvre à davantage que lui, s'abîme tout d'abord dans l'absence de limites animale. Nous nous abîmons, écartant les jambes, béant, le plus possible, à ce qui n'est plus nous, mais l'existence impersonnelle, marécageuse de la chair.

La communication des deux êtres passant par une perte d'eux-mêmes dans la douce fange qui leur est commune... [11]

It is significant that, in this account, Bataille separates the torture scene from its political context: indeed, it is as if there is no political context, merely a religious act of suffering which parallels both Bataille's own inner experience and the sufferings of the Christian saints. At the centre of this representation of a 'supplice', moreover, are two key metonymic figures: 'les yeux blindés' and 'la langue coupée avec une tenaille.' Vision and speech are abolished in sacred violence which paralyses the functions of the subjective consciousness. The Absent God, therefore, is a contiguity whose negative presence is communicated in his silence.

For Bataille, moreover, this inversion of blindness and vision has both a metaphorical and metonymic significance: it is, on the the one hand, an inverted metaphor which, as Bataille indicates in the quotation from Nietzsche's Zarathoustra chosen to preface *L'Expérience intérieure*, 'La nuit est aussi un soleil', functions as a totemic turning toward the darkness and illumination of 'le non-savoir'.

On the other hand, in *Sur Nietzsche*, this trope functions as a metonymic figure which is linked to desire, 'la volonté de la chance', which is the origin and cause of inner experience. Bataille sees 'la chance' as the .central metaphor used by Nietzsche to delineate the circularity of being. Bataille sees in this trope a shift from the metaphorical language of philosphy to the unstable language of 'atheology': the circularity of being inscribes itself into 'volonté de chance'. Blanchot describes this circularity of 'la chance' as a game where 'l'oubli est le maître du jeu': a riddle without an answer. [12] This is not a simplification, but rather a paradox which lies at the centre of

---

[11] *Sur Nietzsche*, *ŒC*,VI, pp.117-118
[12] Op. cit., Maurice Blanchot,'Le Jeu de la pensée', p.737

Bataille and Nietzsche's inner experience, and which annihilates text and vision.

More precisely, as Bataille wrote in a text for Nietzsche's centenary composed at the same time as he was writing *Sur Nietzsche*, the signal importance of Nietzsche's thought is that, like the 'supplice des cent morceaux', or the description in *Le Petit Parisien*, it overwhelms the Hegelian, and therefore Marxist dialectic, with the stringent demands of an economy of suffering.[13] This is the notion that Bataille had been developing in the 1930s in his activities with Acéphale and, to a certain extent, in his contributions to Contre-attaque and his restating of the meaning of revolutionary violence as excessive or ecstatic. Bataille saw that the central problems of politics, and therefore fascism, were essentially religious and therefore could not be resolved by materialist ideologies. This is why Tropmann in *Le Bleu du Ciel*, like Nietzsche, offers a pathological account of the insufficiency of politics. Bataille's political positions in the 1930s, therefore, are not only inextricably linked to his drift away from any form of materialist ethics, but also a series of negative movements which transgress all historical imperatives, and - as demonstrated in the later texts of *Acéphale* - move ultimately towards the empty space of inner experience.

No Man's Land

One of the most important characteristics of Nietzsche's writings for Bataille at this stage, is that they do not offer a critique of politics, but rather a poeticized account of the experience of political catastrophe which finds its fullest and most complete expression in war. Nietzsche's version of the relation between history and politics, between the historical subject and society, is, according to Bataille a form of vision.[14]

---

[13] Georges Bataille, *Choix de Lettres*, ed. Michel Surya (Paris: Gallimard, 1997), pp.217-224

[14] An account of Bataille's relation to Nietzsche's version of the historical subject is given in Jean-Michel Besnier, 'Le Front Nietzschéen', *La politique de l'impossible: L'intellectuel entre révolte et engagement* (Paris: Éditions de la Découverte, 1988), pp.25-37. In particular, Besnier cites the publication in 1914 of the first editions of Charles Andler, *Nietzsche, sa vie et sa pensée* (Paris: Gallimard, 1957) during the battle of the Marne as a decisive influence on Bataille and the rest of his generation. Ibid., p.26.

In *Le Coupable*, Bataille describes how, at the beginning of the war, he had been reading Angela of Foligno's *Book of Visions* at the precise moment that Europe had embarked upon the agony of war: there is a distinct relation, he posits, between the interior experience of the mystic and the larger disaster of war. Three years later, in *Sur Nietzsche*, Bataille develops this notion and writes that the collapse of meaning which is taking place in a literal sense in Europe is, as he decribes inner experience, a 'disintoxication', an almost beatific experience: it is a concrete demonstration of the sacrifice of the subject which occurs in the movement of inner experience.

The 'infinite horror of war' is, however, only analogous to inner experience, in the first instance, in that it brings the subject to an extreme point of suffering which is a form of communication; war, or battle, does not, however, have an exact equivalence with inner experience because although, as an outward catastrophe it exceeds the individual suffering of inner experience in a plurality of forms, it, nonetheless, is linked to the idea of project.

> Dans l'horreur infinie de la guerre l'homme accède en foule au point extrême qui l'effraie. Mais l'homme est loin de vouloir l'horreur (et l'extrême): son sort est pour une part de tenter d'éviter l'inévitable. Ses yeux bien qu'avides de lumière, évitent obstinément le soleil, et la douceur de son regard, à l'avance, trahit les ténèbres, vite venues, du sommeil: si j'envisage la masse humaine, dans sa consistance opaque, elle est déjà comme endormie, fuyante et retirée dans la stupeur. La fatalité d'un mouvement aveugle la rejette néanmoins dans l'extrême, où elle accède un jour avec précipitation.
>
> L'horreur de la guerre est plus grande que celle de l'expérience intérieure. La désolation d'un champ de bataille, en principe, a quelque chose de plus lourd que la «nuit obscure». Mais dans la bataille on aborde l'horreur avec un mouvement qui la surmonte: l'action, le projet lié à l'action permettent de dépasser l'horreur. Ce dépassement donne à l'action, au projet une grandeur captivante, mais l'horreur en elle-même est niée. [15]

For Bataille, therefore, the theme of war is linked to inner experience not as a metaphor but as an equivalent. It is an equivalent which does not exactly match the movement of inner experience, but it is, nonetheless, an experience which undermines all stable referents and introduces suffering as the central principle of social exchange. War is analogous to inner experience in the same way that poetry is

---

[15] *L'Expérience intérieure*, *ŒC*, V, p.58

related to religion: war is the contradiction of social organization as poetry is a sovereign denial of authority or meaning.

Bataille finds support for this encounter with war as a direct contradiction of metaphorized experience in the writings of the German soldier and mystic Ernst Jünger. In particular, in *Der Kampf als Inneres Erlebnis* ('War as Inner Experience'), a book quoted by Sartre in 'Un Nouveau Mystique', Jünger describes the nature of war as the way in which men are brought to a consciousness of 'le réalisme affreux des vieilles images du Crucifié'[16]: in the aftermath of a massacre, the contemplation of slaughter is tragic, in the sense that, as in the Aristotle's definition, of the word, it not only discharges excess but also heightens terror: thus, a massacre, momentarily, returns *ipse* to undifferentatiated versions of itself. Bataille cites a passage from Jünger's *La Guerre, notre mère* (the French translation of *Der Kampf als Inneres Erlebnis* which was readily available in Occupied Paris) in the introduction to *La Limite de l'utile*.

> [...] L'odeur des corps qui se décomposent est insupportable, lourde, douceâtre, repoussante, pénétrante comme une pâte visqueuse. Elle flottait si intensément sur les plaines, après de grandes batailles, que des hommes affamés oubliaient de se nourrir [...] Les champs, couverts d'hommes fauchés par leurs balles, s'étendaient sous leurs yeux. Les cadavres de leurs camarades reposaient à leurs côtés, mêlés à eux, le sceau de la mort sur les paupières. [...] A quoi bon recouvrir les lambeaux de chair avec du sable et la chaux?
> [...] Leur nombre était trop grand. La pioche heurtait partout la chair humaine. Tous les mystères de la tombe se révélaient, si atroces qu'auprès d'eux les rêves les plus infernaux semblaient insigifiants.[17]

Bataille writes that there is an equivalence between war and mystical experience in that they both are forms of useless expenditure which equate to ritual sacrifice: the 'ecstasy' and 'terrors' of both experiences are parallel forms of communication.

For Bataille, however, unlike Jünger who exalts in the heroism of war, the movement of inner experience, once begun, is a movement into excess and discontinuity which is tragic in the specifically Nietszchean sense of intensifying pain, horror, dread or eroticism. Most significantly, Bataille, in his description of the contemplation of the experience of war, distinguishes between 'transcendence' and 'immanence' in a way which dissolves the categorical thnking of

---

[16] Quoted in Surya, op.cit., p.351
[17] 'La limite de l'utile', *ŒC*, VII, p.252

'disintoxicated' thought. More specifically, 'Transcendence' which (from the philosophy of Kant) lies beyond or before experience and is therefore, *a priori*, beyond potential knowledge, falls outside a given set of categories; in the language of theology (of God) transcendent experience has continous existence outside the created world. Immanence, however, is related to the pantheistic notion of God being present throughout the universe: inner experience and immanent versions of experience, such as war or torture, deny the possibility of transcendence.

The 'immanent' nature of the war is such that daily existence cannot be separated from an intense encounter with death or the dead; death is not just a spectacle, but an active sacred presence incorporated into the profane organisation of quotidien existence; Bataille writes of Paris after an air raid:

> Paris est lourd après les bombardements. Mais pas trop. S. quand nous nous quittons, me dit un mot de sa concierge: 'ce qu'il faut voir, tout de même , par ces temps-ci: pensez qu'on a trouvé des cadavres vivants sous les encombres!'. [18]

In the same way, the presence of American soldiers, who represent the imminent presence of that which negates the 'transcendent' forces of Hitlérisme are a literal vision of negation. This 'vision' is at the centre of a section in *Sur Nietzsche* in which Bataille describes the agony of a wound which has been hurting for a long time and which incarnates 'immanent negativity':

> Je rentrai, m'éntendis sur mon lit. Des cris m'éveillèrent d'un demi-sommeil. J'allai à la fenêtre et je vis des femmes, des enfants courir. On me dit en criant que les Américains étaient là. Je sortis et trouvai les blindés entourés d'une foule à peu près foraine mais plus animée. Personne n'est plus sensible que moi à ce genre d'émotions. Je parlais aux soldats. Je riais.
> [...] Les Allemands suent de toute façon la médiocrité transcendée. L'«immanence» des Américains est indéniable (leur être est en eux-mêmes et non au-delà).
> [...] Déchiré, ce matin: ma blessure s'est rouverte au moindre heurt, une fois de plus, un désir vide, une inépuisable souffrance. [19]

Although Bataille is here presumably referring to a real experience of a wound, it is hard to move far away from either the notion of mutilation or wounding as ways into excessive experience: the death of God is a

---

[18] *Sur Nietzsche, ŒC*, VI, p.117
[19] *Ibid.*, p.179

wound which is deepened by the contemplation of his Absence; this is the immanent movement of inner experience beyond Hegelianism into sovereign communication.

In *Sur Nietzsche*, the encounter with excessive experience is itself the void, as immanent experience is substituted for transcendence. Thus, in the same way that the volumes of *La Somme athéologique* not only evoke the *Summa Theologiae* of St.Thomas Aquinas, but also set out to displace their basic tenets by operating in a space which unmakes them, *Sur Nietzsche* was conceived of by Bataille as an interrogation of the primacy of textual experience in the sovereign operation of inner experience: when Blanchot asks whether the writing of sovereignty is blank or neutral, he is not merely interrogating the substance of the experience as a Mallarméan version of aphasia, but also, as he himself says, positing neutrality as the negative side of transgression, the side which reveals the oppositions and contradictions of the 'logos'.[20]

This means that *Sur Nietzsche* is not an interpretation or re-ordering of Nietzsche's thought, nor even a dialogue or asking of questions, but, like the texts of *L'Expérience intérieure*, it functions as a prolonged meditation upon a series of possibilities and unresolvable tensions which defy expression. It is both an irony and shaping circumstance of the book, however, that it is a meditation which is centred upon the 'impossibilities' of the experience of reading Nietzsche in the concrete political context of 1944.

In *Sur Nietzsche*, Bataille also interrogates the irony that one hundred years after Nietzsche's birth, at the precise historical moment that Hitler's Germany was being engulfed in flames, Nietzsche's *amor fati* has collided with the external realities of history; 'Grand Politics' in the Nietzschean sense is also the version of Hegel, propounded by Kojève, who abolishes history in the the realization ('Verwirklichung') of freedom made actual in the social as well personal domain. This realization, however, must necessarily take place in the space opened up by the extreme point of death or inner experience. [21]

---

[20] Jacques Derrida, op. cit., 'De l'économie restreinte à l'économie générale: un hégélianisme sans réserves', p.369

[21] 'La réalité humaine est donc en dernière analyse la réalité objective de la mort: l'Homme n'est pas seulement mortel, il est la mort incarnée: il est sa propre mort. [...] La mort humaine, la mort de l'homme - et par conséquent toute son existence vraiment humaine, sont donc, si l'on veut, un suicide.' Alexandre Kojève, op.cit, *Introduction à la lecture de Hegel*, p.569

136

Sovereignty as a negative assertion of freedom is not, moreover, merely an inversion of Hegel. Thus, although Bataille originally conceived of the book, *Sur Nietzsche*, as the third of the series of *La Somme athéologique* and the volume in which Bataille's notion of 'le non-savoir' would be traced as a 'filigrane' through Nietszche's assault on 'truth', the facts of the German collapse of late 1943 and 1944 are a particularly apposite demonstration of the notion formulated by the Collège de Sociologie - to return to Bataille's position of 1936 and 1937 - that the origins of war lay beyond politics in the domain of religion. The problems of religion are, however, also those of tragedy.

It follows from this that, like *Le Coupable*, *Sur Nietzsche* exists as a fragmented account of subjective experience against objective realities which, as in Bataille's version of Sade, occludes experience in the demands of eroticism, poetry or vision (as observed earlier, it is Angela of Foligno, and not Marx or Hegel, who provides the guiding theory of *Sur Nietzsche* and *Le Coupable*). Secondly, *Sur Nietzsche*, like Nietzsche's own works, is intended as a statement of faith; it thus challenges the very notion of 'philosophy' at the same time as it asserts the negative *credo* of 'atheology'.

As we have already noted in Bataille's vocabulary, the slippage between the words 'atheology' and 'philosophy' is an inverse form of the relationship between 'theology' and 'philosophy' which was such an important theme in Medieval thought. But whereas the Scholastics, by applying rational dialectics to the mysteries of faith, laid the foundations of theology wherein the data of revelation is scrutinised in the light of reason, so that St. Thomas Aquinas can distinguish between theology as the data of revelation, and philosophy as the work of human reason, Bataille emphasises that no distinction can be made between transcendant and immanent criteria. Thus, when Kojève describes how Hegel posits that whilst the theologian conceives of theological discourse as one in which subject (man) speaks to object (God), that theological discourse is in fact a self-reflective process wherein man is both subject and object. Here we find one of the central metaphorical shifts of inner experience.

D'une manière générale, l'anthropologie hégélienne est une théologie chrétienne laïcisée. Et Hegel s'en rend parfaitemement compte. Il répète à plusieurs reprises que tout ce que dit la théologie chrétienne est absolument vrai, à condition que d'être appliqué non pas à un Dieu transcendant imaginaire, mais à l'Homme réel, vivant dans le Monde. Le théologien fait de l'anthropologie sans s'en rendre compte. Hegel ne fait que prendre vraiment conscience du savoir dit théo-logique,

en expliquant que son objet réel est non pas Dieu, mais l'Homme historique, ou. comme il aime à dire: 'L'Esprit du peuple'
Entre autres, cette conception est clairement exprimée par Hegel à la fin des Conférences de 1805-06 (vol, XX, p.268.7-21) [22]

Atheology, however, is not strictly speaking, as Kojève defines it, 'negative theology', in this sense, although, as we have seen there are affinities between the apophatic 'methods' of both Bataille and Blanchot.

As observed earlier, the instability of the 'project' of inner experience, condemned by Sartre as a contradiction in terms, also places in question the 'project' of writing to the extent that, as Nietzsche suggests in *The Gay Science*, the classical opposition between truth and knowledge is also an opposition between text and vision. The 'project' of atheology is, thus, to establish a relation between metaphorical and metonymic versions of the wound opened up by inner experience as 'violence intérieure'; the Hegelian 'Aufhebung' is, thus, discarded in the interiority of the sacrifice of meaning that is inner experience. In the preface to *Daybreak*, Nietzsche talks of the 'self-overcoming' of morality, which he calls *die Selbstaugfhebung der Moral*; this 'self-overcoming' is a central part of inner experience:

As interpreters of our experiences - One kind of honesty has been unknown to all founders of religions and their like - they have never made of their experiences a matter of conscience in knowledge. 'What did I really experience? [...]Was my mind sufficiently alert? Was my will bent against my fantasy? - none of them has asked such questions, none of our dear religious people asks such questions even now: they feel, rather, a thirst for things which are contrary to reason and do not put too many difficulties in the way of satisfying it - thus they experience 'miracles' and hear the voices of 'angels' But we, we others, thirsty for reason, want to look our own experiences as fixedly in the eye as a scientific experiment, hour by hour, day after day. We ourselves want to be our own experiment and vivisectional animals![23]

Inner experience aims at an internal conflict which can have no outcome but the destruction of the individuated self and a sinking into 'le non-savoir'. It follows from this that 'atheology' cannot be related to 'atheist humanism', the inverted theology which replaces the Cartesian

[22] Ibid., pp. 572 -573
[23] Friedrich Nietzsche, *Beyond Good and Evil*, trans. R.J Hollingdale (London: Penguin, 1969), p.65.

notion of God the creator of eternal truths with the Divine freedom of man. The salient characteristic of Humanism is the ambition to attribute divinity to human activity; to incorporate the transcendent into the immanent; this, however, is a species of idealism, Hegelian in its origin, which Bataille refuses to accept. The *via negativa* of Bataille's atheology is in direct contradiction to this movement: inner experience is thus the sacrifice of *ipse* which, in a moment of sovereign communication, brings together subject and object in an immanent, and thus monist, experience which is properly 'mystical' in the sense that it breaks both with metaphorical logic and the interior structure of 'significative discourse'.

> Ce qui désoriente dans ma manière d'écrire est le sérieux qui trompe son monde. Ce sérieux n'est pas menteur, mais qu'y puis-je si l'extrême du sérieux se dissout en hilarité? Exprimée sans détour, une mobilité trop grande des concepts et des sentiments (des états d'esprit) ne laisse pas au lecteur plus lent la possibilité de saisir (de fixer).[24]

'Atheology' is in this sense a negative movement towards annihilation as a 'release from action'. As Bataille indicates, this movement is parallel to the movement towards interiority which is given in Zen Buddhist philosophy as a way of 'retourner chez soi'. Bataille says that the term inner experience can even be substituted by the term *pal* or *zen*, to illustrate the fact that as an experience it is both auto-sufficient and revelatory.[25] This movement, however, is the opposite of a monastic form of ascesis which points to an upward summit to which the mystic aspires; rather, as Bataille indicates by comparing himself with Sartre, inner experience is a reversal which presents itself as its own authority, 'un potlatch d'absurdité.'

> Je hais les moines.
> Renoncer au monde, à la chance, à la vérité des corps, devrait à mon sens donner de la honte.
> Il n'est pas de péché plus lourd.
>
> Heureux de me rappeler la nuit où j'ai bu et dansé - dansé seul comme un paysan, comme un faune, au milieu des couples.

---

[24] *Sur Nietzsche, ŒC*,VI, p.195
[25] 'Je ne veux plus parler *d'expérience intérieure* (ou mystique) mais de *pal*. De même on dit le *zen*.' Ibid., p. 78

Seul? A vrai dire, nous dansions face à face, en un *potlatch* d'absurdité, le *philosophe* - Sartre - et moi.[26]

For Bataille, 'atheology' is not separate from 'philosophy', but it is an active contradiction which undermines the language of 'philosophy' and the possibility of a philosophical project. Thus, the affinities between Blanchot and Bataille outlined above in Chapter three, the pursuit of the displacement and dissolution of knowledge in sacrifice and apophatic method, are predicated upon a specifically Nietzschean account of vision as pure expenditure.

Moreoever, like Aquinas, who held that it was possible, 'in principle', to create a philosophical system which would be conceived outside of knowledge of God and would be therefore incomplete but not false,[27] Bataille maintains that as dicontinuity is revealed in the experience of Absence, the collapse of a metaphysical category for thought, as described in *Sur Nietzsche*, is not only a destabilising of a materialist outlook, but also an encounter with alterity which is the antithesis of Christian theology.

Champ de Bataille

In *Sur Nietzsche,* Bataille is mainly concerned with an examination of the relation between being, or beings, and Good and Evil. Bataille probes the wound opened by the death of God in the loss of self which occurs in the expenditure of sacrificial volence of war. This examination of limit and experience, which lie beyond 'philosophy' itself as Kantian categories or hierarchies of thinking, is precisely what Bataille describes as 'l'impossible': the pursuit of transcendent experience (or 'self-overcoming' in Nietzschean terminology) of the limited being.

This version of Nietzsche is not so very different from the Nietzsche whom Bataille defends against Fascism in the pages of *Acéphale* and whose presence shapes and informs the version of revolutionary violence presented in the debates and papers of Contre-attaque. The singular difference between the Nietzsche whom Bataille sees as an avatar of poetic violence in the 1930s and the version of

---

[26] Ibid., p. 90

[27] This distinction is made clear by Thomas in the section of the *Summa* entitled 'Man's place in Creation.' St. Thomas Aquinas, op. cit., *Summa Theologiae*, edited and translated by Timothy McDermott (Texas: Christian Classics, 1989), pp, 105-108

140

Nietzsche with whom Bataille conducts a dialogue in *Sur Nietzsche* is that, by 1944, the catastrophe has already happened and the world is now on fire.

As we have seen in this chapter, the violence of the external world is matched by one of the central movements of inner experience. War is both a metaphor and a real phenomenon which, when apprehended as both at the same time, releases and discharges sovereign experience: this 'combat intérieur' is one of the central axes of inner experience.

> JE SUIS MOI-MEME LA GUERRE
> Je me représente un mouvement et une excitation humaine dont les possibilités sont sans limite: ce mouvement et cette excitation ne peuvent être apaisés que par la guerre.[28]

The Spanish mystics, in the same way, describe the journey towards the union with God as both an 'interior combat' and a 'dark night of sense' in which 'there can be no concordance between light and darkness; as St. John says: *Tenebrae am non comprehenderunt* (The darkness could not receive the light). According to St. John of the Cross, the reason for this is that '[as philosophy teaches] two contraries cannot exist in the same subject.' The Mystical Union which does take place, the marriage between the bride and the divine *Logos*, is, however, a Union in which contraries are united as 'love effects a likeness between the lover and the Object loved': St John of the Cross quotes David, 'Similes illis fiant qui faciunt ea, et omnes qui confidunt in eis' (Let all who set their hearts on them become like them) to describe this reconciliation.[29]

As observed in the first chapter of the present study, Bataille's first encounter with Nietzsche can be traced back to 1922, the year in which Bataille saw his first bullfight, and lost his Christian faith in a moment where the sun moved into night: subject and object fused in the inner experience of self-blinding. The *envoi* to *Sur Nietzsche*, from John Ford's *'Tis Pity She's a Whore*, resonates throughout the texts on war and chance:

Entre Giovanni avec un coeur au bout de son poignard
GIOVANNI.- Ne soyez pas étonnés si vos coeurs pleins d'appréhensions se crispent à cette vaine vue. De quelle pâle épouvante, de quelle lâche colère, vos

---

[28] 'La pratique de la joie devant la mort', *ŒC*, I, p. 557
[29] Quoted in op. cit. *The Fire and the Cloud: An Anthology of Catholic Spirituality*, ed. David A.Fleming S.M, p. 87

sens n'auraient-ils pas été saisis si vous aviez été témoins du vol de vie et de beauté que j'ai fait! Ma soeur! Oh ma soeur!
FLORIO.-Qu'y a-t-il?
GIOVANNI -La gloire de mon acte a éteint le soleil de midi et fait de midi la nuit...[30]

In this metaphorical inversion of sun into night, Bataille circumscribes the movement of inner experience. Unlike Hegel, however, who in his treatment of Medieval philosophy, allows theology into discourse only so far as it contributes to philosophical thinking, Bataille insists upon the primacy of the experience of silence, or 'la nudité' as central to the movement of inner experience. Most importantly, the sun and the night are abolished in the apocalypse, or war, of inner experience.

Similarly, that the texts of *La Somme athéologique*, in which the shiftings of inner experience are traced and followed to their unresolvable conclusions, were either published or written during the experience of occupation and war becomes, however, not simply an irony, but a central shaping force in the development of Bataille's thinking. Inner experience, in which *ipse* is consumed by its own violence, cannot be separated from the outer world, which in a parallel movement into 'war', is sliding 'into night'.

Bataille describes the composition of *Le Coupable* as an 'expérience mystique hétérodoxe'.The term 'hétérodoxe' at this stage in the development of Bataille's thought, however, like the use of the term 'hétérologie' in the texts written by Bataille for the Collège de Sociologie, has now come to stand for a strategy which would 'join expenditure to the negativity envisaged by Marxism.'[31] In this sense, at least, the 'hétérodoxe' inner experience is a movement beyond the limits of the Hegelian or Marxist version of negativity, that is to say contradiction, into the unmediated negativity which constitutes 'la scission entre haut et bas.' This is, says Francis Marmande, Bataille's most authentic political statement.[32]

The first inspiration behind the *Le Coupable*, Bataille tells us, was the death of Laure in 1938, an experience which left him 'déchiré'. The solitary inner experiences of mourning, guilt and a desire to die are

---

[30] *Sur Nietzsche ŒC*,VI, p.9
[31] Allan Stoekl, 'Introduction', op. cit., Georges Bataille, *Visions of Excess: Selected Writings 1927-1939*, p.xxv, fn.22
[32] Op. cit., Francis Marmande, *Georges Bataille Politique*, p. 50

also measured against a world which is pursuing a movement towards self-annihilation. Inner experience as a 'expérience mystique hétérodoxe' is, thus, also the paradox formulated by Bataille in a text written for the Collège de Sociologie, and at the point where he was turning away from involvement in the outward world of politics, and towards mystical experiment:

> Le monde des amants n'est pas moins vrai que celui de la politique. Il absorbe la totalité de l'existence, ce que la politique ne peut pas faire. Et ses caractères ne sont pas ceux du monde fragmentaire et vide de l'action pratique mais ceux qui appartiennent à *la vie humaine* avant qu'elle ne soit servilement réduite: le monde des amants se construit, comme la vie, à partir d'un *ensemble de hasards donnnant la réponse attendue à une volonté d'être avide et puissante.*[33]

Francis Marmande has described this formula as the defining logic of Bataille's series of political positions during the course of the 1930s and, in particular, the premonition of catastrophe which occurs encounters the failure of politics in *Le Bleu du Ciel*, a book which Bataille had finished (but decided not to publish) before embarking on the project of Contre-attaque.[34] The texts of *La Somme athéologique*, and especially the final book *Sur Nietzsche*, are an engagement with this same paradox: the essential shift in position is that the end of politics, in the tragic experience of war, does finally parallel and match the inner experience, or the world of lovers.

---

[33] 'L'apprenti sorcier', *ŒC*, I, p. 532

[34] Francis Marmande, *L'indifférence des ruines, variations sur l'écriture du Bleu du Ciel* (Marseille: Éditions Parenthèses, 1985), p.82

Chapter Six

An erotics of God:
Divine absence and eroticism

By night on my bed I sought him
whom my soul loveth
I sought him, but I found him not.
Song of Songs, Ch.3. v.1

If the texts of *La Somme athéologique* are, as has been argued in the present study, to be considered, like Aquinas' *Summa*, a compendium of writings which are a disengagement from philosophy and a movement beyond the language of metaphysics into an encounter with divine absence, the question arises of how Bataille can reconcile the thinking subject of 'atheology' with the 'divine object' of his thought. In this chapter I will examine the limits of Bataille's language at the moment of this transgression, the encounter with divine absence.

Although, as we have already noted, Derrida points out that Bataille is often less Hegelian than he thinks, Bataille is nonetheless an assidous reader of Hegel and his reading both shapes and informs not only the content but also the substance of inner experience and its relation to the problem of an 'atheological' method in which agent and object might be dissolved.[1] Bataille's 'method of meditation', therefore, is a trangression of the Hegelian system which, nonetheless, remains faithful to the Hegelian notion of death as an abstract negativity in which self, or in Bataille's terminology *ipse*, becomes aware of its own existence through the contemplation of its destruction.[2]

---

[1] This is presumably why Derrida begins his 1967 essay on Bataille by quoting Bataille's own statement from *Le Coupable*, 'Souvent Hegel me semble l'évidence, mais l'évidence est lourde à supporter.' Jacques Derrida, op. cit., 'De l'économie restreinte à l'économie générale', p.369

[2] This key notion is explained thus by Kojève: 'Hegel dit que l'homme n'est individuel que dans la mesure où il est mortel. Si l'Esprit (qui s'appelle ici Amour) était infini ou immortel, il serait rigoureusement un. Si l'Esprit se réalise comme multiple, sous forme d'être humains qui diffèrent les uns des autres et donc chacun vit une vie individuelle qui lui est propre - c'est uniquement parce que les êtres humains ou 'spirituels' voire 'aimants' sont mortels.' Op. cit., Kojève, *Introduction à la lecture de Hegel*, p.552

Like Rimbaud's famous declaration that 'C'est faux de dire; je pense. On devrait dire: on me pense.[...] Je est un autre',[3] inner experience is not simply a suppression of the rational self, but in fact its annihilation in the movement of negativity away from its origin. In his introduction to *Phenomenology of Spirit*, Hegel explains a parallel process of externalization which is a form of mysticism:

> Mind becomes object, for it consists in the process of becoming an other to itself, i.e an object for its own self, and in transcending this otherness. And experience is called this very process by which the element that is immediate, unexperienced i.e. abstract - whether it be in the form of sense or of a bare thought - externalizes itself, and then comes back to itself from this state of estrangement.
> [...] The dissimilarity which obtains in consciousness between the ego and the substance constituting its objects, is their inner distinction, the factor of negativity in general.[4]

It follows from this statement that Derrida can argue that the Hegelian 'Aufhebung' does not abolish distinction and that the idea of a duality, for Bataille, as for Hegel, is overcome without necessarily being abolished.[5] This means that all notions of inner experience as 'action' or 'project' are not only in direct contradiction to the central movement into 'negativity in general', but also that the sovereign operation of inner experience, wherein *ipse* can only attain the Hegelian totality in its own negation, is predicated upon the possibility of its own failure: 'the subject is absent, the object is dissolved in continuity[...] it is NIGHT, but a night which 'is' not - a night which can only be apprehended by a vision which has been decentered'.[6]

Bataille's 'gnosis', however, transgresses the term 'Aufhebung', in the same way as the opening of the eye into and vision, of text or divinity, becomes a useless, tragic, expenditure. The overcoming of duality, whilst preserving distinction, means that the restricted economy of the Hegelian system is negated by its own movement towards death.

---

[3] Arthur Rimbaud, 'A Georges Izambard', *Collected Poems* (London: Penguin, 1986). p. 5

[4] Georg Wilhelm Friedrich Hegel, *Phenomenology of Spirit*, trans. A.V.Miller (Oxford and New York: Oxford University Press, 1977), p. 89

[5] Op. cit., Jacques Derrida, 'De l'économie restreinte à l'économie générale', p.371-372

[6] Leslie Ann Boldt, 'Introduction ', *Inner Experience* (Albany: SUNY Press, 1987), p.14.

Similarly, as part of his discussion of Hegelian 'negativity', Kojève examines Hegel's philosophy of death, and says that not only is negativity linked to the subject which finds 'self-consciousness' through its opposite, but also that 'negativity', which for Bataille abolishes 'action' through the circularity of its own movement, is linked to determinate being (Dasein), which is itself a manifestation of 'negativity'. [7]

I will consider the slide between experience and non-meaning not only as a moment of blindness in the experience of the sacred, or, as in Klossowski puts it, one of 'ces mouvements du pathos',[8] but also in the terms that Blanchot used, when describing the 'jeu de la pensée' which led Bataille to the 'l'illimité de la pensée qui s'y joue par la parole';[9] the absent God, apprehended by the sovereign subject in erotic experience, is not only an origin but an expenditure.

'La folie de voir'

In his early essay on Hegel, 'La critique des fondements de la dialectique hégélienne', written during his most Marxist period in 1932, Bataille underlines the significance of the negative in the Hegelian dialectic as the beginning of the movement beyond language into experience: this insight, he writes, is in fact what distinguishes the Hegelian mode of thought from Marxism which posits 'la dialectique [...] comme la loi générale d'une réalité fondamentale'.[10] In the total self-clarity of subjectivity which is the Hegelian culmination of philosophy, Bataille asserts that 'expérience vécue' is what escapes all systems and therefore constitutes, in atheological terms, the central insight which defines all other terms; an atheological method thus begins and ends in its own experience of the negative. On a textual level Foucault describes this as follows: 'le geste qui franchit les limites touche l'absence même.'[11]

For Bataille, this movement towards 'expérience vécue', is itself the inner experience of radical discontinuity which defines atheology as

---

[7] Op. cit., Alexandre Kojève, *Introduction à la lecture de Hegel*, p. 570

[8] Pierre Klossowski, 'A propos du simulacre dans la communication de Georges Bataille', *Critique*, 195-196, p. 748

[9] Op.cit, Maurice Blanchot, 'Le jeu de la pensée', *Critique*, 196-197, p.741.

[10] *ŒC,* I, p.278.

[11] Michel Foucault, 'Préface à la transgression', *Critique*, 195-196, p.768.

146

method and principle. That the circularity of the economy of anguish can only be transgressed in the excess of laughter, tears or ecstasy, means that the possibility of a dialectical system is abolished in the need for inner experience.

> Immense aléa.
> L'alternance (du ruisseau qui s'écoule et de l'aigle au-dessus des eaux). Méandres. Indescriptible paysage, touffu, varié, fait de discordance et 'riant'. En lui tout déconcerte. Le malaise suit la détente comme un chien, comme un chien fou, faisant des cercles, apparaissant, disparaissant. Je parle de rire.[12]

The central point of this concentric circle is the point where *ipse*, in the pursuit of the object of atheology, seeks to blind itself in its recognition of itself as its own subject and object; transgression, in this sense, means that the annihilation of the self which occurs in inner experience is a blinding of the self which, as Bataille writes in a text more or less contemporaneous with his early reflections on Hegel, is a definition of the transgressive act of automutilation as 'une impulsion révélée par une expérience intérieure [...] liée à la notion de l'esprit de sacrifice.'[13] However, as Gilles Ernst has pointed out, if transgression is a sacrifice, it, thus, has a double sense;[14] it is, as observed earlier in this thesis, faithful to the Latin cognate of 'going across', or as Ernst calls it 'action de passer de l'autre côté', and it is also the eccecliastical Latin meaning of *lex transgressa*, 'violation de la loi'.

The horror of vision, or 'la folie de voir', is the reason why Bataille's transgression of the dialectical system in the sacrifice of *ipse* is centred on the key image, in his fictions and in *La Somme athéologique*, of the sun. This is the theme of a famous early essay on Picasso:

> Le soleil, humainement parlant (c'est à dire en tant qu'il se confond avec la notion de midi) est la conception la plus élevée. C'est aussi la chose la plus abstraite, puisqu'il est impossible de le regarder fixement à cette heure-là. Pour achever de décrire la notion de soleil dans l'esprit de celui qui doit l'émasculer nécessairement par suite de l'incapacité des yeux, il faut dire que ce soleil-là a poétiquement le sens de la sérénité mathématique et de l'élévation d'esprit. Par contre si, en dépit de tout, on le fixe obstinément, cela suppose une certaine folie et la notion change de sens parce que, dans la lumière, ce n'est plus la production qui apparaît, mais le déchet,

---

[12]*Le Coupable, Œuvres complètes,V, p.335.*
[13] 'Soleil Pourri', *ŒC*, I, p.264.
[14] Gilles Ernst, *Georges Bataille: Analyse du récit de mort* (Paris: Presses universitaires de France, 1993), pp.84-87.

c'est à dire la combustion, assez bien exprimée, psychologiquement, par l'horreur qui se dégage d'une lampe à arc en incandescence.[15]

This paradox is the central image of Bataille's thought. More specifically, it is the image which initiates what Stoekl calls in Bataille's thinking the 'fall of allegory', [16] that is to say the disruption of any hierarchy of meaning which might privilege one object (filth, ruptured eyes, the sun) over another (the head, God, vision). This disruption is not, however, a simple inversion: the world in which 'disruptive low matter' works against any transcendental project is also a world in which, as meaning is destabilized, no new hierarchy can be established. Bataille writes,

> Le Soleil aime exclusivement la Nuit et dirige vers la terre sa violence lumineuse, verge ignoble, mais il se trouve dans l'incapacité d'atteindre le regard ou la nuit bien que les étendues terrestres nocturnes se dirigent continuellement vers l'immondice du rayon solaire.[17]

'La conception la plus élevée' which produces 'le déchet' is not only the summit but its opposite; the fall of that summit. In the same way that Kojève's version of negativity in the Hegelian dialectic posits itself as the element which moves the dialectic forward, so the radical heterogeneity of base matter, for Bataille, mitigates against the possibility of the sun being recuperated in an inverse system. Stoekl describes how Bataille, as a medievalist aware of the theoretical implications of allegory, recognises that the 'fall of the elevated and noble threatens the coherent theory of allegory itself' and that, as a result, allegory is not abolished but, rather, replaced by a 'headless allegory' in an 'incessant and repetitious process' which projects a symbolic language as a metonymic substitute for the loss of a stable system of referents;[18] the meaning of language is thus sacrificed in the pursuit of 'le bas matérialisme'. The negative movement from vision to blindness does not abandon the dialectical process, but overcomes it in destructive expenditure. 'The fall of allegory' in determining relations between objects and their subjects, thus denies the stability of an

---

[15] 'Soleil Pourri', Œ*C*, I, p. 231.

[16] Op. cit., Allan Stoekl, 'Introduction', Georges Bataille, *Visions of Excess: Selected Writings 1927-1939*, pp.xiii-xv

[17] 'L'Anus solaire', Œ*C*, I, p.86

[18] Op. cit., Allan Stoekl, *Visions of Excess*, pp.xiii-xv

inverse hierarchy, such as the replacement of God with excrement: Bataille's *gnosis*, the revelation received in the illumination of the anal sun, is that God, who in traditional Christian mystical experience is 'Pure being', is 'L'immondice du rayon solaire.'[19]

Divine Rags

The collapse of meaning into tragic expenditure which is defined by atheology is also the central movement described Bataille's erotic fictions, texts which Surya describes as 'la clé lubrique' of inner experience.[20]

Most significantly, Bataille links the potential collapse of the poetic image - in this case the metonymic chain which proceeds in both directions from excrement to God - to the sacrifice of meaning in the 'fall of allegory'. The same disintegration of vision in ecstasy occurs in the allegorical closure when Simone temporarily terminates the linear motion of the narrative of *Histoire de l'oeil* by inserting the priest's eye into her vulva.

> Simone regarda l'extravagance et finalement la prit dans la main, toute bouleversée; mais elle n'avait pourtant pas d'hésitation et elle s'amusa tout de suite à se caresser au plus profond des cuisses en y faisant glisser cet objet qui paraissait fluide. La caresse de l'œil sur la peau est en effet d'une douceur complètement extraordinaire avec en plus un certain cri de coq horrible, tellement la sensation est étrange.
>
> Simone, cependant s'amusait à faire glisser cet œil dans la profonde fente de son cul et s'étant couchée sur le dos, ayant relevé les jambes et ce cul, elle essaya de l'y maintenir par la simple pression des fesses, mais tout à coup il en jaillit, pressé comme un noyau de cerise entre les doigts, et alla tomber sur le ventre maigre du cadavre à quelques centimètres de la verge.
>
> [..] Mettez-le moi dans le cul, Sir Edmond, cria Simone. Et Sir Edmond faisait délicatement glisser l'œil entre les fesses.[21]

There is an ambiguity in this text, however, which precludes any reading which might ascribe a simply Freudian value to Simone's (and the other participants') actions in this scene. Bataille emphasised that the act of 'énucléation' cannot simply be measured against Freud's theory of Oedipal symbolic castration, but that it also has a religious

---

[19] 'L'Anus solaire', *ŒC*, I, p.86.

[20] Op. cit., Surya, p.374.

[21] *Histoire de l'œil*, *ŒC*, I, p.68

value which recuperates the eye as the metonymic contiguity of the all-seeing God. Thus when Bataille added onto the text of *Histoire de l'oeil* an explanation of how he came to write the text and says that he was greatly troubled as a child and an adolescent by the blindness of his syphilitic father, he is offering the image of the blind father as a metaphorical substitution for God.

> Je suis né d'un père syphilitique (tabétique). Il devint aveugle (il l'était quand il me conçut) et quand j'eus deux ou trois ans, la même maladie le paralysa. Jeune enfant j'adorais ce père. Or la paralysie et la cécité avaient ces conséquences entre autres: il ne pouvait comme nous aller pisser aux lieux d'aisance; il pissait devant son fauteuil, il avait un récipient pour le faire. Il pissait devant moi, sous une couverture qu'aveugle il disposait mal. Le plus gênant d'ailleurs était la façon dont il regardait. Ne voyant nullement, sa prunelle, dans la nuit, se perdait en haut sous la paupière: ce mouvement se produisait d'ordinaire au moment de la mixtion. Il avait de grands yeux tres ouverts, dans un visage émacié, taillé en bec d'aigle. Généralement, s'il urinait, ces yeux devenaient presque blancs; ils n'avaient pour objet qu'un monde que lui seul pouvait voir et dont la vision lui donnait un rire absent. Or c'est l'image de ces *yeux* blancs que je lie à celles des œufs; quand, au cours du récit, si je parle de l' œil ou des œufs, l'urine apparait d'habitude.[22]

The castration of the subject which takes place here also occurs on a textual level in *Histoire de l'oeil*; Simone's insertion of the priest's eye into her vulva, and the goring and enucleation of the bullfighter Granero, the erotic and sacrificial object, are ecstatic experiences of blindness; castration is not forgotten or sublated, rather the self-reflecting cogito of the Cartesian model is here annihilated in the transparency of the object; the self is literally obliterated by the blank eye of the Other.

For Bataille, the intimation of the tragic in sacrifice is thus pure expenditure. The subject is consumed, or consumes itself, before the the blank eye of the sun; the opening of the eye to the sun, especially at its apex at midday, invites obliteration; the dialectical process, either the Hegelian model of knowledge, or the Freudian one of therapy, is wiped away into insignificance by the blinding brilliance of the sun. Foucault writes of this 'folie de voir':

> Peut-être définit-il l'espace d'une expérience où le sujet qui parle, au lieu de s'exprimer, s'expose, va à la rencontre de sa propre finitude et sous chaque mot se trouve renvoyé à sa propre mort. Un espace qui ferait de toute oeuvre un de ces

---

[22] 'Réminiscences', *ŒC*, I, p. 607

gestes de 'tauromachie' dont Leiris parlait, pensant à lui-même, mais à Bataille sans doute aussi. C'est en tout cas dans la plage blanche de l'arène (oeil gigantesque) que Bataille a fait cette expérience, essentielle pour lui et caractéristique de tout son langage, que la mort communiquait avec la communication et que l'oeil arraché, sphère blanche et muette, pouvait devenir germe violent dans la nuit du corps, rendre présente cette absence dont n'a cessé de parler la sexualité, et à partir de laquelle elle n'a cessé de parler. [23]

In the same way that the actions of Simone, who by consuming the contiguity of vision of the divine - literally, the priest's eye - in the night of orgasm, trangresses metaphor into 'headless allegory', Madame Edwarda provides a vision and experience of Divine Absence in which the object ('Dieu-qui-n'est-pas Dieu') and the subject (Pierre Angélique, the martyred 'saint') are sacrificed in a ritual series of events which lead to a 'noche oscura' in which subject and object are consumed.

Both Simone and Edwarda, 'voyantes', are mirrors of male desire who offer a pathway to the unlimited experience of the sacred. In particular, the literal, visual experience of the absent God which Edwarda offers is significant because it not only abolishes language but also brings together the materiality of the body and the immanent experience of the Divine *Logos* in one image:

De mon hébétude, une voix, trop humaine, me tira. La voix de Madame Edwarda, comme son corps gracile, était obscène:
-Tu veux voir mes guenilles? disait-elle.
Les deux mains agrippées à la table, je me tournai vers elle. Assise, elle maintenait haute une jambe écartée: pour mieux ouvrir la fente, elle achevait de tirer la peau des deux mains. Ainsi les 'guenilles' d'Edwarda me regardaient, velues et roses, pleines de vie comme une pieuvre répugnante. Je balbutai doucement:
-Pourquoi fais-tu cela?
-Tu vois, dit-elle, je suis DIEU...
-Je suis fou...
-Mais non, tu dois regarder: regarde!
Sa voix rauque s'adoucit, elle se fit presque enfantine pour me dire avec lassitude, avec le sourire infini de l'abandon: 'Comme j'ai joui!'[24]

Edwarda's orgasm, in which Pierre Angélique is consumed, has both the erotic quality ascribed to Bernini's 'Extase de sainte Thérèse' and an experiential 'oceanic' quality which Angela describes as 'a

---

[23] Michel Foucault, 'Préface à la transgression', *Critique*, 195-196, p. 768

[24] *Madame Edwarda*, *ŒC*, III, pp.20-21

plenitude of which I cannot speak'.[25] The events of *Madame Edwarda*
are also constructed as an acephalic mass in the course of which the
central figure 'Pierre Angélique', (like the second century martyr
beheaded on the hill of Montmartre by the Parisians whom he had been
sent to convert, and after whom the Rue St. Denis was named), is
called to the presence of God. In the moment of communion, or more
properly in Bataillien language communication, like Thomas - who
before the figure of Christ on the Cross was called upon to kiss the
dying God's open wound - 'Pierre' must affirm his 'faith' in Divine
Absence by putting his lips to 'la plaie vive' of Edwarda; this act is, in
acephalic terms, a celebration of 'la Négativité pure' in which
negativity is not 'sublated' but embraced as the first principle of
atheology; the word of Absence. Pierre is, thus, both celebrant and
mystic in a Communion in which he is simultaneously wretchedly
abject, and like Edwarda, 'voyant'. His vision is equivalent to that of
Angela of Foligno who '[reports] the lucid vision in which she
perceived this truth: the twofold revelation of an Absolute at once
humble and omnipotent, personal and transcendent - the unimaginable
synthesis of 'unspeakable power' and 'deep humility'.[26]

Like Angela, 'Pierre Angélique' has 'the eyes of his soul opened' in
vision. It is, however, a degraded vision centred on a negativity
without reserve. Bataille quotes Angela to explain the sovereign and
visionary aspects of this displacement.

'Au lieu où j'étais, je cherchais l'amour et ne le trouvais plus. Je perdis même celui
que j'avais traîné jusqu'à ce moment et je fus faite le non-amour.' (Livres des
visions XXVI, trad. Hello).
, Angèle de Foligno parlant de Dieu parle en esclave. Ce qu'elle exprima,
toutefois, peut m'atteindre et jusqu'au tremblement. Je balbutie. Je ressens la sainte
comme un autre balbutiement. Je ne m'arrête pas à ce qui peut être le reflet d'états
de choses dont le temps a disposé, d'enchaînements déchaînés aujourd'hui
(refermés d'une autre façon).[27]

Mysticism and eroticism are, for the most part, indistinguishable in
Bataille's atheological method; they are central to the shifts in inner
experience which lead to the the self-annihilation of the subject. The

---
[25] Quoted in Evelyn Underhill, op. cit., *Mysticism, A Study in the Nature and Development of Man's Spiritual Consciousness*, p.345.
[26] Ibid., p.345.
[27] *Le Coupable, Œuvres complètes, V*, p.251

reality of the experiences of the Christian mystics is, for Bataille, 'un mouvement d'amour ivre.'[28] 'Sainthood' is, however, project and therefore in direct contradiction to the negative method of atheology wherein language exhausts itself and collapses into non-meaning. 'Pierre', who is brought to the sacred experience of Absence is, in these terms, an acephalic saint. However, in the movement towards the 'angelic' experience, Bataille offers neither a dialectical nor a poetic resolution to the meaning and nature of 'Pierre's' experience of transgression; this is how the central point of sovereign experience, indeed sovereignty itself, can be thus described by Bataille as 'blessure béante'.[29]

Le 'mime'

For Klossowski, the central point of the instant of possible communication in Bataille's inner experience is 'the emptiness' which awakes in 'the Other' ('l'autre') the complicity preliminary to the sacrifice of meaning. Klossowski thus uses the term 'simulacrum' to describe the 'risk' of inner experience, which is a simulation of death, and is predicated upon the potential failure of communication. [30]

But if the 'project' of inner experience is a 'simulacrum', a way of 'experiencing the fall without actually falling', asks Klossowski, how can the object of atheological mysticism, communication, be possible, as Bataille asserts is the case ('Immense aléa'), in the instant of sovereignty? As communication is dispersed into fragments of undifferentiated being, the very movement into communication is an experience of *aporia*, a blind spot, which renounces death as it risks itself in the subversion of all potential systems; this is the point at which atheology recognises itself as a system beyond all systems.

Qui dit athéologie se soucie de la vacance divine, soit de la 'place' ou du lieu spécifiquement tenu par le nom de Dieu - Dieu garant du moi personnel.

Qui dit athéologie dit aussi vacance de moi - du moi dont la vacance est éprouvée dans une conscience laquelle pour ne point être ce moi en est elle-même la vacance.

Que devient la conscience sans suppôt?

---

[28] 'Notes', *ŒC*, VI, p.483

[29] Ibid., p.366

[30] Pierre Klossowski, 'A propos du simulacre dans la communication de Georges Bataille', *Critique*, 195-196, pp. 742-748

[...] Le recours au simulacre ne recouvre cependant pas une absence d'événement réel ni le succédané de celui-ci; toutefois dans la mesure où quelque chose doit arriver à quelqu'un pour qu'on puisse dire qu'il y a expérience, le simulacre ne va-t-il pas s'étendre à l'expérience même, tant que Bataille l'énonce nécessairement comme vécue dès qu'il en parle quitte à se réfuter lui-même en tant que sujet s'adressant à l'autre.[31]

In the same way that the paradox of the reduction of metaphysics to language occludes the mystery of God in syntax, atheology, as an exercise in pure self-consciousness, gives meaning to esctatic experiences only to the extent that *ipse* negates itself in a moment of pure expenditure; Bataille's method of meditation is thus, for Klossowski, an inverse form of poetic creation wherein the thinking subject extinguishes itself in in the blinding darkness of sovereign experience.

This is, for Bataille, the movement of *ipse* into an affirmation of pure negativity in which God is abolished and replaced by *ipse'*s consciousness of itself as unrestricted, and therefore 'Divine', subjectivity. The simulacrum collapses into pure negativity, the experience of 'le non-savoir'.

Si je 'mime' le savoir absolu, me voici par nécessité Dieu moi-même (dans le système il ne peut, même en Dieu, y avoir de connaissance, allant au-delà du savoir absolu). La pensée de ce moi-même - de l'*ipse* - n'a pu se faire absolue qu'en devenant tout. La Phénoménologie de l'Esprit compose deux mouvements essentiels achevant un cercle: c'est achèvement par degrés de la conscience de soi (de l'*ipse* humain), et devenir tout (devenir Dieu) de cet ipse achevant le savoir (et par là détruisant la particularité en lui, achevant donc la négation de soi-même, devenant le savoir absolu). Mais si de cette façon, comme par contagion et par mime, j'accomplis en moi le mouvement circulaire de Hegel, je définis, par-delà les limites atteintes, non plus un inconnu mais un inconnaissable. Inconnaissable non du fait de l'insuffisance de la raison mais par sa nature (et même, pour Hegel, on ne pourrait avoir souci de cet au-delà que faute de posséder le savoir absolu...) [32]

Unlike 'rational atheism', which is no more than an inverse form of monotheism, atheology is predicated upon and has as its centre the abolition of its own subject; the collapse of meaning inherent in the sovereign operation is a collapse into discontinuity which annihilates thought and abolishes the possibility of fixed referent: the simulacrum,

---

[31] Ibid., p.742
[32] *L'Expérience intérieure, ŒC*, V, p. 127.

or 'mime' has authority because it is, as Bataille writes 'une extrême déchirure, si profonde que seul le silence de l'extase lui répond.'[33]

> Bataille souligne qu'à l'inverse de la création poétique les contenus de l'expérience que se propose sa méthode de méditation modifient le sujet qui s'y exerce, donc altèrent son identité. Cette méthode devrait amener à la disparition du sujet pour qu'aucun suppôt ne limitât plus par la conscience de soi la souveraineté de ces contenus d'expérience.
>
> [...] L'athéologie se voudrait ici soustraire au dilemme qui apparaît maintenant: l'athéisme rationnel n'est rien d'autre qu'un monothéise renversé. Mais Bataille ne croit guère à la souveraineté du moi que l'athéisme propose. De là que la seule vacance répondant à la vacance de Dieu constituerait le moment souverain.[34]

More importantly, because sovereignty is a sacrifice in which the communicant becomes lost in waves of eroticism which exceed enclosure, the 'simulacrum' of inner experience, Klossowski concludes, is nonetheless an affective experience; because it is predicated upon absence, inner experience exceeds and undermines discourse which would immobilize the 'poetic' experience in syntax.

Perte de vue

Bataille himself quotes from Blanchot's *Aminadab*, to show how this relation, or movement, between the discontinuity of the subject and the 'experience' of its own negation, can be immobilized in a frozen instant of communication. The 'divine object', which is the pursuit of atheology, is, thus, in the first instance, an Absence which apparently abolishes the possibility of communication; like the poetry of St. John of the Cross, who constantly interrogates the meaning and substance of *El Cántico* in his own exegis, or indeed 'the darkness of God' in Eliot's 'East Coker', who reduces human expression to the unknowable, the language of atheology is not opposed to the language of atheism. It is, rather, literally a *paradox* in its original, Greek, sense: experience which stands beyond thought or the expression of that thought in language other than the sacred. Thus through a recurring pattern of images, centred upon a matrix of codified language around the notion of 'la nuit', Bataille refers back to versions of religious experience

---

[33] ibid., p.128

[34] Op. cit., Pierre Klossowski, 'A propos du simulacre dans la communication de Georges Bataille', p.750

which displace philosophy. Specifically, Bataille refers to the image of 'night', which for Dionysius the Areopagite, and then St. John of the Cross, is a fundamental experience of non-categorical, that is to say immanent experience. Indeed, although Bataille denies the potential of transcendent experience, the paradox of the possibility of metaphysical, or religious spheres of experience, being extinguished in night, in darkness, is in itself an awakening to Absence which confirms the thinking subject's existence in the circularity of negation.

Within Eliot's 'the darkness of God' in 'East Coker' is a subject which, like the *ipse* of inner experience, negates itself in its own self-consciousness.

> I said to my soul be still, and let the dark come upon you
> Which shall be the darkness of God.
> [...] Wait without thought, for you are not ready for thought:
> So the darkness shall be the light, and the stillness the dancing.
>
> [...] To arrive where you are, to get from where you are not,
> You must go by a way wherein there is no ecstasy.
> In order to arrive at what you do not know
> You must go by the way of ignorance.
> In order to possess what you do possess
> You must go by the way of dispossession
> In order to arrive at what you are not
> You must go through the way in which you are not.
> And what you own is what you do not own
> And where you are is where you are not.[35]

For Eliot, however, the apophatic reduction of God, Spirit and mystical experience to language is a closed system which destroys itself in its circularity and denies the possibility of revelation or transcendence. The apophatic method is a snare rather than an awakening.

For Bataille, on the other hand, the 'mise en jeu' of an apophatic 'monde vu de la nuit du non-savoir' is the awakening to excessive experience which, although contrary to the enclosed system of Christianity, or for that matter the Hegelianism which posits spirit above substance, is, nonetheless, 'le sommet', even if it is, in its transgression of all systems, the summit of a disaster. Bataille quotes Blanchot:

---

[35] T.S Eliot, 'East Coker', *Selected Poetry* (London: Faber, 1965), p.78.

De toute façon, qu'un homme ne vive pas avec la pensée incessante de l'inconnu fait d'autant plus douter de l'intelligence que le même est avide, mais aveuglément, de trouver dans les choses la part qui l'oblige d'aimer, ou le secoue d'un rire inextinguible, celle de l'inconnu. Mais il en est de même lumière: les yeux n'en ont que des reflets.

'[...] Jamais la philosophie n'avait paru plus fragile, plus précieuse, plus passionnant qu'à cet instant où un bâillement faisait évanouir dans la bouche de Bergson l'existence de Dieu.'[36]

The *via negativa* of dislocation and introjection in Blanchot's version of the self in *Thomas L'Obscur* can be traced back though this original apophatic movement towards '[le] moment tragique' : it is also the same movement of *ipse* towards its own annihilation. In the immanent movement of inner experience, language is itself no less a barrier to communication than the lived experience of silence. In *Aminadab*, Blanchot inscribes loss of vision and the anguish of death into the title of the novel, which is, in part, a borrowing from St. John's *Cántico Espiritual*.[37]

In this poem, St. John describes Aminadab - the reference itself an exotic cipher taken from the *Song of Songs* - as the spiritual representive of demonic forces, a negative presence who might rupture the dialogue between the divine Logos and the faithful soul. There is a momentary loss of vision, in which Aminadab, who does not come, is mentioned as a dangerous possibility.

> Que nadie la miraua,
> Aminadab tanpoco merecia,
> Y el cerco sosegaua,
> y la cauallería
> A uista de las aguas descendía
>
> (For nobody was looking...
> Nor did Aminadab appear;
> And the siege was subsiding,
> and the cavalry
> in sight of the waters was descending.)[38]

---

[36] *L'Expérience intérieure*, *ŒC*, V, pp.119-120

[37] It has also been suggested that the title of *Aminadab* was taken by Blanchot from Emmanuel Lévinas' younger brother, Aminadab, who died in Lithuania at the hand of the Nazis in 1941. See Leslie Hill, op. cit., *Blanchot: Extreme Contemporary*, p.11

[38] 'El Cántico Espiritual', *Obras Completas de San Juan de la Cruz* (Madrid: Espasa-Calpe, 1936), p.34.

At this point in the *Cántico*, the enigmatic nature of the poem has touched its most mysterious point; Aminadab is introduced casually, 'almost as an old friend'[39] who the narrator is waiting for, but his identity as a shadowy Other is not explained, except that he is felt to be undesirable. The military imagery which accompanies his non-presence further indicates a rupture with the calm which thus far prevails in the poem.

It is, moreover, significant that the 'ecstatic consciousness is not self-conscious: it is intuitive, not discursive '[...] possessed by a great Idea, it has become a single state of enormous intensity'.[40] For St. John this means that the negative presence of Aminadab is in contradiction to the ascent of the Soul to the 'abraço de Dios' ('Embrace of God') which is the culmination of the mystical experience and at the end of the radiant night.

However, for Blanchot, the unseen Aminandab is not only a metaphor for the loss of the subject in its Other, but also, as it was for the the Spanish mystics, who talk of the 'mystical night' and whom Bataille cites in *La Somme athéologique* as mystical exemplars, the experience of loss itself.

Mysticism reveals the opacity of night as the transparency of the divine object. More specifically, when, in the *Cántico Espiritual*, St. John of the Cross refers to night in three different forms as 'noche sosegada' ('night of sin'), 'las noches veladores' ('Night of grief') and 'noche serena' ('calm night'), he only reaffirms, for Blanchot and Bataille, not only the metaphorical but also the metonymic relation between 'darkness' and 'le non-savoir' which are at the centre of inner experience. The impossibility of communication is, thus, posited in direct contradiction to the Surrealist absolute or primal unity. For Bataille, as for Blanchot, the blinding moment of communication is also a blind spot; the Hegelian movement comes to a standstill. Thus Bataille can concur with Aquinas' argument about the distinction between substance and experience in the *Summa*, 'Utrum opponantur unum et multa'('Nothing is composed of its opposite').

---

[39] Marc Bloch, *Saint John of the Cross: Poet and Mystic* (London: Macmillan, 1971), p. 98.

[40] Op.cit., Evelyn Underhill, *Mysticism, A Study in the Nature and Development of Man's Spiritual Consciousness*, p.345

'L'Alleluiah'

Although the 'impossible' which Bataille meditates upon is enclosed, at least for the most part, within the textual drama of the Hegelian system, Bataille also 'laughs' at philosophy and says that it is this movement into 'excessive awakening' which undermines Hegelianism and the discipline of the dialectical process. This is the potential rupture which is a displacement, or a mime, of sacrificial ecstasy. The movement into impossibility is a 'simulacre' of the unthinkable. This is how, in the 'simulated' representation of 'le non-savoir', the blind spot of philosophy is reduced to a negative economy of anguish.

Kojève translates the Hegelian term 'Aufhebung' as 'suppression-dialectique' and uses this term to describe the way in which two terms can remain, but their opposition is overcome: it is this 'reconciliation' which allows God, for Hegel, and Kojève, and Bataille, to be 'desacralized' (*entgöttern:* literally, the 'taking away of God') as part of the essential movement towards sovereignty rather than, as in classical atheism, discarded.[41]

The absent God is thus a negation which overflows from discourse, as does erotic experience, for example, into an existential constitution of non-meaning. Bataille's transgression of the Hegelian 'Aufhebung' into the circularity of an unrestricted negativity is, therefore, not only the 'desacralization' of God, which links God to non-meaning in a movement which constitutes excess, but also, more importantly, an erotic meditation upon the vacant space of 'Deus Divinus' in which the object gazes back in a moment of communication and rapture: the 'headless allegory' is a moment of reversal wherein subject and object exchange places: '-Tu vois, [...] je suis DIEU...' says Madame Edwarda.[...].[42] Vision and blindness are interchangeable experiences in a system in which, as Kojève explains, opposes the Hegelian exigency to sidestep the logic of historical temporality in 'angelic

---

[41] Op. cit., Alexandre Kojève, *Introduction à la lecture de Hegel*, p. 555-556
[42] *Madame Edwarda, Œ C*, III, p.20

timelessness' or 'La liberté qui est la manifestation de la négativité:[43] '[...] tu dois regarder: regarde', says Edwarda.[44]

In the language of *La Somme athéologique* Bataille, thus, not only traces the the dislocation of self in inner experience, but, at the very level of the text, re-enacts the drama of the sacrifice of meaning into non-meaning. This means, in the first instance, that although Bataille, as a medievalist, would have recognised that there is no fixed line between allegory and symbolism, nonetheless in certain of the texts *of La Somme athéologique* language functions at an allegorical level, that is to say that at a level which immobilizes meaning in what Hegel calls an 'abstract negativity'. The individual's struggle against the 'négativité sans emploi', which is the desire for continuity and the recognition of discontinuity, is an open wound in being which cannot be resolved in representation of that struggle in art or religious language; the Hegelian 'Vorstellung' is undermined by Absence in the same way that the 'Aufhebung' is transgressed in a moment of communication predicated upon the very negativity Hegel sees as central to the dialectic:

> Ultime possibilité. Que le non-savoir soit encore savoir. J'explorerais la nuit! Mais non, c'est la nuit qui m'explore. La mort apaise la soif de non-savoir. Mais l'absence n'est pas le repos. Absence et mort sont en moi sans réplique et m'absorbent cruellement, à coup sûr.[45]

Thus, the encounter with Divine Absence, which is the centre of inner experience is a displacement of spiritual language which, although it transgresses all transcendent versions of religious experience, nonetheless remains faithful to the vocabulary of experience which it denies.

The 'alleluiah', or 'awakening to laughter', or eroticism, or tears, is a mystical experience which is as much a displacement of the structures of philosophy as well as being the 'trial by death'. For Bataille, the opening to ecstasy is an experience of pure negation which overwhelms the limit, or limits, because it belongs to an economy

---

[43] Op. cit., Alexandre Kojève, *Introduction à la lecture de Hegel*, p.555
[44] *ŒC*, III, p.21
[45] *L'Expérience intérieure*, *ŒC*, V, p.130

which renounces meaning and knowledge in the name of an impossible unrestricted negativity.

As we have seen, this movement towards the collapse of meaning in *La Somme athéologique* is often described in terms of the transparency of darkness, 'la nudité de la nuit'. In the language of Bataille's fictions, however, there is a shift from allegory, or indeed a collapse, towards a form of symbolic language, or 'langage devoyé' as Barthes puts it,[46] which itself recreates the moment of collapse into inner experience; the 'darkness of unknowing' is also the 'night which is a sun'. This movement from night to sun, or sun into night, is not, as we have seen a simple inverse hierarchy, an allegory of reversal; nor is it a 'mime' of 'the fall of allegory'. Inner experience is the central point of an erotic encounter, a transgression, which collapses all fixed points of reference in experience which survives being sublated.

This is, it has been argued, the final significance of Bataille's inner experience. It is a process, it has been argued, constituted out a discontinous negative movement from metaphor to real experience. Inner experience is, therefore, a movement which not only transgresses the limits of fiction, poetry, politics and philosophy, but which is undermined itself in this movement.

Inner experience is also a trangression which, like erotic feeling, can only be translated into language through a framework and vocabulary which it actively denies. However, although inner experience ruins and discards the language of religious mysticism, it is faithful to the notion of experience rather than thought as the most essential defining feature of discourse; this is, indeed, the central importance of an atheological method as opposed to a philosophical system. This is also - as the wound of being is opened in the transgressive, erotic movement towards experience beyond language[47] - the largest religious significance of Bataille's description of inner experience as 'le cri d'une bête blessée.'[48]

---

[46] Roland Barthes, 'La Métaphore de l'oeil', *Critique*, 195-196, p.777

[47] It is specifically the erotic nature of mystical language which Bataille defines as the point of transgression: '[...]Quoi qu'il en soit du langage érotique des mystiques, il faut dire que leur expérience, n'ayant pas de limitation, déborde ses prémices et que, poursuivie dans l'énergie la plus grande, elle ne garde pour finir de l'érotisme que la transgression à l'état pur.' *Histoire de l'érotisme, ŒC*, VIII, p.149.

[48] 'Notes', *ŒC* VI, p.423

Conclusion

La pensée comme une tauromachie

El sol es el mejor torero
Spanish Proverb

The aim of the present study has been to trace the shifting meaning of the term 'expérience intérieure' across the texts of *La Somme athéologique*. The principal argument has been that through each of the texts which make up *La Somme athéologique*, as well as the notes and addenda which surround them, the inner experience described by Bataille is to be understood as a real phenomenon as well as a metaphor. The main framework for this argument has been developed from a consideration of the vocabulary which Bataille uses to describe the inner experience. This vocabulary is directly related to phenomena such as laughter, tears, orgasm. These experiences are physical experiences as well as intellectual events and as such they are, in Bataille's terms, transgressive instants which lie beyond discourse. They are moments of excess which are firmly rooted in authentic experience.

In the same way, it has been argued, whether Bataille uses or appropriates the vocabulary of Christian mysticism, Oriental meditative techniques, Nietzschean or Hegelian philosophy, the end-point of inner experience is a moment which defies reduction or mediation. The inner experience is thus a movement from metaphor to real experience which parallels traditional mysticism because it is an encounter which stands outside discourse. The inner experience, most importantly, is an encounter with absence which, as is the case in traditional mysticism, alters the thinking subject.

It has been significant to this study that Bataille's interest in 'mysticism' stands in dialectical relation to his anti-idealism, inherited from Kojève, whose 'terrorist' version of Hegel presents a world without any teleological shape or structure, and who destroys the humanist account of moral history. Most significantly, like Kojève's Hegel, Bataille attacks the nature of objective truth with an extreme form of Pyrrhonism, or epistomological nihilism. This is paradoxically rooted in reason, and a weapon to be wielded against the falsity of Kantian hierarchies of thinking.

162

It is, however, one of the defining characteristics of Bataille's inner experience that the 'sacrifice de soi', which renders the nature of the inner experience 'mystical', is also shaped as an inverse form of the Thomist adage 'ex nihilo, nihil fit.' For Sartre, it flowed from this logic that Bataille's relation to the language of inner experience is contradictory ('C'est à regret, d'ailleurs, que M.Bataille use du discours,' writes Sartre, 'Il le hait et à travers lui, le langage tout entier').[1] In *Sur Nietzsche*, Bataille, however, formulated a response to Sartre in which he emphasises that inner experience is a form of meditation or thinking which cannot be reduced to philosophy.[2] Inner experience is, moreover, for Bataille, to be understood as a phenomenon beyond existential categories and indeed beyond the language of existentialism. The substance of inner experience is not only analogous to Christian mysticism but it is also, in a negative sense, a response to the demands of Christianity, and other religious systems. Inner experience is, therefore, a refutation of the closed system of existentialist thinking which finds its authority, like the authority given to spiritual experience in the Church, within its own substance.

In a 1944 debate organized by Marcel Moré, attended by Sartre and Gabriel Marcel amongst others, Bataille's inner experience was discussed by a Catholic priest, Jean Daniélou. In his *exposé*, Daniélou traced the movement of inner experience as being a movement parallel to that of Christian mystics, in the sense that, like the experiences of the neo-Platonist philosophers who founded the Christian mystical tradition, Bataille's inner experience is a 'double expérience' which resists interpretation at the same time as it offers knowledge of the Divine.[3] This 'double experiénce' means that not only does inner experience elude the logic of Sartrean existentialist humanism, but that it also replaces the external ordering logic of rational systems with an interior, subjective perspective which shatters conceptual language.

Le Père Daniélou says this duality gives to the inner experience a 'mystical' content which, although it lies outside the authority of the Church, has a religious significance: 'Je pense qu'il y a dans la négativité, l'excès, la communication, le sacrifice, des valeurs mystiques que M. Bataille peut contribuer à remettre en valeur. Je

---

[1] Jean-Paul Sartre, op.cit, 'Un nouveau mystique', *Situations I*, p.133
[2] 'Réponse à Jean-Paul Sartre', *Sur Nietzsche, ŒC*, VI, pp.195-196
[3] 'Exposé du R.P.Daniélou', *ŒC*, VI, p. 323.

pense que ces valeurs ne prennent leur sens plein que dans la mesure où elles ont de la mystique, non seulement la forme, mais le contenu.'[4] Bataille himself acknowledged this parallel. In response to Le Père Daniélou, although he described his relation to Christianity as 'pur et simple d'hostilité', he conceded to Daniélou a unity in the debate which arose from the fact that 'vous placez la vie mystique avant l'Église, ce qui est au fond exactement l'essentiel de ma position.'[5]

As we have observed in the present study, in the 'Mystical Theology', as it was understood by Dionysius the Areopagite and the Spanish Mystics, as well as the methods of meditation practiced by Oriental mystics, Bataille is interested in the way that factual knowledge is dispersed in meditation by feeling and emotion in both the theory and practice of meditative technique. This study has shown that inner experience, in its pursuit of 'le non-savoir' across the texts of *La Somme athéologique*, entirely matches these processes and methods.

The study has also concerned itself with the question of the relation between philosophy and mysticism. More specifically, if inner experience is closer to the experience of traditional religious mystics than it is to the problems of contemporary philosophy, how, then, can Bataille state, as he does in the opening section of *L'Expérience intérieure*, that he holds inner experience as an apprehension of the unknown which, in the Hegelian terms defined by Kojève, stands in a dialectical relationship to the thinking subject?

As we have seen, this paradox is a key theme in the fictive representation of inner experience which takes place in the early novels of Maurice Blanchot. More particularly, for both Blanchot and Bataille, inner experience is 'tragic' communication in the sense that it is self-reflective; the thinking subject finds only silence as a response to its communication of non-meaning. There can be, therefore, no dialectical resolution to the problems that this double bind creates.

However, in the same way that Bataille asserts that poetry introduces the strange by way of the familiar, inner experience links experience of 'le non-savoir' with *ipse* by a 'un fil tenu [...] un fil [qui] lie l'appréhendé au moi.'[6] For Blanchot and Bataille, as we have observed in Chapter three, this means that the failure of

---

[4] Ibid., p.327
[5] Ibid., p.358
[6] *L'Expérience intérieure, ŒC*, V, p.17

communication which takes place in inner experience is, in itself, a form of communication which abolishes and transgresses the dialectical movement between subject and object. Blanchot represents this collapse of meaning by inscribing it into the text of his fictions. Bataille engages with this failure as a lack of textual authority which undermines the possibility of inner experience as merely metaphorical event. It is, indeed, as observed in Chapter four, in poetic experience that the thinking subject encounters itself as a pure, irrecuperable negativity.

Whereas poetry, in the Surrealist sense, aims at a moment of illumination, for Bataille it offers direct experience of negation. This experience not only immobilizes the dialectical movement but also trangresses metaphorical order. It is a dispersal of categories which, like Blanchot's opposition to textual experience, negates itself as an action or project. This explains not only André Breton's hostility to Bataille's formulation of symbolic language, as described, for example, in 'Le Langage des Fleurs', as an inverse hierarchical system, but also Breton's attitude towards Bataille's pursuit of poetry as a sacrifice rather than a transcendent point of revelation.

The text of inner experience is, however, an account of *ipse*'s encounter with 'le vide' in which a zero point is reached which destroys objective truth as it simultaneously affirms the reality of inner experience as communication. In this sense, inner experience is not a 'parody' of Surrealism but, indeed, its opposite: a method which undermines all stable symbolic structures by replacing language with experience of negation.

It is important, however, that inner experience, in this context, is defined by Bataille as a meeting point between thought and feeling which abolishes individuality in favour of a pure expenditure of the self. This is why, in the final chapters of this study, the movement of inner experience in *La Somme athéologique* was measured against either the outward reality of war, or the internal apocalypse which occurs during sexual excess. Catastrophe and erotic excess are, as Bataille puts it, the 'antipodes' of spiritual experience in that they are experiences which cannot lead to a tragic discharge which, as Aristotle has, it 'purges pity and terror'. Rather, as Nietzsche advocates, the true meaning of the tragic experience for Bataille, is to be found in the intensification of suffering and pain.[7]

Inner experience is, then, not a catharsis but an ascesis. In this sense also, inner experience ceases to be a textual drama. Although the inner experience is founded on negative principles, it stands, thus, as an authentic engagement with essential aspects of existence. Most importantly, this is how inner experience can only be expressed by Bataille in conceptual terms which lie outside the parameters of categorical thinking.

'La cicatrice intérieure'

Although, as we have observed, Bataille disdained any description of himself as a 'mystic', it has been one of the further objectives of this study to demonstrate that the central urgency of Bataille's writings from the late 1930s onwards is rooted in the paradox that one can be both religious and an atheist. Bataille was not alone in fixing the contradiction of the presence of divine absence as the central motif of his thought. Few members of the European generation which encountered Surrealism in the 1920s and participated in the activities of its renegade outgrowths in the 1930s did not see, in the chiliastic spirit of the age, the question of spiritual experience in a godless universe as central to artistic or political activity. However, in his activities with the Acéphale group, his talks and lectures for the Collège de Sociologie, and finally the texts for the journal *Acéphale* which immediately preceded the composition of *L'Expérience intérieure*, Bataille was perhaps alone in his insistence that the contradiction of religious feeling and rational atheism could be met, if not reconciled, in a concrete experience which might be described, albeit in a refracted fashion, as 'mystical'.

---

[7] Nietzsche explains his opposition to Aristotle in *Beyond Good and Evil*: 'Almost everything we call 'higher culture' is based on the spiritualization and intensification of cruelty.[...] That which constitutes the painful voluptuousness of tragedy is cruelty; that which produces a pleasing effect in so-called tragic pity, indeed fundamentally in everything sublime up to the highest and most refined thrills of metaphysics, derives its sweetness solely from the ingredient of cruelty mixed in it. What the Roman in the arena, the Christian in the ecstasies of the Cross, the Spaniard watching burnings or the bullfight [...] what all of these enjoy and look with secret ardour to imbibe is the spicy potion of the great Circe 'cruelty'. Friedrich Nietzsche, 'Our Virtues', *Beyond Good and Evil*, trans, R..J. Hollingdale (London: Penguin, 1973), p.140

This explains, in part, the hostile or sceptical critical reaction to the publication of the first texts of *La Somme athéologique*. It does not explain, however, the extent to which a good deal of contemporary criticism, with honourable exceptions, has either overlooked or sidestepped the question of Bataille's 'mysticism'. In the introductory chapter of this study, the inner experience was described as the fundamental paradox of Bataille's philosophy. The inner experience is a transgression which, when translated into language, subverts the stable referents of philosophy. It has been argued, from this notion, that this is how Bataille's inner experience, in a movement cherished by his post-modernist admirers, takes the thinking subject towards the apex of philosophy and literature, at a point where movement towards one form of expression undoes the systematic totality of the other.

This movement, it has been argued in the present study, has above all a religious significance. The inner experience pursued by Bataille has as its goal the putting to death of God in the form of a sacrifice. This sacrifice causes the simultaneous opening of a wound in the experience of one who commits this sacrifice. This is what lies at the heart of inner experience. Bataille's 'mysticism' is not, therefore, parodic in the sense that it is merely a textual dramatisation which borrows the language of 'real' mystics who belong to an established Church or religion.

However, given Bataille's passionate disregard for closure or completion, it is unsurprising that the project of *La Somme athéologique* was never completed. The ideas on experience, mysticism, poetry, communication which Bataille pursued through the texts of *La Somme athéologique* were, however, defining points in his intellectual itinerary. In *Méthode de Méditation*, most significantly, Bataille asks the question whether philosophy, if it is stretched towards its limit, towards transgression, death, has any real meaning in a personal or social sense. This is a question which, although unresolved and unresolvable, has a clear impact on Bataille's later writings on questions of economics, ethnology and political science.

It is equally important for the present study, however, that the central question which is set by mysticism, if it is detached from a theological function, is whether it has any meaning outside of the subjective experience of the mystic. Inner experience, Bataille tells us, is a moment, at once poetic, oneiric and erotic, which has no authority or reference other than itself. What, then, is the significance of an impossible experience which can neither be communicated nor understood? This study has argued that the truest function of the experience described in texts of *La Somme athéologique* is as a form of self-laceration which opens up a wound in thought or being. The texts of *La Somme athéologique*, and in particular *L'Expérience intérieure*, are conceived of as a response to an exigency to open this 'wound in thought' to unfathomable depths. The texts occupy a fragile space wherein inner experience is not only a theoretical confrontation with the void, but also a practical exploration of the limitless possibilities of 'non-savoir' as an expression of 'souveraineté'.

In this sense, at least, Bataille's 'mysticism' functions as an experience which is at the same time spectacle and ritual. The clearest analogy is that of a corrida, in which the torero is both the sacrificial victim and monstrous destroyer. This is a parallel drawn by Michel Leiris, with a reference to the paintings of André Masson which might equally well apply to the writings of Georges Bataille .

> Par le truchement des courses de taureaux, André Masson nous mène au point crucial de l'art: guerre inexpiable du créateur avec son œuvre, du créateur avec lui-même et du sujet avec l'objet, dichotomie féconde, joue sanglante dans laquelle l'individu entier est engagé, ultime chance pour l'homme - s'il consent à s'y risquer jusqu'à ses os - de donner corps à un sacré.[8]

Michel Leiris compares the artist to the bullfighter because he seeks to abolish death in a duel; this, says, Leiris, is an act of dizzying and severe beauty. Like the Icarian figure of the bulllfighter Granero, who in the central scene of *Histoire de l'œil* is blinded and sacrificed in a tragic festival, Bataille, in a parallel manner, in the texts of *La Somme athéologique*, stares at the sun and risks death in the name of sacred experience.

Bataille's encounter with absence in the movement of inner experience is as visceral as Granero's encounter with the 'monstre solaire' in the form of the bull. The sacred event which takes place in this section of *Histoire de l'œil* is, thus, both a metaphysical and physical reality. In the same way, the inner experience described in *La Somme athéologique*, as a sacred and transgressive movement, occurs at a mythic and a literal level. Like the corrida, it demands a response from its audience which transgresses the possibility of ethical

---

[8] Michel Leiris, *Brisées* (Paris: Gallimard, 1971), p.65

categories and moves into the domain of religious experience. Inner experience is, therefore, 'mystical' in the sense that it is a moment which opens up to blinding vision. However, the truest significance of the inner experience is that, unlike the Christian's mystical encounter with the figure of Christ on the Cross, it leaves, in the experience of those who are touched by its searing, blinding intensity, a scar which will not heal.

BIBLIOGRAPHY

1. Manuscripts

Bibliothèque Nationale de Paris

Papiers Georges Bataille

-*Correspondance Ambrosino-Kojève, cote N.a.f. 15853*
-*Correspondance Lacan-Weil, cote N.a.f. 15854*
-*Papiers des groupes 'Contre-Attaque' et 'Acéphale', cote N.a.f. 15952*

2. Complete works of Georges Bataille

Each of these volumes is published by Éditions Gallimard, Paris.

Œuvres Complètes, tome 1, Premiers écrits 1922-1940, introduction by Michel Foucault (1970)
Histoire de l'œil: L'Anus solaire: Sacrifices:
Textes et articles: *Aréthuse: Documents: La Critique Sociale; Acéphale: Contre-Attaque: Collège de sociologie*
Annexes: Notes

Œuvres Complètes, tome II, Écrits posthumes 1922-1940, (1972)

Œuvres Complètes, tome III, Œuvres littéraires (1973)
Madame Edwarda: Le Petit: L'Archangélique: L'Impossible: Haine de la poésie: L'Orestie: La Scissiparité: L'Abbé C: L'Être indifferencié n'est rien: Le Bleu du ciel
Notes

Œuvres Complètes, tome IV, Œuvres littéraires posthumes (1973)
Poèmes: Le mort: Julie: La maison brûlée: La tombe de Louis XXX: Divinus Deus (Ma mère -Charlotte d'Ingerville -Sainte) -Ébauches
Notes

Œuvres Complètes, tome V, La Somme athéologique, tome I (1973)

170

L'Expérience intérieure: *Méthode de Méditation*: *Post-scriptum 1953*:
Le Coupable: *L'Alleluiah*: *Catéchisme de Dianus*
Notes

Œuvres Complètes, tome VI, La Somme athéologique, tome 2 (1973)
Sur Nietzsche: *Memorandum*
Annexes: Notes

Œuvres Complètes, tome VII (1976)
L'Économie à la mesure de l'univers: *La Part maudite*: *La Limite de
l'utile*: *Théorie de la religion*, Conférences (1947-1948)
Annexes: Notes

Œuvres Complètes, tome VIII (1976)
L'Histoire de l'érotisme: *La Part maudite II*: *Le Surréalisme au jour le
jour*: Conférences 1951-1953: *La Souveraineté*: *La Part maudite III*
Annexes: Notes

Œuvres Complètes, tome IX (1979)
La Peinture préhistorique: *Lascaux ou la naissance de l'art*: *Manet*: *La
Littérature et le mal*: *Dossier de 'Lascaux'*: *Dossier William Blake*
Notes

Œuvres Complètes, tome X (1987)
L'Érotisme: *Le Procès de Gilles de Rais*: *Les Larmes d'Éros*: Dossier
de *L'Érotisme*: Dossier des *Larmes d'Éros*: Hors *Les Larmes d'Éros*.
Notes

Œuvres Complètes, tome XI (1988)
Articles 1. Année 1944-année 1949.
Notes

Œuvres Complètes, tome XII (1988)
Articles 2, Année 1949-année 1961.
Notes

3. Books by Georges Bataille

Notre Dame de Rheims (Saint-Flour: Imprimerie du Courrier d'Auvergne, 1918)

Les Monnaies des Grands Mogols (Paris: J. Florange, 1928)

Histoire de l'œil, under the pseudonym of Lord Auch, illustrated with eight lithographs by André Masson, (Paris: René Bonnel, 1928)

Histoire de l'œil, édition de Séville, illustrated with six etchings by Hans Bellmer (Paris: Éditions 'K', 1944)

Histoire de l'œil, édition de Burgos, illustrated with six etchings by Hans Bellmer (Paris: Jean-Jacques Pauvert, 1952)

Histoire de l'œil (Paris: Jean-Jacques Pauvert, 1967)

L'Anus solaire, illustrated with six drawings by André Masson (Paris: Galerie Simon, 1931)

Sacrifices, illustrated with five etchings by André Masson (Paris: G.L.M, 1936)

Madame Edwarda, under the pseudonym Pierre Angélique (Paris: Éditions du Solitaire/Robert Chatté, 1941)

Madame Edwarda, under the pseudonym Pierre Angélique, illustrated with etchings by Jean Fautrier, under the pseudonomyn Jean Perdu (Paris: chez le Solitaire, 1945)

Madame Edwarda, under the pseudonym Pierre Angélique, preface by Georges Bataille (Paris: Jean-Jacques Pauvert, 1956)

Madame Edwarda, illustrated with twelve plates by Hans Bellmer, (Paris: Jean-Jacques Pauvert, 1966)

L'Expérience intérieure (Paris: Gallimard, 1944)

172

Le Petit, under the pseudonym Louis Trente (Paris: Robert Chatté 1944)

Le Coupable (Paris: Gallimard, 1944)

L'Archangélique (Paris: Messages, 1944)

Sur Nietzsche, volonté de chance (Paris: Gallimard, 1945)

L'Orestie (Paris: Éditions de Quatre-Vents, 1945)

Dirty (Paris: Éditions Fontaine, 1945)

L'Alleluiah, catéchisme de Dianus, accompanied by lithographs by Jean Fautrier (Paris: Auguste Blaizot, 1947)

L'Alleluiah, catéchisme de Dianus, accompanied by lithographs by Jean Fautrier (Paris: Éditions 'K', 1947)

Méthode de méditation (Paris, Éditions Fontaine, 1947)

Histoire de rats (journal de Dianus), illustrated with three etchings by Alberto Giacometti (Paris: Éditions de Minuit, 1947)

Haine de la Poésie (Paris: Éditions de Minuit, 1947)

La Part maudite, essai d'économie générale, I. La consumation (Paris: Éditions de Minuit, 1949)

Éponine (Paris: Éditions de Minuit, 1949)

L'Abbé C (Paris: Éditions de Minuit, 1950)

L'Expérience intérieure, revised edition, accompanied by *Méthode de Méditation* and

Post-scriptum (Paris: Gallimard, 1954)

La Peinture préhistorique, Lascaux ou la niassance de l'art (Genève: Skira, 1955)

La Littérature et le mal (Paris: Gallimard, 1957)

Le Bleu du ciel (Paris: Jean-Jacques Pauvert, 1957)

L'Érotisme (Paris: Éditions de Minuit, 1957)

Les Larmes d'Éros (Paris: Jean-Jacques Pauvert, 1961)

L'Impossible (Paris: Éditions de Minuit, 1962)

Le Mort (Paris: Jean-Jacques Pauvert, 1967)

5. Introductory chapters and prefaces to books by Georges Bataille

'Laure' (also known as Colette Peignot), *Le Sacré*, accompanied by *Poèmes* and *Divers écrits* (Paris: Private Edition,1939)

'Laure' (also known as Colette Peignot), *Histoire d'une petite fille* (Paris: Private Edition, 1943)

Michelet Jules, *La Sorcière* (Paris: Éditions des Quatre-Vents, 1946)

Nietzsche Friedrich, *Memorandum*, ed. Georges Bataille (Paris: Gallimard, 1945)

Sade Donatien-Alphonse-François, Comte (also known as Marquis de), *Justine ou les malheurs de la vertu* (Paris: Presses du Livre Français, 1950)

Sade Donatien-Alphonse-François, Comte (also known as Marquis de), *Justine ou les malheurs de la vertu* (Paris, Jean-Jacques Pauvert, 1955).
Procès de Gilles de Rais, ed. Georges Bataille, (Paris: Club Français du Livre, 1959)
Max Ernst (Paris: Gonthier-Seghers, 1960)

6. Translations by Georges Bataille

Chestov Léon, *L'idée de bien chez Tolstoi et Nietzsche (philosophie et prédication)*, translated from the Russian by T.Beresovski-Chestov and Georges Bataille (Paris: Éditions du Siècle, 1925)

7. Selected Letters

Georges Bataille, Lettres à Roger Caillois, 4 août 1935-4 février 1959, ed. Jean-Pierre Le Bouler, introduction by Francis Marmande, (Rennes: Éditions Folle Avoine, 1987)

Choix de Lettres, 1917-1962, ed. Michel Surya, (Paris: Gallimard,1997)

8. Other works with significant contributions from Georges Bataille.

Acéphale, religion-sociologie-philosophie, 1936-1939, introduction by Michel Camus. (Paris: Jean-Michel Place, 1980)

Le Collège de sociologie 1937-1938, introduction by Denis Hollier, (Paris. Idées/Gallimard, 1979)

La Critique sociale, revue des idées et des livres, introduction by Boris Souvarine, (Paris: Éditions de la Différence, 1983)

Documents, ed. Bernard Noël, (Paris, Mercure de France, 1968)

Documents, Doctrines - Archéologie-Beaux Arts-Ethnothographie, année 1929, tome I: introduction by Denis Hollier, (Paris: Jean-Michel Place, 1992)

Documents, Archéologie - Beaux Arts-Ethnographie -Variétés, année 1930, tome II, introduction by Denis Hollier, (Paris: Jean-Michel Place, 1992)

L'Affaire Sade, Compte rendu exact du procès intenté par le ministère public, (Paris: Jean-Jacques Pauvert, 1957)

9. Collections of critical essays on Georges Bataille

Bataille, actes du colloque du Centre Culturel International de Cerisy-la-Salle (Paris: 10/18 U.G.E., 1973)

Bataille après tout, ed. Denis Hollier, coll. L'Extrême contemporain (Orléans: Éditions Belin, 1995)

'Bataille' *L'Arc, 44* (1971)

Bataille: Writing the Sacred, ed. Carolyn Bailey Gill, (London: Routledge, 1995)

Écrits d'ailleurs, Georges Bataille et les ethnologues (Paris: Éditions de la Maison des Sciences de l'Homme, 1987)

'Georges Bataille' *L'Arc*, 32 (1967)

'Georges Bataille, une autre histoire de l'oeil', *Cahiers de l'Abbaye de sainte Croix*, 69, (1991)

'Georges Bataille', *Revue des sciences humaines*, 206 (1987)

'Georges Bataille' *La Ciguë*, 1 (1958)

Georges Bataille, une liberté souveraine, ed. Michel Surya (Orléans:Ville d'Orléans/Fourbis, 1997)

'Georges Bataille, la littérature, l'érotisme et la mort,' *Magazine littéraire*, 234, (1987)

'Hommage à Georges Bataille', *Critique*,195-196 (1963)

'Kojève's Paris/Now Bataille' *parallax, 4*, (1997)

October, 36, (1986)

'On Bataille', *Stanford French Review*, no 12 (1988)

'On Bataille' *Yale French Studies*, no. 78 (1990)

On Bataille: Critical Essays, ed. Lesie-Anne Boldt-Irons, (Albany: SUNY Press, 1995)

10. Books on Georges Bataille

Arnaud, Alain and Excoffon-Lafage, Gisèle, *Bataille* (Paris: Éditions du Seuil, coll. Écrivains de toujours 101, 1978)

Audoin, Philippe, *Sur Georges Bataille*, (Paris: Actual/Le temps qu'il fait, 1989)

Besnier, Jean-Michel, *La Politique de l'impossible: L'intellectuel entre révolte et engagement*, (Paris, Éditions de la Découverte, 1988)

Bosch, Glòria, *André Masson et Georges Bataille*, (Vic: coll. Complicitats, Eumo Editorial 1983)
   - *'L'Abbé C' de Georges Bataille: Les structures masquées du double*, (Amsterdam: Rodopi, 1983)

Cels, Jacques, *L'Exigence poétique de Georges Bataille*, (Bruxelles: Éditions Universitaires De Boeck, 1989)

Chatain, Jacques, *Georges Bataille* (Paris: Seghers, 1973)

Dean, Carolyn Janice, *The self and its pleasures: Bataille, Lacan and the history of the decentered subject*, (Ithaca: Cornell University Press, 1985)

Didi-Huberman, Georges, *La Ressemblance informe: ou le Gai-Savoir visuel selon Georges Bataille*, (Paris: Macula, 1995)

Durançon Jean, *Georges Bataille*, (Paris: Gallimard,1976)

Ernst, Gilles, *Georges Bataille: Analyse du récit de mort*, (Paris: Presses Universitaires de France, 1993)

Fardoulis-Lagrange, Michel, *G.B. ou un ami présompteux*, (Paris: Éditions Le Soleil Noir, 1969)

Feher, Michel, *Conjurations de la violence: introduction à la lecture de Georges Bataille*, (Paris, Presses Universitaires de France, 1981)

Fiat, Christophe, *Texte au supplice*, (Colleville-Montgomery: Éditions 23, 1998)

Fitch, Brian T., *Monde à l'envers, texte réversible: la fiction de Georges Bataille*, (Paris: Lettres Modernes/Minard, 1982)

Gallop, Jane, *Intersections: A Reading of Sade with Bataille, Blanchot and Klossowski* (Lincoln, Nebraska and London: University of Nebraska Press, 1981)

Hawley, Daniel, *L'Oeuvre insolite de Georges Bataille. Une hiérophanie moderne*, (Genève/Paris:Slatkine Champion, 1978)
-*Bibliographée annotée de la critique sur Georges Bataille de 1929 à 1975*, (Genève/Paris,Slatkine/Champion, 1976)

Heimonet, Jean-Michel, *Le Mal à l'oeuvre, Georges Bataille et l'écriture du sacrifice*, (Paris:Éditions Parenthèses, 1987)

Hollier, Denis, *La Prise de la concorde. Essais sur Georges Bataille* (Paris: Gallimard, 1974)

Ishaghpour, Youssef, *Aux origines de l'art moderne: Le 'Manet' de Georges Bataille* (Paris: Éditions de la Différence, 1989)

Land, Nick, *The Thirst for Annihilation: Georges Bataille and Virulent Nihilism*, (London: Routledge, 1992)

Limousin, Claude, *Bataille*, (Paris, Éditions Universitaires, coll. Psychothèque, 1974)

Magné, Gilles, *Eroticism in Georges Bataille and Henry Miller*, (Birmingham: Summa, 1993)

178

Marmande, Francis, *L'Indifférence des ruines*, (Paris: Éditions Parenthèses, 1985)
-*Georges Bataille politique*, (Lyon: Presses Universitaires de Lyon, 1985)

Palumbo, Pietro and Ecoloeo, Marisa, *Su Bataille: prospettive ermeneutiche*, (Palermo: STAS, 1985)

Pefanis, Julian, *Heterology and the postmodern: Bataille, Baudrillard and Lyotard*, (Durham N.C.: Duke University Press. 1991)

Perniola, Mario, *Georges Bataille e il negativo* (Milano: Feltrenelli, 1977)
L'instant éternel - Bataille et la pensée de la marginalité (Paris: Méridien/Anthropos 1982)

Prévost, Pierre, *Pierre Prévost rencontre Georges Bataille* (Paris: Éditions Jean- Michel Place, 1987)

Rella, Franco, *The Myth of the Other: Lacan, Deleuze, Foucault, Bataille* (Washington DC: Maisonneuve Press, 1993)

Renard, Jean-Claude, *'L'Expérience intérieure' de Georges Bataille ou la négation du Mystère* (Paris. Éditions du Seuil. 1987)

Richardson, Michael, *Georges Bataille* (London: Routledge, 1994)

Richman, Michèle H., *Reading Georges Bataille: Beyond the Gift* (Baltimore, John Hopkins University Press, 1982)

Sasso, R, *Georges Bataille: le système du non-savoir. Une ontologie du jeu.* (Paris: Éditions de Minuit, coll. 'Arguments', 1978) Shapiro, Steven, *Passion and Excess: Levinas, Blanchot, Bataille and communication* (The Hague: M.Nijhoff. 1982)

Stoekl, Allan, *Politics, Writing, Mutilation: The Cases of Bataille, Blanchot, Roussel, Leiris and Ponge* (Minneapolis: University of Minnesota Press, 1985)

Surya, Michel, *Georges Bataille: La Mort à l'œuvre* (Paris: Gallimard, 1987)

Teixera, Vincent, *Georges Bataille, La part de l'art: La peinture du non-savoir*, (Paris: L'Harmattan, 1997)

Warin, François, *Nietzsche et Bataille: la parodie à l'infini*, (Paris, Presses Universitaires de France, 1994)

11. Theses, monographs, essays and articles on Georges Bataille

Abel, L, 'Georges Bataille and the repetition of Nietzsche', *View 6*, 2-3, (1946), pp. 42-45

Alberes, R-M., 'Une mystique littéraire du mal', *Combat*, 4149, (1957), p.6

Alexandrian, Sarane, 'Bataille et l'amour noir', pp.256-280, *Les libérateurs de l'amour*. (Paris: Éditions du Seuil, 1977).

Alhau, M., 'Georges Bataille', *Sud*, 21, (1977), p.129.

Amer, H., 'Le bleu du ciel', 'La littérature et le mal', 'L'érotisme', *NRF.*, 61 (1958), pp.138-142.

Arban, D. 'Cinq minutes avec Georges Bataille', *Le Figaro Littéraire*, 117, 17 July, 1948, p.5.

Aubral, F., 'La crue', *Cahiers du chemin*, 18 (1973), pp.116-1222.

Audoin, Philippe, 'Un saint enragé', *Le Nouvel Observateur*, 90, 3-9, (1966), pp.26-27

August, M., Liddle S.: 'Artaud/Bataille: Three views of the Colloque of Cerisy', *Sub-stance*, 5-6, (1973), pp.199-236.

Autie, D., 'Deux inédits de Georges Bataille: Notre Dame de Rheims et son commentaire; La théorie de la religion', *Le Monde*, 6 September, 1974, p.7

-'Une relecture de la 'Somme athéologique'. Un païen exemplaire: Georges Bataille', *Le Monde*, 23 August, 1973 , pp.7-8.

Baudrillard, J, 'Quand Bataille attaquait le principe métaphysique de l'économie', *La quinzaine littéraire*, 1 June 1976, pp.21-24

Baudry, J.L, 'Bataille et l'expérience intérieure', *Tel Quel*, 55, 1973, pp.63-76.
-'Bataille et la science: introduction à l'expérience intérieure', *Bataille, actes du colloque du Centre Culturel International de Cerisy-la-Salle*, (Paris: 10/18 UGE, 1973), pp.127-146.
-'Écriture - fiction- idéologie', *Tel Quel/Théorie d'ensemble*, (Paris: Éditions du Seuil, 1968)

Beaujour, M., 'Eros and Nonsense: Georges Bataille, *Modern French Criticism*, ed. John K.Simon, (Chicago: University of Chicago Press, 1972), pp.149-173

Belay, Boris, 'That obscure Parallel to the Dialectic', *parallax,* 4 (1997), pp.55-70

Bellour, R, 'La place de Dieu', *Les Lettres Françaises,* 1142, 28 July (1966), pp.23-25.

Bermejo, J-M, 'La experiencia interior', *Estafeta literaria,* 519, 1 July, (1973), pp.1388-1389.
-'La literature y el mal', *Estafeta literaria*, 483, 10 January (1972), pp.808-809

Bernard, M. 'Georges Bataille était l'homme d'une folle chevauchée', *Arts* 878, 18-24 July, 1962, p.9.

Barsani, J., 'Georges Bataille', pp.440-446, in *La Littérature en France depuis 1945*, (Paris: Bordas, 1970), pp.440-446.

Besnier, Jean-Michel, 'Le système (de l')impossible', *Esprit,* 38, (1980) pp.148-164.

Bisiaux, 'Notes pour mémoire: Georges Bataille', *Arts* 424, 14-20 August, 1953, p.5.

Blanchot, M. 'L'Expérience intérieure', *Journal des Débats*, 5 May, 1943. reprinted in *Faux-pas* pp.51-56 (Paris: Gallimard, 1943.
- '*Pierre Angélique*: *Madame Edwarda*', *NRF,* no. 43, July 1956, pp.148-150
- 'Le Récit et le scandale', *NRF,* no. 43, July 1956, pp.148-150, reprinted in *Le Livre à venir* (Paris: Gallimard, 1959) pp.213-233
- 'L'Amitié: pour Georges Bataille', *Les Lettres Nouvelles*, no. 29, October.1962, pp.7-12. reprinted in *L'Amitié* (Paris: Gallimard, 1971)
- 'L'Expérience-limites', *NRF,* no. 118, October 1962, pp.577-592. reprinted in *-L'Entretien infini* (Paris: Gallimard, 1969) pp.330-313
- 'Le Jeu de la pensée', *Critique*, nos. 195/196, August-September, 1963, pp.313-322
-Preface to the Italian edition of *Sur Nietzsche: Nietzsche, il culmine e il possibile* (Milano: Rizzoli, 1970)

Blanzat, R. 'La Haine de la poésie', *Arts et Lettres 3* (12), 1948, p.60-66.

Boldt, Leslie-Anne, 'Translator's introduction to *Inner Experience*', in Georges
    Bataille, *Inner Experience*, trans. Leslie-Anne Boldt (Albany: SUNY Press, 1988)

Bonesio, Luisa, *La stile della filosofia: estetica e scrittura da Nietzsche a Blanchot*, (Milano: Fr Angeli, 1983).

Borch-Jacobsen, Mikkel, 'The Laughter of Being, *Modern Language Notes*, 102 (1987), pp.737-60.

Borderie, R. 'Georges Bataille' *Littérature de notre temps 3*, (Tournai: Casterman, 1968), pp. 9-12

182

Botting, Fred, 'Relations of the Real in Lacan, Bataille and Blanchot, *Sub-stance*, 73 (1994), pp.24-40
-'Signs of Evil: Bataille, Baudrillard and Postmodern Gothic', *Southern Review*, 27 (1994), pp. 493-510

Botting, Fred and Wilson, Scott, 'Literature as Heterological Practice: Georges Bataille, Writing and Inner Experience', *Textual Practice*, 7 (1993), pp.195-207
-'Pow, Pow, Pow: Hamlet, Bataille and Marxism Now, *parallax*, 4 (1997), pp.119-36

Boudet, J., 'Une Mystique de la souillure: Georges Bataille, in *Souillure et pureté*, ed. Michel Adam (Toulouse: Privat, 1972) pp. 204-210.

Boudot, P. 'Nietzche et l'au-delà de la liberté, in *Nietzche et les écrivains français de 1930 à 1960* (Paris: Aubier-Montaigne, 1970), pp.107-115.

Bounoure, G. 'Georges Bataille, poète maudit', *Mercure de France, no.* 1194, February 1963, pp.196-203.

Bowie, Malcolm. 'La Crue de L.Finas.', *French Studies*, no. 30, 1976, pp.496-497.

Brochier, Jean-Jacques, 'La littérature érotique aujourd'hui, *Magazine littéraire,* no.13, December 1967, pp.14-16
-'Bataille était le contraire d'un écrivain', *Magazine littéraire,* no.45, October 1970, pp.8-18

Bruno, Jean., 'Bruits de la ville,' *Le Nouvel Observateur*, 13-19 July 1966, pp.26-27.

Butor, M. 'Le Mariage de l'archangélique et du félin. Bataille et Jacques Hérold', *NRF.*, no. 319, 1 August 1979, pp.159-160.

Caillois, R., 'The Collège de sociologie: Paradox of an active Sociology', *Sub-stance,* 11-12 (1975), pp.61-61.

Calas, Nicolas, 'Acephelic mysticism', *Hemisphères II*, no.6, 1945, pp.2-13.

Camus, Michel, 'L'Acephalité ou la religion de la mort, *Cahiers Obliques I*, no. I, 1980, pp.23-28.

Caplan, J., 'La Beauté de la mort, *Dada/Surréalisme*, no. 5, 1975, pp.37-43.

Carroll, David, 'Disruptive Discourse and Critical Power: The Conditions of Archaeology and Genaeology', *Humanities in Society*, 5 (1982), pp.175-207.

Carrouges, M., 'La Signification de L'Expérience intérieure, in *Jeux et poésie* (Liège:Éditions du Cerf et la pensée catholique, 1944), pp. 157-162.

Chapsal, Madeleine, 'Georges Bataille', *L'Express*, 23 March 1961, pp.34-36.
-'Entretien avec Breton', *Quinze écrivains, Entretiens* (Paris: Juillard, 1963) pp. 35-44
-'Georges Bataille', *Quinze écrivains, Entretiens* (Paris: Juillard, 1963) pp.9-22
-'Georges Bataille et les maudits', *L'Express*, 21 May 1967, p.42
-'Le Droit d'aller jusqu'au bout', *L'Express*, 21 June 1970, pp.39-40
-'Georges Bataille à l'étal', *L'Express*, 16 May 1971, pp.49-50.

Collier, P., 'Théorie de la religion', *French Studies*, 32 (1978), pp.359-360
-'La Prise de la Concorde', *French Studies*, 32 (1978), pp.490-491

Comay, Rebecca, 'Gifts without Presents: Economies of 'Experience' in Bataille and Heidegger', *Yale French Studies*, 78 (1990), pp. 66-80

Coudol, J, 'A propos de la réédition du Coupable', *Tel Quel*, 5 (1961), pp.54-55

Cuzin, F., 'L'Expérience intérieure', *Confluences*, 27 (1943), pp.746-753, reprinted in *L'Arc*, 44 (1971), pp.189-191.

Derrida, Jacques, 'De l'économie restreinte à l'économie générale: un hégélianisme sans réserves.' *L'Arc*, 32 (1967), pp.24-25, reprinted in *L'Écriture et la différence* (Paris: Éditions du Seuil, 1967) pp.369-409

Dubief, H. 'Extrait du Journal de Maurice Heine', *Textures*, 6 (1970), pp.49-51
'Témoignages su Contre-Attaque', *Textures*, 6 (1970), pp. 52-60

Dumur, G., 'Les larmes d'Éros', *France Observateur*, 31 August 1961, p. 16.
-'Le bibliothécaire du diable', *Le Nouvel Observateur*, 28 June, 1970, pp. 40-42.

Duras, Marguerite, 'Bataille, Feydeau et Dieu', *France Observateur*, 12 December, 1957, pp.20-21.
-'A propos de Georges Bataille', *La Ciguë*, 1 (1958), pp.32-33.

Duvignaud, J. 'Usage de richesses', *L'Arc*, 32 (1967), pp.71-72.

Engelstein, J.-C. 'Zigzag (*La Crue*, de Lucette Finas), *Critique*, 319 (1973), pp.1075-1101.

ffrench, Patrick, 'The Corpse of Theory', *parallax*, 4 (1997), pp.99-118

Filloux, J.-C. 'L'Expérience intérieure selon Georges Bataille', *Méridien,* 11 (1944), pp.10-14.

Finas, Lucette, 'Bataille forcé', *Le Quinzaine littéraire*, 30 June, 1970, pp.10-11.
-'La Crue', *Critique*, no. 286 (1971), pp.241-263
- *La Crue. Une lecture de Bataille: Madame Edwarda*. (Paris: Gallimard, 1972)

Flay, Joseph C., 'Hegel, Derrida and Bataille's Laughter', in *Hegel and his Critics*, ed. William Desmond (Albany: SUNY Press, 1989), pp.163-73

Fraenkel, Theodore, 'Georges Bataille, mon ami' *Les Lettres Françaises*, no. 935, 18 July 1962, pp.1-12

Galletti, Marina, 'Masses: A failed Collège?', *Stanford French Review*, 12 (1988), pp. 49-73

Gill, Carolyn Bailey, 'Bataille and the Question of Presence', *parallax*, 4 (1997), pp.89-98

Golding, Sue, 'Solar Clitoris', *parallax*, 4 (1997), pp.137-150

Goux, Jean-Joseph, 'General Economics and Postmodern Capitalism', trans. Kathy Ascheim and Rhonda Garelick, *Yale French Studies*, 78 (1990), pp.206-24

Grenier, Jean, 'Une Nouvelle religion', *Commeodia*,103 (1943), p.2
-'L'expérience intérieure', *Revue d'histoire de la philosophie et d'histoire générale de la civilisation*, 38 (1944), pp.175-177

Guerlac, Suzanne, 'Recognition by a Woman!: A reading of Bataille's L'Érotisme', *Yale French Studies*, 78 (1990), pp. 90-105

Habermas, Jürgen, 'The French Path to Postmodernity: Bataille between Eroticism and General Economics, trans. Frederic Lawrence, *New German Critique*, 33 (1984), pp.79-102, reprinted in *Bataille: A Critical Reader* (Oxford: Blackwell, 1997), ed. Fred Botting and Scott Wilson, pp.167-191

Heimonet, Jean-Michel, 'From Bataille to Derrida: Différance and Heterology', trans, A. Engstrom, *Stanford French Review*, 12 (1988), pp.129-47
-'Recoil in Order to Leap Forward: Two Values of Sade in Bataille's Text'. trans. Joanicho Kohchi, *Yale French Studies*, 78 (1990), pp.227-36

Henric, Jacques, 'Bataille', *Tel Quel*, 84 (1980), pp.68-71.

Hollier, Denis, *Bataille entre deux guerres*, Thèse 3e cycle, Université Paris-X, Nanterre, 1973
    -'Le Matérialisme dualiste de Georges Bataille', *Tel Quel*, 25 (1966), pp.44-54
    -'La Tache aveugle', *L'Éphémère*, 3 (1967), pp.8-13
    -'Le Savoir formel', *Tel Quel*, 34 (1968), pp.18-20
    -'Le Dispositif Hegel/Nietzsche dans la bibliothèque de Bataille', *L'Arc*, 38, 1969, pp.35-47
    -'Bataille paraît', *Le Quinzaine littéraire*, June 1970, pp.5-6.
    -'La Copulation labyrinthinque (un détail d'interférences'), *Les Lettres Françaises*, no. 1249, 29 March 1972, pp.14-15
    -'On Equivocation (Between Literature and Politics), trans. Rosalind Krauss, *October*, 55, (1990), pp.3-22.
    -'The Use-Value of the Impossible', *October*, 60 (1992), pp.1-25
    -'About Some Books Which Bataille Did Not Write', *parallax*, 4 (1997), pp.151-66

Houdebine, J-L, 'L'ennemi du dedans', *Tel Quel*, 52 (1972), pp.49-73.

Hussey, Andrew, 'The Black Surrealist of Catastrophe', *The Times Higher Educational Supplement*, November 11, 1994, p.33
    -'Beau comme un guêpe', *Littérature et cruauté: Actes du sixième colloque annuel de littérature française, francophone et comparée de Columbia University*, (New York: Columbia University, 1996), pp.62-79
    -'Fanatics of the Apocalypse: Traces of the End in Debord and Bataille', *Space and Culture*, 2, 1997, pp.85-95
    -'Elision and paradox', *The Times Literary Supplement*, May 22, 1998, p.31

Hussey, Andrew and Stubbs, Jeremy, 'Tempête de flammes', *parallax*, 4 (1997), pp.151-166.

Jay, Martin, 'The Disenchantment of the Eye: Bataille and the Surrealists', in *Downcast Eyes: The Denigration of Vision in*

Twentieth-Century French Thought (Berkeley: University of California Press, 1994) pp.211-263

Jouffroy, Alain, 'La plus noire figure.' *L'Express*, 27 June 1965, pp.84-85
- 'Bataille et Breton', *La quinzaine littéraire*, 1 August 1967, pp.9-10
- 'Société secrète de l'écriture', *Change*, 7, 1970-71, pp.30-45
- 'Un Aragon, des Aragons', in *Louis Aragon, Du surréalisme au réalisme socialiste*, ed. Gavin Bowd and Jeremy Stubbs, (Manchester: AURA, 1997), pp. 1- 13

Jourdain, S. 'Une unique expérience', *Tel Quel*, 21, 1965, pp.41-60.

Klossowski, Pierre, 'L'Expérience de la Mort de Dieu chez Nietzsche et la nostalgie d'une expérience authentique chez Georges Bataille', in *Sade, mon prochain* (Paris: Éditions du Seuil, 1947) pp.155-183
- 'A propos du simulacre dans la communication de Georges Bataille', *Critique*, 195/196 August-September 1963, pp.742-750
'La Messe de Georges Bataille', in *Un si funeste désir* (Paris: Gallimard, 1963) p.121-132

Klossowski, Thadée, 'Le Ciel', *L'Arc*, 32, (1967)

Kojève, Alexandre, 'Préface à l'œuvre de Georges Bataille', *L'Arc*, 44, 1971, p.36

Krauss, Rosalind, 'Antivision', *October*, 60 (1992), pp.151-66

Kristeva, Julia, 'Bataille, l'expérience et la pratique', in *Bataille à Cerisy*, (Paris: U.G.E, coll.10/18, 1977), pp. 267-301

Lala, Marie-Christine, 'The Conversions of Writing in George Bataille's L'Impossible', trans. Robert Livingston, *Yale French Studies*, 78 (1990), pp. 237-45

Larmore, Charles, 'Bataille's Heterology', *Semiotext(e) 2*, 2, (1976), pp. 87-104.

188

Lechte, John, 'An Introduction to Bataille: The Impossible as (a Practice of) Writing', *Textual Practice*, 7 (1993), pp.173-94

Leiris, Michel, 'De Bataille l'impossible à l'impossible *Documents*,' *Critique*, 195/196,(1963), pp.685-693, reprinted in *Brisées* (Paris: Mercure de France, 1966
  -'Du temps de Lord Auch', *L'Arc*, 32, (1967), pp. 6-15.

Libertson, Joseph, 'Bataille and Communication: From Heterogeneity to Continuity', *Modern Language Notes*, 89 (1974), pp.669-98

Lotringer, Sylvère, 'Artaud, Bataille et le matérialisme dialectique', *Sub-stance*, 5-6 (1973), pp.207-225.

Macherey, Pierre, 'Georges Bataille: Materialism Inverted', in *The Object of Literature* (Cambridge: Cambridge University Press, 1995), pp.112-31

Marcel, Gabriel, 'Le Refus du salut et l'exaltation de l'homme absurde', in *Homo viator*, (Paris: Aubier), 1945, pp. 259-279

Marmande, Francis, *Bataille Politique*, Thèse d'État (lettres), Université de Paris VIII, 1982

Mascolo, Dionys, 'Du jeu, de l'érotisme', *France Observateur*, 20 February 1958, pp.16-17.

Masson, André, (Inspecteur général des bibliothèques), 'Georges Bataille', *Bulletin des Bibliothèques de France* 7, 7 (1962), pp.457-477.
  -'Georges Bataille, *Bibliothèque de l'École des Chartes*, 122 (1964), pp.330-384

Masson, André (Artist), 'A propos de Georges Bataille', *La Ciguë*, (1958), p.40.
  Entretiens avec Georges Charbonnier (Paris: Juillard, 1958), pp.53, 56, pp.137-138, 179-181.
  -'Le Soc de la charrue', *Critique*, 195/196 (1963), pp.701-705.
  Le rebelle du surréalisme, (Paris: Hermann, 1976)

Mehlman, Jeffrey, 'Ruse de Rivoli: Politics and deconstruction', *Modern Langauge Notes*, 91, (1976), pp.1061-1072

Metraux, Alfred, 'Rencontre avec les ethnologues', *Critique,*195/196 (1963), pp.677-694

Michelson, Annette, 'Heterology and the Critique of Instrumental Reason', *October*, 36 (1986), pp.111-27

Mishima, Yukio, 'Essai sur Georges Bataille', *NRF*, 256 (1974), pp.77-82.

Monnerot, Jules, 'Sur Georges Bataille', *Confluences*, 8/9 (1945/1946), pp.874-8882, 1009-1018.

Moré, Marcel, 'Georges Bataille', *Cahier des saisons*, 38 (1964), pp.357-361, reprinted as 'Georges Bataille en présence de la mort', in *La foudre de Dieu* (Paris: Gallimard, 1969), pp.210-215
 -'Georges Bataille', in *Écrits de Laure*, ed Jérôme Peignot (Paris:Jean-Jacques Pauvert, 1971) pp.123-129

Nadeau, Maurice, 'Georges Bataille et *La Haine de la poésie'*, *Combat,*1073 (1947), reprinted, in *Littérature présente*, (Paris: Corrêa,1952) pp.314-319
 -'Après le rire, la mort. Avec Georges Bataille disparaît un prodigeux excitateur', *L'Express*, 19 July 1962, pp.20-21.
 -Le Roman français depuis la guerre (Paris: Gallimard, 1963), pp.135-137

Nancy, Jean-Luc, 'La Communauté désœuvrée', *Aléa*, 41(1983), pp.11-49

Noël, Bernard, 'Poésie et expérience', in Georges Bataille, *L'Archangélique et autres poèmes* (Paris: Mercure de France, 1967) pp.9-17
 -'Sur Documents', in Georges Bataille, *Documents* (Paris: Mercure de France, 1968) pp.9-13
 -'L'In-fini de Bataille', *La quinzaine littéraire*, 14 July, 1973, pp.6-7.

'La Dent malade', *Gramma*,1 (1974), pp.163-177.

-'Georges Bataille et l'intimité', *La quinzaine littéraire*, 1 sept. 1974, pp.3-4.

-'Quelques sorties', in Georges Bataille, *Le Dictionnaire Critique*, (Paris: L'Écarcalate, 1993), pp.9-12

Pawlett, William, 'The Use-Value of Georges Bataille', *parallax*, 4 (1997), pp.167-74

Pefanis, Julian, 'The Issue of Bataille', in *Postmodern Conditions*, ed. Andrew Milner, Philip Thomson, and Chris Worth (New York, Oxford and Munich: Berg, 1990), pp. 135-55

Peignot, Colette ('Laure.'), *Écrits de Laure*. (Paris: Jean-Jacques Pauvert,1971), reprinted as *Écrits de Laure*, (Paris: U.G.E, coll. 10/18, 1978)

Peignot, Jérôme, 'Ma Mère diagonale', *Change,* 7 (1970-71), pp.162-172, reprinted in *Écrits de Laure*. (Paris: Jean-Jacques Pauvert 1971), pp.9-22.

Perniola, Mario, 'Il negativo e la poesia in Georges Bataille', *Rivista di estetica*, 16 (1971), pp.342-370.

-'Interpretazioni di Bataille', *Rivista di estetica,* 18 (1973), pp.138-176.

Piel, Jean, 'Bataille et le monde: de la *Notion de dépense* à *La part maudite*', *Critique,* 195/196 (1963), pp.721-733.

Pierssens, M, 'Notes sur Bataille, la guerre, l'Espagne', in *Les écrivains et la guerre d'Espagne*, ed. Marc Hanrez (Paris: Panthéon, Coll. 'Les Dossiers H', 1975), pp. 223-230

Pleynet, Marcelin, 'Les problèmes de l'avant-garde', *Tel Quel*, 25, 1966, pp.77-86.

'L'Orestie', *Bataille à Cerisy* (Paris, U.G.E., coll. 10/18, 1977). pp.107-119

Pont, J, 'Bataille o la transgression', *Revista de literatura,*13 (1974), pp.17-19.

Popowski, M. *Lisibilité et illisibilité*, Thèse de 3e cycle, Université de Paris X, 1981.

Queilles, G, A. *Breton et Georges Bataille: Le rapport à Hegel*, Thèse de 3e cycle, Université de Paris IV, 1979.

Queneau, Raymond, 'Première confrontation avec Hegel', *Critique*, 195/196 (1963), pp.694-700

Rainord, M., 'La Communication', *L'Arc*, 32 (1967), pp.73-74

Richman, Michèle H.,'Introduction to the *Collège de Sociologie*: Postructuralism before its time?', *Stanford French Review*, 12 (1988), pp.79-95
   -'Bataille Moralist? Critique and the Postwar Writings', Yale French Studies, 78 (1990), pp.143-68

Risset, Jacqueline, 'De Monsieur Teste à Acéphale, in *L'invenzione e il modelo*, Roma: Bulsoni, 1973.

Rollin, J-F. 'Ma Mère', *Esprit*, 345 (1966), pp.715-718.

Ronse, H, 'Georges Bataille', *L'Arc* 32 (1967), pp.1-4.
   -'L'Apprenti sorcier', *L'Arc* 44 (1971), pp.1-2.

Sartre, Jean-Paul, 'Un Nouveau mystique', *Cahiers du Sud*, 260, 261, 262 (1943), pp.783-790, 866-886, and 988-994, reprinted pp.143-188, in *Situations I*, (Paris: Gallimard, 1947) pp.133-175

Sasso, R, 'Hegel-Bataille, ou l'enjeu philosophique', *Études Philosophiques,* 33, 1978, pp.465-479.

Short, Robert Stuart, 'Contre-Attaque', in *Entretiens sur le surréalisme,* ed. Ferdinand Alquié (Paris, La Haye, Mouton, 1968) pp.144-175

Sollers, Philippe 'De Grandes irregularités de langage, *Critique*,195/196 (1963) pp.795-802

-'Le Toit', *Tel Quel*, 29, 1967, pp.24-45, *L'écriture et l'expérience des limites*, (Paris: Éditions du Seuil, 1971) pp.104-138.

-'Le Récit impossible', *La quinzaine littéraire, 1st September,* 1966

-'Le Coupable', *Tel Quel*, 45 (1971), pp.97-100.

-'L'Acte Bataille', *Tel Quel,* 52 (1972), pp.41-48.

-'Pourquoi Artaud, pourquoi Bataille', *Artaud à Cerisy* (Paris: U.G.E, coll.10/18, 1973)

-'Une Prophétie de Bataille', *La Guerre du Goût*, (Paris: Gallimard 1997)

Sontag, Susan, 'The pornographic imagination', *Partisan Review,* 34 (1967), pp.151- 212.

Stoekl, Allan, 'Le Système du non-savoir-compte rendu', *Modern Language Notes*, (1979), pp.1261-1264.

'The Death of Acéphale and the Will to Chance: Nietzsche in the Text of Bataille', *Glyph*, 6, (1979), pp.42-67.

-'Hegel's Return', *Stanford French Review*, 12 (1988), pp.119-28.

-'Truman's Apotheosis: Bataille, 'Planisme', Headlessness', *Yale French Studies*, 78, 1990, pp.246-62

Suleiman, Susan Rubin, 'Pornography, Transgression and the Avant-garde: Bataille's Story of the Eye', in *The Poetics of Gender*, ed. Nancy K.Miller (New York: Columbia University Press, 1986), pp.117-38

Verneaux, R, 'L'Athéologie mystique de Georges Bataille', *Recherches de Philosophie,* 3-4 (1958), pp.125-158.

Wahl, Jean, 'En lisant la littérature et le mal', *La Ciguë,*1 (1958), pp.41-46.

'Le Pouvoir et le non-pouvoir', *Critique,* 195/196 (1963), pp.778-794.

Waldberg, Patrick, 'Vers un nouveau mythe?' Prémonitions et défiances', *V.V.V.*, 4 (1944), pp.41-49.

'Notes sur Georges Bataille', *L'archangélique*, (Paris: Nouveau cercle parisien du livre, 1967)

Weiss, Allen S., 'Impossible Sovereignty: Between The Will to Chance and The Will to Power', *October*, 36 (1986), pp. 129-68

9. Other works consulted

Ades, Dawn, *Masson*, (New York: Rizzoli, 1994)

Aquinas, Thomas, *Summa Theologiae*, edited and translated by Timothy McDermott (Texas: Christian Classics, 1989)

Aristotle, *Poetics*, trans. F. Copleston (Washington: Image, 1961)

Barillé, Élisabeth, *Laure, La Sainte de l'abîme* (Paris: Flammarion, 197)

Blake, William, *Selected Poetry*, ed. W.H Stevenson, (London: Penguin, 1988)

Blanchot, Maurice, *Thomas l'Obscur*, (Paris: Gallimard, 1950)
    -*Faux Pas* (Paris: Gallimard, 1943)
    -*L'Espace littéraire* (Paris: Gallimard, 1955
    -*L'Entretien infini* (Paris: Gallimard 1969)
    -*L'Amitié* (Paris: Gallimard, 1971)
    -*La Communauté inavouable* (Paris: Éditions de Minuit, 1983)
    -*L'Instant de ma mort* (Montpélier: Fata Morgana, 1994)

Bloch, Marc, *Saint John of the Cross: Poet and Mystic* (London: Macmillan, 1971)

Bowie, Malcolm, *Lacan* (London: Fontana, 1991)

Breton, André, *Œuvres Complètes*, tome 1 (Gallimard, 1988)
    -*Manifestes du surréalisme* (Paris: Jean-Jacques Pauvert, 1962)
    -*Le Surréalisme et la peinture*, Paris: Gallimard, 1965

194

Clement of Alexandria, *Opera Omnia*, trans. W.Wilson, 2 vols. (Edinburgh, 1867)

Coomaraswamy, Ananda, *The Darker Side of Dawn* (London: Abraxas, 1935)

Derrida, Jacques, *De la Grammatologie* (Gallimard: Paris, 1967), p.214.
-*Psyché, Inventions de l'autre* (Paris: Galilée, 1987)

Dionysius the Areopagite, *The Divine Names and Mystical Theology*, Dionysius, trans. by C.E. Holt (London: Methuen, 1920).

Eliot, T.S, *Selected Poetry* (London: Faber, 1965)

ffrench, Patrick, *The Time of Theory* (Oxford: Clarendon Press, 1995)

Forest, Philippe, *Histoire de Tel Quel* (Paris: Éditions du Seuil, 1995)

Hegel, Georg Wilhelm Friedrich, *Phenomenology of Spirit*, trans. A.V Miller (OUP, 1977)

Hill, Leslie, *Maurice Blanchot: Extreme Contemporary* (London: Routledge: 1997)

Hussey, Edward, *The Presocratics* (London: Duckworth, 1972)

Jakobson, Roman, *Essais de linguistique générale* (Paris: Éditions de Minuit, 1964).

James, William, *Varieties of Religious Experience* (New York, 1902)

Jay, Martin, *Downcast Eyes* (Berkeley and Los Angeles: University of California Press, 1994)

Jouve, Pierre-Jean, *Vagadu*. (Paris: Gallimard, 1985)

Kojève, Alexandre, *Introduction à la lecture de Hegel*, ed. Raymond Queneau (Paris: Gallimard, 1947)

Laure, *Écrits, fragments, lettres*, (ed.) Jérome Peignot (Paris: Jean-Jacques Pauvert, 1978)

Leiris, Michel, *L'Age d'homme* (Paris: Gallimard, 1988)

Mehlman, Jeffrey, *Legacies of Anti-Semitism in France* (Minneapolis: Minnesota University Press, 1983)

Nadeau, Maurice, *Histoire du surréalisme* (Paris: Éditions du Seuil, 1964)

Nietzsche, Friedrich, *Complete Works*, trans. Walter Kaufman (New York: Random House, 1974)

Norris, Christopher, *Derrida* (London: Fontana, 1987)

Pascal, Blaise, *Pensées*, texte de Léon Brunschvig (Paris: Nelson, 1955)

Polizzotti, Mark, *Revolution of the Mind, The Life of André Breton* (London: Bloomsbury, 1995)

Rawson, Philip, *Tantra: The Indian Cult of Ecstasy* (London: Thames and Hudson, 1993),

Rimbaud, Arthur, 'A Georges Izambard', *Collected Poems* (London: Penguin, 1986).

Roudinesco Élisabeth, *Histoire de la psychanalyse* en France, tome 2 (Paris: Fayard, 1994)

Sartre, Jean-Paul, *L'Être et le néant* (Paris: Gallimard, 1973)

Steiner, George, *Real Presences* (London: Faber, 1989)

St. John of the Cross, *El Cántico Espiritual*, coll. Clásicos castellanos (Madrid: Espasa- Calpe, 1944)

Taylor, Charles, *Hegel* (London: Cambridge University Press, 1975).

196

Unamuno, Miguel de , *The Tragic Sense of Life* (London: Macmillan, 1921),

Underhill, Evelyn, *Mysticism: A Study in the Nature and Development of man's Spiritual Consciousness* (London: Methuen, 1930)

Vivekananda Swami, 'Commentaires sur les aphorismes de Pantanjali', *Les Grands maîtres spirituels dans l'Inde contemporain* (Bruxelles: Éditions Ayden , 1938)

INDEX